NEWS AT TEN

FIFTY YEARS WITH STAN CHAMBERS

NEWS AT TEN
FIFTY YEARS WITH STAN CHAMBERS

STAN CHAMBERS
INTRODUCTION BY HAL FISHMAN

CAPRA PRESS
SANTA BARBARA

Cover design by Frank Goad.
Typography by Jimmy O'Shea.
Amanda Jones, editor.

LIBRARY OF CONGRESS CATALOGING-IN-PUBLICATION DATA
Chambers, Stan, 1922-
News at ten : fifty years with Stan Chambers.
p. cm.
ISBN 0-88496-386-1 : $14.95
1. Chambers, Stan, 1922- . 2. Television journalists—United States
—Biography. 3. Television broadcasting of news—United States.
I. Title.
PN4874.C597A3 1994
070'.92—dc20   94-15284
[B]   CIP

CAPRA PRESS
P.O. Box 2068
SANTA BARBARA, CA 93120

CONTENTS

INTRODUCTION
BY HAL FISHMAN

I've been anchoring the news in Los Angeles for 35 years. That must be some kind of record for longevity in a business known for its revolving-door policy on anchors and reporters. Nevertheless, when I started back in 1960, Stan Chambers had already been on television for 13 years! He was there when it all began and is still there, reporting news in the morning and in the evening from all over Southern California. Viewers wonder if he ever rests.

The story of Stan Chambers is the story of television news. When Stan joined KTLA, Los Angeles was just beginning to emerge from its small-town mentality and was viewed world-wide as some kind of lotus-land populated by retirees, citrus growers and movie stars. Stan's career is congruent with Los Angeles becoming the megalopolis it is today. Stan was a television news reporter when the Big Red Cars traversed all of Southern California and trolleys ran along Hollywood Boulevard. And he was there as Los Angeles became the second most populous city in the country, capital of the Pacific Rim and leader in aerospace and high-tech research and development. Stan was also reporting to the people of Southern California during the tough times as well. Many readers will recall those powerful television images of the attempted rescue of little Kathy Fiscus. When you think about the Bel Air fire, the Baldwin Hills dam disaster, the Watts riots, the Sylmar earthquake, the airplane in the wires, the Laguna and Malibu fires, the Los Angeles riots, the Northridge quake among a thousand other stories, you should know that only one reporter in the history of television covered them all, and his name is Stan Chambers.

Stan has also reported for us from Poland and Moscow. He covered the Pope's 72-hour visit to Los Angeles, and is known, recognized and respected not just locally, but all over the world.

This book is not merely a series of anecdotal presentations. It's essential and exciting reading for all who live in Southern California and wish to gain a rare insight to their community and their own lives in relation to this vast multicultural society we call Los Angeles. It is also essential reading for anyone who watches television news anywhere in America. This book provides fascinating revelations into how news is gathered and presented to the public. After all, there is no more important source of information in our democratic society than television news, and the reader will find "News At Ten"a truly exciting book.

I can personally report to you that Stan Chambers is the same person off the air as you see on TV. His intelligence and boundless energy, his news judgment and professionalism, have helped make "News At Ten" the most successful prime time news program in the history of Los Angeles television. Most importantly, Stan is a true gentleman and deeply caring individual.

An inevitable result of being seen on TV every night is that so many people recognize you. And when you have worked as long and as close with someone as I have with Stan Chambers, occasionally someone will greet me with "Hi, Stan." Usually, I don't correct them—you see, I consider it a great compliment.

FOREWORD

Local television news is the people's news, the electronic equivalent of the home-delivered newspaper, the day-to-day diary, the theme of human activity that runs through our times.

When you report news in Los Angeles, you are broadcasting to the biggest hometown in the country. Los Angeles is a collection of almost a hundred independent cities and communities, just like the ones back home. The L.A. residents came here from all over the country. It is the same story today as it has been year after year. People pack up the family, load up their belongings, say goodbye to friends and move to Los Angeles.

We Angelenos have been through a lot together. Watching local newscasts has been a unifying experience. Everyone watches in disbelief and suffers through the tragic, illogical L.A. riots; the devastating brush fires that ravaged the beach, mountain and suburban communities of Laguna, Bel Air, Malibu and Altadena; the earthquakes that shook the region and crumbled homes and hospitals in Northridge, Sylmar and San Fernando.

Reporting local news is the same all over the country. Reporters and their camera crews are recording the stories in the field where news is happening. Editors under heart-pounding pressures are back at the station bucking the deadlines of the evening newscast. Somehow, every night, they overcome the stress, iron out problems and bring everything together to broadcast a near-flawless newscast.

How many times have you heard your local reporter end his story with something like "Stan Chambers, Channel 5, News At Ten." Similar sign-offs are repeated every day, over and over again, in every television city in America.

The news stories I cover, and the situations I get into, are similar to what local reporters encounter all over the country. We are an interesting breed. Local reporters are recognized wherever they go. We are seen on the evening news so often, we almost become family. Not stars or celebrities, we are friends. People are interested in what we do, because we are a part of what is going on in the city. When something happens, we rush to the scene. I have been one of these local reporters for nearly 50 years. I started at KTLA just after it became the first commercial television station in the West in 1947 and have been there ever since.

This is not a history, but rather a personal perspective drawn from those years of reporting. I have tried to recapture some of the past to show what it was like to be there in the beginning of television news and how it evolved into what it is today.

Since I have been on the air for so many years, I often meet people who become misty-eyed when they say they enjoy watching me on the news, because I remind them of the days when their children were little and still at home. I often meet those grown children, now with families of their own, who tell me I was one of the first people they had ever seen on the TV screen when television was so new and they were so very young. I feel fortunate to be included in their television memories. Many were with me through rough times and good times and remember many of the times when things went wrong.

1.

RODNEY KING
AND THE LOS ANGELES RIOTS

Our helicopter whirled in a tight circle over Florence and Normandie in South Central Los Angeles. Pilot Mike Tamburro kept the ship at a constant bank. I was in the left seat next to the pilot and had a clear view of the rampaging clutter on the street below. Cameraman Martin Clancey, strapped in a shoulder harness, was hanging out of the helicopter. He had opened the left side door, placed his mini-cam on his shoulder and was recording the helter-skelter action. This was the early evening of April 29, 1992. The Los Angeles riots were erupting below us.

We began to get more reports of scattered violence shortly after we had watched on television the barbaric videotape of motorists being ripped out of their cars, hammered, pounded and chased by rock-throwing men on the ground. The image of a man, later identified as Reginald Denny, being pulled from his truck by thugs, still burned in my mind. My memory was seared by the vivid imprint of the motionless, beaten man, lying on the ground, being kicked and brutalized. I was still filled with rage at the sight of one of the assailants picking up a large piece of cinder-block and throwing it at Denny's apparently lifeless body, smashing him in the head. After the savage beating, the attacker appeared to do a dance, raise his hands towards the helicopter overhead and flashed a gang sign. Then, to my utter disbelief, another person on the street reached into the pocket of the fallen driver and stole his wallet.

This was my television memory; now I was seeing first hand what was really happening.

I peered through my side-window as the copter continued to circle in a steep bank. I could see that traffic was moving through the intersection below us. I watched as various cars whipped a U-turn to avoid the chaos ahead. There were clusters of people milling around. They were throwing rocks and bottles at the passing cars. There were no police around, just an unruly mob venting hate on innocent motorists who happened to find themselves in the wrong place at the wrong time.

Other figures on the street were darting in and out of a liquor store at the corner, taking what they wanted. The looting, the beating and the hysteria was going on right below me.

My mind went back 27 years to when I covered the Watts riots in 1965. I tried to draw similarities that might help my reports on what was going on below. I remember telling myself that the big difference was that in Watts, they had fires.

Soon after, I noticed white smoke beginning to build in the street at the corner. A single overturned car had just been torched and was beginning to smoke and burn. Within moments, I could see more smoke pouring out of the front windows of the liquor store where looters were still running wild. It was a light smoke, wispy and barely visible from 700 feet above.

As we circled, Martin, peering into the viewfinder of his Sony camera, shouted over the radio communications system, "I think that liquor store is on fire."

Our pilot nodded and refocused the flight circle to the smoking corner building below. Things began to develop in a chaotic and rapid manner. An appliance store just east of Normandie, a short distance from the liquor store, showed the tell-tale light white smoke.

It wasn't long before large flames were shooting out the doors and windows of the first liquor store. The overturned car continued to burn. The appliance store seethed with heavy white smoke that slowly turned to rolling black clouds fed by billowing flames eating their way through the collapsing roof.

My thoughts again flashed back to 1965. I remember being in the newsroom and watching pilot-reporter Larry Scheer in the KTLA Telecopter broadcasting the first fire pictures from Watts. My reaction tonight was the same as it had been a quarter of a century ago: I can't believe this is happening, but I am afraid it's only going to get worse. The light of dusk was now completely gone, the sky was black and the lights of South Central Los Angeles sparkled below.

By this time, the station had pre-empted all programs and was in full riot coverage. Hal Fishman, Larry McCormick and Jann Carl were at the anchor desks, Ron Olson was in the middle of the rioting crowd outside police headquarters at Parker Center, and Steve Lentz and Marta Waller were covering other parts of the city as the riots seemed to spread.

Fires were breaking out over a widespread area below our helicopter. Dark plumes of smoke were ominously spreading to different spots of the city. New fires exploded on Manchester, Vermont, Figueroa, Martin Luther King Jr., Crenshaw, Jefferson, Rodeo and Century Boulevards. Our pilot broke off from our tight flying circle as we spotted flare-ups. He pulled the stick in one direction and cut a diagonal path across the sky to the next erupting blaze.

Each one was a startling surprise. The numbers of separate fires grew from five or six to a dozen, to two dozen. They were now breaking out over a wide part of the city. This was not Watts of 1965 where the fires erupted in a relatively small area. These conflagrations were not limited to Watts and South Central Los Angeles. Roaring, rolling, intense flames were burning in all directions. The targets were varied, but very much the same. Supermarkets, Thrifty Drug Stores, Chief Auto Parts, liquor stores, swap meets, Korean businesses, restaurants and mini-malls miles apart ignited under the arsonist's torch.

Often, our copter would arrive when a fire was just starting. We watched countless buildings where the light wisps of smoke smoldered then grew heavy, then went gray, then black, then erupted into consuming flames of intense orange. It didn't take long. Flames would roll through the roof of one building, then the fire would spread to a structure next door. Many mini-malls were completely wiped out when fire exploded in one of the stores, then raced through the attic which adjacent businesses shared.

Firemen could not respond to many of these early fires because snipers were shooting at them. Later, police escorts went in with them. KTLA remained on the air for hours. Countless times during the night, I kept repeating to myself: I can't believe this is happening.

I have lived all my life in Los Angeles and know it well. So many places I grew up with were burning. It was heart-rending to be over my city as these structures melted down into ash heaps. So many buildings had been erected in the last few years, a hopeful sign that, at last, something was happening: a new shopping center here, a new mini-mall there, an old building rehabilitated across the street with a new business opening up inside. All the progress since the fires of Watts seemed lost in the heat of this night.

I kept remembering the stories we did in Watts after the 1965 riots. I vividly recalled the twisted, shattered buildings that had burned to the ground. One by one, clean-up crews had come in, leveled the structures, and hauled away the debris, leaving nothing but weed-filled lots. Those lots had remained vacant for years after the tragedy of Watts, a wounded community with no places of business, just block after block of vacant lots. It was so sad. Here tonight, each one of these fires was burning up not only the buildings, but the jobs and futures of so many people who lived in the community. Now, there would be no work, no places to buy anything, no hope, no future. All because of these fires of April, 1992. For years to come, sociologists will be trying to find out why this happened. What ignited this tragedy, this rebellion? There will be many questions and many answers. However, there was really only one, immediate cause: the jury in the televised trial of the four officers accused in the beating of Rodney King announced they had found the officers "not guilty."

*   *   *

A pickup truck with its motor running was in my parking place when I arrived on the KTLA lot that afternoon in March 1991. A free-lance camera-man had borrowed my space while he ran a videotape of a late news story to the newsroom. I waited for about thirty seconds. He came racing out the door and waved an apology.

"Sorry, Stan, I think Rosalva will like the house fire I just brought her. Fire through the roof, good action."

"No problem," I waved back as he got into his car.

There are several of these cameramen who make a living shooting news stories and selling them for $125 each to the different television stations. They drive their own camera cars, listen to police scanners and chase after breaking news stories.

He slammed his truck door shut, backed out much too fast, then raced out of the parking lot to go to another television newsroom with a copy of his latest story.

I had no idea that another one of those unexpected moments that report-ers encounter frequently was about to hit me. They say we should always expect the unexpected, but I have never been able to take those moments in stride.

The newsroom was busy when I entered. I reached into my coat pocket and pulled out my press pass. I keep it on a chain so I can put it around my neck when I am on stories where they must be worn. I also keep a few keys on the chain, one for the news van, others for my desk and mail box. I opened the narrow, book-like, metallic door of the mail box and took out a weekly paper from Taiwan, a letter from the German Consulate, three inter-office memos and my paycheck. I closed the door, always hard to relock, and went across the lobby to the glass-encased bulletin board. Yesterday's program ratings are posted there each morning. There aren't many businesses where you get a daily report card on how well you did the day before. It is another computer tracking of our daily lives. It is a rather humbling experience, an instant gauge on how the television viewers accept you. It is best not to lose too many days in a row.

"News At Ten" had a six rating. The other three newscasts against us had between a one and a three. That was good news, but how long could we keep it up?

My three-to-eleven o'clock shift is always full of surprises. Most of the scheduled stories have already been covered, so we turn our attention to what has just happened. I never know what my assignments are going to be when I drive to work listening to the news radio stations. I don't know if the people at the all-news stations, KFWB or KNX, have any idea how important their newscasts are to those of us who are field reporters. Their local news stories set the tone of the day and give us a feeling of what has happened and what might happen that night.

Our assignment editor, Rosalva Skidmore, looked up from her phone call, smiled and waved a greeting. I scanned the newswire copy on her desk while she finished the call. Rosalva is a pretty brunette with a wonderful smile and great enthusiasm. She is great to work with, very pleasant and professional. She handles stress well and refuses to let deadlines get her down.

"Stan, when you get a chance, will you take a look at this freelance video that we got today and see what you think we can do with it. It's an amateur home video, but it is really quite powerful. Take a look at it."

It was an unusual request so I put it in a play-back video unit right away. I looked at the pictures and felt a flow of adrenalin surge through my body. I had never viewed anything like this before. Although shot the night before in the San Fernando Valley Foothill Police Division, it looked like something that might have happened in Tiananmen Square in Beijing or in a poor black township in South Africa but not in Los Angeles.

The first part of the video was blurred and it was difficult to tell what was happening, but when the photographer found his focus, I saw an incredible scene of police officers hitting a man with batons, over and over again. The beating didn't stop. It continued at a frenzy. The man was on the ground reeling around. He seemed submissive, but the blows continued. I put the VCR in reverse and watched the blows bounce away from the victim. Then I put it on "play" and looked in disbelief as they pounded him again and again.

"How did we get this?" I asked.

"Some guy with a new home video camera shot this from his patio and he wants to sell it to us as a freelance news story," Rosalva answered.

I kept running the tape back and forth. More than a dozen officers had surrounded the person and three of them were hitting him with batons or kicking him. The others just seemed to stand around.

"Are we the only ones to have it? What's the background?" I asked.

"There was a pursuit on the Foothill Freeway. The guy tried to get away. When he finally stopped, he got out of the car and tried to take on the whole force," she answered.

Several others in the newsroom came over, clustered around the monitor and watched the videotape playback over and over again. Everyone had a pained expression.

"Better show this to the police first. We've got to get their reaction," I said to Rosalva.

The tape had been left off at the main gate by a viewer named George Holliday. He had taken the video when he heard shouting and yelling on the street in front of his apartment. He began videotaping the action and the violent beating sequence unfolded in front of him. Our news director, Warren

Cereghino, had watched it many times before I saw it. He agreed that we had to show it to the Police Department brass before we put it on the air.

I called Lieutenant Fred Nixon in the press relations department and told him what we had.

"Bring it down Stan. I'll have some of the staff take a look at it with me."

Commander Bill Booth, who had been head of press relations for years, had just been promoted to deputy chief. So this was the first day on the job for his replacement, Commander Robert Gil. Viewing this explosive package would be Commander Gil's baptism by fire.

The officers were waiting for me when I arrived with a copy of the tape at their sixth floor office of Parker Center about six o'clock that evening. They watched silently as the tape was played and replayed. It seemed to me they could not believe what they were seeing, but their official reaction was calm and noncommittal.

Lieutenant Nixon did an on-camera interview with me and said that they would have to investigate the circumstances to try to determine what had happened. He said there was no way he could comment on the tape until he knew more about the circumstances. It wasn't much of a reaction from the Police Department, but we could use it on the air when we ran the tape that night. Several other high-ranking officers saw the tape before I left that evening. These screenings gave the department a chance to get ready for the storm that was about to engulf them. I left a copy of the tape and was assured that the investigation would start immediately.

I had no idea about the impact of the beating tape, but I knew it would be bad.

I asked Nixon, "Why don't you suspend everyone involved and then worry about the circumstances later?" He nodded his head but didn't give me any response.

A *Los Angeles Times* news photographer, Mike Meadows, was in the police press office that night and jumped on the story early.

I filled him in on some of the details and he told his city desk about the existence of the tape. Mike came over to our newsroom and photographed stills of the video on one of our television monitors. He would have his pictures in time for the morning edition of the *Times*.

I left Parker Center about seven that night. I caught up with my camera crew and drove to George Holliday's condominium in Sylmar. Rosalva had set up an interview with the man who shot the tape.

It was raining while we searched for the correct address in the condominium complex. It was a large, gated community. We followed directions, but lost our way through the maze of buildings. We had to retrace our steps a few times before we found the right unit. George Holliday answered the door and introduced us to his wife. Both were from Argentina, but had lived in this country for many years. George managed a plumbing company.

I looked around his condo. His new camera was still in the white, foam protective packaging. The new camera box was nearby, as well as a scattering of video tapes and cables and connectors.

George told me he was just learning how to use it. He had shot it only a few times. "There was an Arnold Schwartzeneger movie filming down the street last week," he told us. "I took the video camera and got shots of Arnold and some of the other members of the cast. It was good experience and I enjoyed it."

"How did you happen to take this video?" I asked.

His wife answered. "The sirens and copter noise woke me up. I went out on the balcony and saw all the commotion and called George. Maybe you should get the new camera. There's a lot going on out there on Foothill."

"I found the camera. It took a little time to get it ready and for me to start shooting. I just followed the action," Holliday added.

George Holliday had no idea of the impact of what he was videotaping. He didn't have any plans to contact a television station, because he wasn't sure if anyone would be interested. It wasn't until the next morning, when his wife called the Foothill Station and inquired about the man arrested outside their condo the night before, that they considered doing anything about it. "The policeman on the phone gave me the run-around. He wouldn't give me any information at all, so I asked George if maybe we should give it to a news station. I was a little scared about doing it. Because of the way they talked on the phone we decided to call you," she told me as we sat in their living room.

The Hollidays said they had watched KTLA a lot and knew that we did these late-breaking action stories and figured that we might be interested. They called, talked to our assignment desk and were asked to drop the tape off with the security officers at the KTLA main gate. The rest is history.

It was still raining when we left the Hollidays. I knew this would be a difficult story. It was brutal and violent and would offend a lot of people. I decided to use that as a peg for my narration. I had an umbrella out as I put my notes together and decided to use it while I told the story.

I wanted to be as objective as possible and not sensationalize something as devastating as the tape. I wanted people to see it and make up their own minds.

I did the on-camera portion of my story and then went back to the news-room to finish up the rest.

There was some concern for the safety of George Holliday as we put the finished tape together. Would we make him a marked man if his face went on the air? How important was his on-camera appearance to our presentation?

While we were getting the tape ready for our ten o'clock broadcast, I was paged over the newsroom loudspeaker.

It was Assistant Police Chief Bob Vernon. "Stan, I want you to know that we have already sent investigators out to the site where the videotape was shot. They are working in the rain talking to witnesses right now. All we are interested in is the truth. Let the chips fall where they may."

I thanked the chief. We now had a strong reaction from the Police Department. We could tell the viewers what immediate steps the police were taking. Vernon also told me that Police Chief Daryl Gates was out of town. I later learned that he was attending a police seminar in the East, and wouldn't be back in Los Angeles until the next morning.

Tony Fote went over and over the tape in his editing room. He is an expert at working under deadline pressure and getting the heart of a story in the finished edit. The first ten seconds or so were out of focus as Holliday started shooting his new camera. There were images there, but you could not tell what was happening. Once he was in focus, the images were clear and the action mesmerizing. We decided to pick it up there. The officers swarmed around Rodney King. We let the tape play until the beatings stopped. The tape was so brutally powerful, we just used Holliday's voice as he described what he saw. That is the way it went on the air that night. Of course, the tape could not show what had gone on before. The camera wasn't rolling during the high-speed police pursuit down the San Fernando Freeway. The large number of officers at the scene were there because they were part of the pursuit and follow up. The camera did not show that Rodney King threw off four officers who tried to subdue him after the freeway chase. The camera did not show Sergeant Stacy Koon use a taser gun twice in an effort to subdue Rodney King. Nothing that preceded the beatings on the tape had been recorded except the out-of-focus footage taken by George Holliday before the clear pictures appeared in his view finder. The fact that the officers thought King was on PCP, a drug that seems to give super-strength to someone under its influence, was of course not apparent on the videotape.

The beating that happened in San Fernando was seen all over the world and had a devastating impact.The tape was played over and over again on television. It incited anger, rage, sorrow and pain. Police Chief Daryl Gates called it an aberration.

It took almost a year before the trial of the four officers accused of beating Rodney King began. There was wide media coverage of the trial. Many stations did live broadcasts from the courtroom. One station, KTTV in Los Angeles, televised the day-by-day proceedings of the entire trial. All the media in Los Angeles and most of the country followed every development of the trial. Those interested in the minute details of the legal arguments had access to the complete story. Defense attorneys were able to raise doubts in the minds of the jurors about the actions they saw on the tape.

Some officers testified they were frightened by the way King was acting. Some said they feared for their lives. Defense attorneys talked about "tunnel vision," where a person is so intent on what is happening directly in front of him that he has no idea about what is around him. The fact there were a lot of officers there didn't enter into the mind of those faced with an aggressive, possibly PCP-drugged assailant. They talked to the jury about the escalation of force. They listened to experts who said it was necessary to go all the way short of shooting to subdue the man. They had the jury look at "freeze frames" of the tape and had experts say various blows were according to regulation. Many disagreed with the testimony of some of the witnesses, but the jury could not find criminal fault and the officers were found not guilty of the charges. When the jurors returned with that innocent verdict on three of the accused officers and were unable to reach a decision on the only remaining count against the fourth officer, the backlash slammed into the city.

Reporters covering the trial rushed to their live cameras, their microphones and their computer terminals to tell the world about the decision.

During the trial, Brian Jenkins, a black reporter for KCOP television, and Michael Ambrosini, an anchorman for KNX newsradio, were fixtures in the media room of the Simi Valley courthouse. They were in the middle of everything every day covering the controversial trial. Both of them were among the two or three dozen reporters who spent weeks in the small converted courtroom, crammed with desks, monitors, chairs, computers and telephones. They were not far from the small work space that Eric Spillman and I shared while covering the trial. Brian's makeshift desk was at the end of one cluttered table. Michael sat behind an old-fashioned typewriter about two dozen feet away. They were almost chained to their computers and typewriters while the trial droned on in the courtroom down the hall. They listened intently to the slow-moving developments in the court, condensing important issues for their audiences. Michael had to do updates for KNX radio a dozen times a day. He was always over his workstation mumbling to himself.

When the riots exploded, both were caught up in the surge of violence and both of them found themselves playing the unanticipated role of hero.

Brian Jenkins was with Bob Quinlan in a KCOP camera car parked on a street in the riot zone. They were stunned by what they were seeing. At one point they saw a white man running frantically, chased by four black youths. The assailants caught up and tackled the man right in front of the KCOP car. Bob Quinlan had his camera on his shoulder and was shooting through the car's windshield. When the four young men pounced on the victim, Brian Jenkins opened the door, raced from the truck, and began pulling them off of the man. Quinlan was taking pictures of everything that was happening.

Jenkins wasn't fighting them. He was pleading with them and trying to keep them from hurting the man, but he kept pulling them off as he tried to reason with the hot tempers.

"Come on guys, leave him alone. He didn't have anything to do with the decision. He hasn't hurt anyone. Don't pick on him just because he's white."

Somehow, it worked. They grudgingly stopped as the imposing figure of Brian Jenkins, who talked to them like a big brother, swung the tide away from further violence. Brian took the beating victim into his camera car.

I talked to Brian a few days later on a hostage-barricade story we were both covering. He said, "When I saw the videotape that my cameraman shot of me running into the fight, I couldn't believe I did it. I guess it was something inside of me that said I had to do something, so I just ran out there and tried to stop the guys from beating him." Brian was able to rescue the man, get him into their KCOP car and rush away from the scene. The victim was a photographer from France who was trying to get pictures of what was happening that chaotic day in South Central Los Angeles.

Brian's partner at the Rodney King trial table, Michael Ambrosini, also found himself thrust into a volatile situation as the riots broke out around him near the corner of Vermont and Martin Luther King Boulevard. A microwave television news crew from KCAL-TV was under attack. Reporter Bill Gephardt and cameraman Chris Torgerson had been interviewing looters when several men came rushing out of the crowd and chased them. Gephardt was hit by a flying bottle. At one point he slipped and fell; the pursuers were on top of him. He was hit on the side of the face so hard, some of his teeth were loosened. They viciously kicked him in his side. Others tried to steal the television camera. In the scuffle that developed over Torgerson's camera, Gephardt was able to get up and start running through traffic in the middle of the street. The four assailants finally were able to grab the KCAL-TV camera from Torgerson and took up the chase after Gephardt. As the pair weaved in panic through traffic in the middle of the street, they spotted Ambrosini's KNX car. The car hardly stopped, the door swung open, both men jumped inside. Ambrosini tried to pull away but the car got jammed in the heavy traffic. The attackers pounded on the windows, grabbed the locked doors and shook the van trying to get at the fleeing newsmen. The moment Ambrosini found an opening, he cut the car free and the three of them fled the scene. Bill Gephardt had to be taken to a local hospital. The KCAL-TV microwave truck had to be abandoned on the street.

A KTTV television truck had to be deserted at another riot scene. Mobs were running randomly through the parking lot of a Fedco Store. Some of them vented their anger when they spotted a television crew huddled inside the big, white truck. A few rushed over and banged on the doors, others tried to rock it back and forth, some pelted it with anything they could get their hands on. One man swinging a two-by-four, shouting and glaring menacingly at the engineers inside the cab, let loose a vicious blow to the windshield and the side of the truck. The glass shattered but did not break. Still, it was almost impossible to see through the windshield.

The crew had hoped to ride out the storm, but now it was developing into a desperate situation. Their only hope was to get out of there. They decided to start the truck and race away from the threatening crowd.

What the engineers didn't know was that the heavy blow by the two-by-four hit a tender target, the "kill switch" in the dashboard, making the truck inoperable. The switch is there to prevent fires that might be caused by a serious collision. The frightened crew was now stranded among the rioters. Mobs seem to have a guiding force of their own. Anger erupts in waves. New targets drew their attention. There were too many other things to do at that Fedco store and the attacking mob lost interest in the truck and turned their attention to looting.

At the right moment, when the action had turned elsewhere, the engineers opened the door and fled the scene. The grandmother of one of the engineers lived a half mile away. Her house was their only nearby haven of safety. They abandoned the truck and ran to her place, where they stayed the rest of the day.

For months after the looting and burning, local newsmen spoke of their close calls in the riots. I remember a November afternoon in 1992 at the Los Angeles County Courthouse. A bunch of reporters and cameramen were standing in the hallway outside a courtroom where the local teachers were arguing their salary situation before a judge.

I saw Marco Peterson, a black cameraman from KTTV, sitting on a nearby bench reading a newspaper. He turned out to be the hero in this abandoned microwave truck story. Marco was the one who volunteered to go back to the Fedco parking lot to try to salvage the truck.

I sat next to him and asked why he offered to do that.

"Stan, did you know that was my son's truck?" Marco answered. "He just started working at the station. I wanted to help out. You know Robert Campbell. Well, he and I went down to the Fedco parking lot to see if the truck was still there."

Marco told me how he tried to blend in as he walked through the crowd of looters to the truck. He made believe that he was trying to jimmy the front door open.

"I had my secret key hidden in my hand and got the door opened. I got some cheers when I got into the front seat. They thought I was trying to steal the truck. I put the key in the ignition, but no luck. I tried and tried but it just wouldn't start. I kept doing it until the battery died. Robert and I drove down in a big pick-up truck, so we decided to try to push the KTTV truck out of the parking lot." While this was going on, looters were running out of the Fedco Store carrying dresses, shoes, lamps, television sets and anything else they could get their hands on. Many had driven their cars on to the parking lot and were filling them up with the stolen merchandise.

"With all of this chaos going on, Robert drove the pick-up truck behind the disabled vehicle and started pushing it slowly. The crowd started cheering us on thinking they were trying to make off with it."

"Keep going, Brother, it's all yours."

"That's the way. You're taking the big one."

"Good going. That's what I like to see," the voices in the crowd laughed approvingly.

Marco and his friend waved back to the crowd as the two trucks eased off the parking lot to a quiet part of the neighborhood where a tow truck could be called in.

"That tow truck cost the station $500," Marco told me.

A few weeks after the riots, I was in Simi Valley. About a hundred people had gathered outside the courthouse to denounce the decisions in the Rodney King case. They shouted their speeches over an amplified speaker. Many were angry, but the rally was peaceful. Local police in riot gear were inside the building and were ready to move into action in case things got violent. One of my colleagues also covering the story was James Bartholomew, a freelance journalist who often works for the *New York Times*. Bart still had a badly bruised jaw from the riots. He had been taking pictures at Florence and Normandie when he got caught in the flash point of the outbreak, and he was attacked and beaten by an angry crowd. Someone grabbed a large stick and smashed him in the face. Others took his cameras and trashed his car. A man watching the attack was able to get to Bartholomew and helped him get back into his car. When other rioters saw this, they attacked the car again, pulling the doors open, rocking it viciously and jumping on top of it. Not only did they almost total his car, they also stole thousands of dollars of cameras and photographic gear. Despite it all, Bart got his pictures of the start of the riot and they were published in the *New York Times*. They showed police trying to arrest a man while a large hostile crowd surged around them.

Bart was out of commission for a few days, but was back here in Simi Valley with cameras strapped around his neck, covering the news.

There were many heroes among the cameramen and reporters who covered the riots. Many were beaten, had their cameras stolen, vehicles damaged, rocks and bottles thrown at them. But there were no fatalities. The Greater Los Angeles Press Club saluted all of the joournalists who covered the riots during the burning, looting and vandalizing. At its 1992 Headliners dinner, it honored "The Media 500," those members of the news media who survived the Los Angeles riots.

At least three of the helicopters that flew over the fires and rioting were hit by gunfire. The KCOP and KNBC copters had bullet holes in their fuselage and my copter was nicked in the rotor blades by a bullet from the ground.

Los Angeles still lives with the scars of the worst uprising in this country since the Civil War. The charred debris from the fires has now been cleared, but many empty lots remain. Bare, upright, exterior walls still stand, constant reminders of the days of fury. Fifty-three people died in the violence, more than 600 buildings burned and damage to the city was over $1 billion. It will take a long time for the heart and spirit of Los Angeles to recover.

This riot would have been incomprehensible to people of Los Angeles in the 1930s or 1940s. They could understand the possibility of a Japanese air raid over Los Angeles, but could not imagine the people of Los Angeles rioting. In fact most of us in 1992 were shell-shocked by what happened. The world has changed dramatically in those five decades. What we are today is far different from those innocent pre-war years when radio dominated our leisure time and television was just a dream.

Some of the Chambers family guest on Skipper Frank's Cartoon Carousel in 1957. Stan Jr. and brother David are sitting front row center with daughter Beverly wearing bunny ears behind them. Baby Nancy is on her father's lap.

Dick Lane, one of L.A. television's first major stars, covering the Tournament of Roses Parade in 1952.

Stan Chambers in his only motion picture role as a KTLA reporter in *The Return of the Amazing Colossal Man* in 1958.

In 1952, KTLA cameras were ten miles from ground-zero when the A-bomb tests were televised from the Nevada desert.

In 1954, Chambers was emcee of "Frosty Frolics," a weekly musical ice show televised from the Winter Garden in Pasadena.

Vice President-elect Richard Nixon and wife Pat being interviewed at the 1953 Rose Parade. Nixon was Grand Marshall in 1959 and 1960.

In 1958, final preparations for the first flight of the KTLA telecopter were underway. Chief engineer John Silva, designer and builder, is at left.

In August 1965, the first fires of the Watts Riots were televised live from the KTLA telecopter. This photo was shot by cameraman Harold Morby while reporter-pilot Larry Scheer broadcast the startling events.

A helicopter hovers over a major oil refinery blaze in El Segundo, 1967.

Flood waters burst out of the mountains washing out bridges in the Sunland-Tujunga
flood area during a storm in 1969.

Freeway bridges near Newhall Pass destroyed in the 1971 San Fernando-Sylmar earthquake. Photo by Harold Morby.

Chambers is frequently on the air moments after reaching the scene of a breaking news story, as he was in this 1989 bus accident.

In 1979 Walter Cronkite was the main speaker at the Sigma Delta Chi dinner when Stan Chambers was named "Broadcaster of the Year."

With Pope John Paul II at the Vatican in 1987 as part of an hour-long special on the life of the Pope. It was shown on KTLA during the Pope's visit to Los Angeles and later became a video release.

Fire rages behind Chambers in this 1993 brush fire near Claremont.

The KTLA "News at Ten" team in 1990. Anchors Hal Fishman and Jann Carl in front. Stan Chambers, Larry McCormick and sportscaster Stu Nahan in back.

2.

THE THIRTIES AND FORTIES:
DEPRESSION DAYS, RADIO DAYS

I grew up in the mid-Wilshire section of Los Angeles, attending St. Brendan's Grammar School during the 1930s and graduating from Loyola High School in 1941. I hardly remember my father, who died when I was four years old. My mother raised my brother Dave and me, working as an extra and actress in the motion picture industry. I remember her waking early in the morning, picking up the telephone and dialing over and over again the busy central casting phone number to see if they had any movie parts for her that day. During those difficult years, extras made $3 a day. The depression kept a choke-hold on the city. Twenty-five dollars a week was a good wage. You could buy a good dinner for under $2. A dollar bill went a long way at the grocery store. Candy bars were three for a dime, coffee five cents a cup, malted milks and hamburgers about a quarter.

We lived in one of those six story, middle-class apartment buildings on one of the streets that cross Wilshire Boulevard. There are dozens of them with grand names like The Asbury Arms, The Langham, The Ambassador Gardens, The Louetta, The Graystone Manor, The Oldfield or The Windsor.

They were wonderful places, with green lawns and patios, recreation rooms and incinerators on every floor where you could toss out your paper trash. Each apartment had a small compartment in the kitchen wall big enough for a garbage can, with a door on the outside wall. As a little boy, I remember opening the door, putting the garbage in and locking it. In the morning, one of the caretakers would open the door accessible from the hallway, take away the garbage and replace it with an empty container. The apartments were completely furnished and painted and carpeted on a regular basis. Of course you had to pay for all of these amenities. The rent was about $25 a month, but that included linens and weekly maid service. However, there were no garages. Few of the residents had cars. To get to work, most took the streetcar or the bus, where tokens were three for a quarter. Taking the bus on Wilshire Boulevard was a real adventure. They were open, double-decker buses where one would climb winding stairs to get topside. The upper deck was breezy and cold in the wintertime, but it offered a beautiful windswept view of the sights of the Boulevard.

I especially enjoyed sitting up there in the open air and looking at the passing sights. My favorite part was when the bus drove through Westlake Park and the lake was on both sides of the street. During the 1930s, part of the lake had been filled in so that Wilshire Boulevard could cut straight through the park and be a direct link from downtown Los Angeles to the Pacific ocean in Santa Monica.

The steeples of Immanuel Presbyterian and other churches dominated theBoulevard. The tower of the art deco Bullocks Wilshire building shared the skyline.

The elegant Ambassador Hotel was the gem of the Boulevard. Vast acres of green lawn facing Wilshire framed the hotel that was set back almost a block from the street. The Ambassador had the famous Coconut Grove, known around the world as one of the favorite night clubs of the reigning movie stars of Hollywood. It had a large movie theater that people in the neighborhood often attended. The hotel had its own post office, zoo, convention hall, tennis courts and swimming pool.

There was a full size driving range just west of the hotel. Riding by on the bus, you could see the golfers polishing up their game with long drives that were always kept in by the towering mesh fences around the range. Across the street and just off the Boulevard was the Chapman Park Hotel. It had been the headquarters for the women athletes who competed in the 1932 Los Angeles Olympic Games.

At Mariposa and Wilshire across from the Ambassador, was the showroom for the sleek sportscars, the Auburn and the Cord. They were the rage for those who could afford them. On the second floor, above the showroom, were the broadcast studios of radio station KFAC. This is where I made my radio debut. In 1937, my teacher at St. Brendan's, Mrs. Avis, produced a weekly children's program and used her students as the actors. About a dozen of us would go over to KFAC and perform in various children's dramas. It was an exciting experience for us to be on the radio and have our parents tell us how good we were. The thing I remember most vividly was clipping the pages of my script onto pieces of cardboard, just before air time. I would carefully put paper clips on all four edges of the script, affixing the pages to the cardboard so that the paper wouldn't rattle while we were reading our parts during our live broadcasts. I was able to play many different characters during its semester run.

Local radio was diversified in those years. I was entranced with all of the radio equipment, the studios and the grown-ups who had regular jobs there.

I remember a sportscaster sitting in a small announce booth in the KFAC studio and broadcasting baseball games that were being played hundreds of miles away. All he had was a teletype machine.

Someone at the park sent him a pitch-by-pitch account of the game, on the teletype. The sportscaster had small scraps of paper with the basic facts, but he had to enhance the game to keep the audience interested. The snap of the bat, the well-hit ball and the sounds of the fans were all re-created for the listener. In the booth, he had a baseball and bat to smack together when someone got a hit and a sound effects record of cheering crowds to capture the excitement of the game. Ronald Reagan was probably the most famous sportscaster who re-created the games. The future President was doing games in the Midwest, about the same time the KFAC sportscaster was capturing the sounds of home runs in Los Angeles and bringing baseball fans realistic descriptions of all their games. I always thought that would be a great job.

Since he re-created real games, I used to re-create imaginary ones. I cut out cardboard racing cars and pushed them around a racetrack on my carpet and announced the races. If radio broadcasters could re-create sports events, so could I.

I had my radio turned on every night. I had my school work arranged so that I could listen to the shows and do my homework during the commercials. "Jack Benny," "Bing Crosby," "Inner Sanctum," "Fred Waring," "Jack Armstrong, The All American Boy," "One Man's Family," "Amos and Andy" and countless other broadcasts like the "Richfield Reporter," "Walter Winchell," and "Your Hit Parade" were there to help me do my homework every week.

I enjoyed public speaking at Loyola High School. My speech teacher, Father Doyle, was a rigid taskmaster who insisted that we memorize everything and, most of all, pronounce distinctly every syllable of every word when reciting before the class. This was followed by more speech classes at Loyola University. I wrote a column for the school newspaper, but never considered journalism as a possible career.

The big change came when I joined the Navy's officer training program and was transferred to USC for my senior year. We were encouraged to take various electives in addition to our regular courses. I took advantage of the opportunity and appeared in a couple of college plays. It opened a new world to me and I relished the challenge of the stage and the pressures of performing. The smell of the ropes and curtains, of stored props and mothballed costumes, still triggers memories of that backstage world I had become a part of. It opened so many other worlds.

It was my first experience with scripts, blocking of scenes and memorization of lines. I especially enjoyed the rapport between cast members and the enthusiasm all of them showed as we went through rehearsals in the weeks before opening night. The experience was a taste of make-believe that stayed with me during my Navy years.

I remember that June morning in 1944 when all of my newly graduated classmates from USC assembled at Union Station in downtown Los Angeles for a coast-to-coast train ride to Pre-Midshipmen School at Asbury Park, New Jersey.

We lined up in the large north patio of the newly constructed station. It was teeming with servicemen and families as we answered roll call and prepared to board the troop train.

A railroad station during the war was always the busiest place in the city. Nearly everyone was in uniform and each had his orders close at hand. There were duffle bags and suitcases stacked everywhere and a continual ebb and flow as servicemen arrived or said good-bye. This was the closest contact with wartime realities that families would experience. It was that moment when their sons actually marched through the heavy gates of Union Depot to their troop trains beyond. It was the final good-bye. The excitement of the moment would soon pass and their sons would be gone.

I still remember the excitement, the bewilderment and the taste of adventure as we finally moved through the long passenger tunnel to our tracks, marched up the narrow ramp through steam-spewing trains on all sides and slowly boarded the reconfigured troop train with crowded bunks from floor to ceiling. It was a long, uncomfortable, five-day train ride to Asbury Park. The Navy had taken over two large seaside hotels that were formerly filled with summer vacationers. Now they were packed with hundreds of apprentice seamen waiting for their next orders to Midshipmen's school.

Classes started the next day. For all practical purposes, we were whipped into the regimen of Midshipmen. We were going to be "90-day wonders," ensigns by the end of the year.

I received orders to Columbia University in New York City. The mid-city campus was ideal. The student dormitory towers were well equipped to handle the constant influx of trainees from across the country. We were caught up in the training system from the first day.

I remember one night, climbing into bed, completely exhausted, hardly able to move and telling myself that there was no way I could repeat tomorrow what I had been through today. I think all of us felt that way, but somehow most of us survived the incessant drilling, lengthy classes, frequent inspections and a scattering of demerits.

As we moved closer to graduation, officers talked to us about possible assignments. One night, a training officer just back from the South Pacific spoke to us about becoming fighter directors." He said there was a great demand out there. A fighter director would land on an island in a rubberized boat. He would have portable radio equipment with him and try to find a high vantage point where he could see how the guns from navy ships were doing against specific targets. He would have radio contact to help direct the fire.

Looking back, I find it hard to believe, but I volunteered to be trained as a Fighter Director. Upon graduation, I received orders to report to Gulfport,

Mississippi for Aircraft Recognition School. This was the first step of training. It consisted mostly of spending hours each day before a slide projector as various Japanese planes were flashed on and off the screen. The class would sit there and watch the small dots that were enemy aircraft and try to identify them. After several weeks, I became rather proficient.

In August, 1945, the country was startled to hear that a new powerful atom bomb had been dropped on Hiroshima, Japan. It would probably mean the end of the war. When the second bomb was dropped over Nagasaki, the end was at hand. I remember the boisterous, exuberant, jubilant V-J day demonstration down the streets of Gulfport. It had happened so fast, I couldn't believe that the war was really over.

My orders changed within a couple of weeks: instead of "Fighter Directors School" in Hollywood, Florida, I was shipped to Newport, Rhode Island, to train new crews being assigned to their new ships.

I knew little more than the new sailors, but I always tried to stay a few pages ahead of them. We took our crews on training vessels on the high, wind-swept seas off Newport. They were all uncomfortable adventures, but gave each of us a taste of what was ahead. The war was over, but there was still much to be done.

After only a few months at Newport, I received new orders to go to the Naval Training Station at Bainbridge, Maryland, and I was assigned to the Naval Academy Pre-Midshipmen's School. Our assignment was to train sailors from the fleet who were selected to attend the Naval Academy at Anapolis. We offered a refresher course for the candidates and helped prepare them for admission to the Academy.

I taught American History to the new students. The school had a rolling, tree-lined campus in the woods above the Susquehanna River. Its academic atmosphere was perfect for the pre-midshipmen. The campus was separate from the Navy Base. There were a half dozen magnificent, old federal style buildings surrounding a grass playing field in the center of campus. All of the classes were held in these pillared, southern style school buildings that were, at one time, the classrooms of the Tome Academy, an exclusive boys school near Port Deposit, Maryland.

There were a couple dozen young ensigns on the faculty. All of us enjoyed being back on a college campus once again. In our spare time, we played football and baseball, went sailing, hiking and spent time on the tennis courts.

One of my good friends was Ed Murtaugh from Harvard. He was a supply officer on the base and a good baseball player. After one of our games on the picturesque field on campus, we were talking about what we would do when we got out of the service. Ed's dad was a lawyer and he hoped to follow in his footsteps at Harvard. My mind was far from being made up. I told Ed of visiting a radio station in New Haven while I was there to see a Yale football game a few weeks ago. I told him how intrigued I was with the news operation. Ed seemed to understand my interest.

"I have a new unit that would be great for you, Stan. It's a wire recorder. You could practice your news broadcasting on it." I had never heard of a wire recorder. I only knew that you could record on records.

"It is something new that I have in the office," he went on. "You talk into it and it records your voice on a spool of thin wire. You can record over it as many times as you like. Come on over to my office later tonight and I'll show it to you."

I took Ed up on his offer. Several nights a week I would bring a copy of the *Wall Street Journal* over to his office and practice reading the news into the microphone of his wire recorder.

Wire recorders didn't last long. They were soon replaced by tape recorders, but that experience in Ed Murtaugh's supply office gave me a direction that I followed after I got out of the Navy.

*   *   *

It was an exciting adventure to be in college in the late 1940s. Lives were starting all over again. Servicemen threw their discharge papers into dresser drawers and stuffed their uniforms into duffle bags forever. Most of them became civilians with great enthusiasm and hope for the future.

Just being on campus buoyed our spirits. There was emotion, a rush, a zeal that permeated the ivy covered walls and rolling hills of colleges all over the country. The war was a thing of the past. All of the rigidity and restraints of the war years were broken. Dreams and opportunities could now become realities.

Jobs weren't on our mind in those days. Getting started and getting ahead were. The GI Bill enabled hundreds of thousands of veterans to go to college without cost. This grand concept in social engineering was, perhaps, the most successful welfare project in the history of the world.

Congress channeled these new forces to the college campuses and gave the returning veterans a domestic Marshall Plan that helped get them started. And start they did!

Men, who had looked forward to returning to their jobs at the corner drug store, market or gas station, now saw possibilities they never dreamed existed. They became the new breed of college men who had caught the gold ring. They could chase careers and reach goals unheard of by their parents. This generation would revitalize and change America forever.

Old social bonds had been broken during the war years. The military camps, the traveling, the fighting, the camaraderie and the dying molded this new generation that would not be content with what was.

They would leave the campuses trained, educated and motivated. They met the challenge of a career with a fervor few generations have mustered.

The new freedom of the campus was easy after years of the military. The change was invigorating, a time of a great revival for the individual. The soldier, who had grown tired of being just a number and a member of a squad, became his own master, judge and trailblazer.

The new soldier-students enjoyed the luxury of being able to spend hour after hour with the poets and teachers of ancient Greece, with the thinkers of the Middle Ages, with the scientists of the Age of Realism. They had time to make the transition from soldier to student.

Teachers were overwhelmed with the motivation and learning ability of the new breed. Learning was not a toy, an interim between high school and work. It was a calling, a life-style and an opportunity for these new students.

Money from the GI Bill gave the veteran an entirely new independence. There was enough cash to pay the rent and bills, even to buy a car. Money was available to all of those veterans who had agreed to accept the challenge of college. The system was not designed as a hand-out, but it was an incentive to help veterans get back into the mainstream and make the smooth transition to being a civilian once again.

They brought with them the know-how and practicality that they had demonstrated so vividly in the service. They were no wild, bored, young high school freshman going to college because it was the thing to do. These veterans were mature men who knew where they had been and where they were going. Most of them made their mark. The GI Bill made it possible.

I was swept up into this creative atmosphere. Of course, at the time, I was not aware of the unique situation and the changes it was brewing.

I remember, vividly, the great number of engineering students on the USC campus. They always carried their bulky drafting boards and slide rules as they strode from class to class. I wondered how so many engineers could find jobs when they graduated.

I recall looking out of a fourth story window of the Student Union building at the ebb and flow of the stream of students passing below. I felt a surge of contentment, an emotion of reassuring warmth, knowing I was a part of their parade. It was a buoyant fulfillment knowing that I belonged to the group. Each person down there had his own world to conquer and I, somehow, shared vicariously in the adventure. There was nothing I enjoyed more on campus than being a part of what was around me.

I ran down the steps with a zestful bounce through the bookstore on the first floor, then out the door. I glanced at the shading sycamore trees above the lush, green park around Doheny Library across the street. If I hurried, I still had time before class for an English muffin and a cup of coffee at The Horse, our favorite hangout a block up the street. The world was never more beautiful. Registration for classes was set for tomorrow. Although I hadn't made up my mind completely, I thought law school was my best bet. Under the GI Bill, I could sign up for almost anything, so why not law? Bridge Hall was just down the street behind me at the south end of the campus, Exposition Park and the Coliseum just beyond. I found a counter seat, but The Horse filled up quickly a few minutes later. All the conversation seemed to focus on registration. Catalogues and notebooks were still being scanned, although everyone seemed to have made up his mind about the courses. I told everyone I was going to try Law. I got encouragement and it helped me make up my wavering mind— Law School. I'd register first thing in the morning.

Registration day is always a chaotic time. I never cared for chaos, especially if I could avoid it. As I walked down busy University Avenue, past the cool shade of Doheny Library, I saw a long line ahead of me at Bridge Hall. It looked ominous and strange. I stared at the students standing in single file. The line poured out of the front door and wrapped around the outside of the building. As I walking by the Hancock Science Building, I began to understand that the line was going through the front door of the Law School. It hit me hard and I felt a surge of anger, a feeling that I had, somehow, been betrayed.

One of the promises I made to myself after getting out of the Navy was never to stand in another line. In the service it was always, "Hurry up and wait." I had done that for the last time. I made a quick, illogical, but final command decision. The line was too long. I didn't need it. My law career stopped before it even began.

I wasn't especially bitter, but I felt I had been cast adrift by the system. I was pensive as I walked around the campus, past the old buildings and the newer ones under construction. The quiet, small campus I remembered from before the Navy had changed considerably and I knew I had to change with it. But that didn't mean I had to stand in long lines. I was reassured when I saw one of the old Victorian buildings on a side street. It had been there since the 1890s and had not been taken care of since it was built. It bore a small makeshift sign saying, "KUSC-FM." After what I had been through, the idea of majoring in Radio seemed interesting. I went in, met Dr. William Sener and decided this might be for me.

In the end, I hedged my bet by minoring in Radio Broadcasting and working on a Masters in History.

At USC, I realized the best job was something you did because you liked it, a complete change of form for me. It became a guideline I followed from then on.

The radio classes were exciting. They were like workshops. We read scripts, broadcast over microphones, produced radio plays and were immersed in the basics of the profession.

USC brought the professional radio world into the classroom. Los Angeles was the radio production center of the nation; professionals from the industry taught our courses. Our teachers were the men and women who wrote, produced, acted and announced the programs we listened to nightly. Radio was still the major source of entertainment for most people across the country. Television was practically unknown.

These instructors were celebrities who had successful careers and were great role models. They helped many USC students bridge the gap from the college campus to the professional broadcast world.

Art Gilmore was one of these outstanding professionals. He was one of the best announcers in the business. His voice was known to everyone. All of his students were impressed by his human qualities. He really cared about us. He always had a smile in his voice. He never told jokes, but he always captivated the students by what he said and how he said it. He was tall, thin and imposing, and impeccably dressed, but completely friendly. He shared his expertise and insights. Students were impressed that, despite his busy schedule, he found time to teach these courses. He was the perfect blend of master teacher and industry professional.

The turning point in my student career came when Art Gilmore told me he thought I had the ability to make it in radio. You can imagine my reaction. Here was the best in the business telling me I had a chance. I was taking his courses because they were fun and I enjoyed being in them. I never expected to get a job because of them.

That one conversation with a great teacher changed my entire outlook. I took his advice and decided to aim for broadcasting as a career, something I enjoyed doing. I no longer worried about getting a job to make a living. I now worried about getting a job that would make me happy.

I distinctly remember being in a KUSC broadcast studio one night listening to the talk show, "Tonight in Los Angeles." They were talking about one of the local television channels, W6XYZ, expanding its broadcasting schedule from two to six nights a week. I didn't even know there were stations on the air in 1946, but I thought this would be an excellent time for me to come up with some program ideas for television.

I called KTLA from a phone booth next to the old Capitol Records Building at Sunset and Vine, just across from the old NBC Studios. I talked to Gordon Wright, the Program Director. I was surprised when he showed some interest, but he told me he was too busy to talk because this was T-Day. It was a big television promotion geared to KTLA's expansion to 28 hours of broadcasting each week. He asked me to call back later.

I did not realize it at the time, but this was only six weeks after KTLA had become a commercial station. The door was open slightly and I made my first overture to television.

Gordon Wright and I had a meeting a few days later over coffee and bran muffins at Oblath's Restaurant next to KTLA, and we worked over the idea for the broadcast. He suggested that we plan just one show for the moment and then see how it went.

My idea was to use an issue of *Campus Magazine* that I helped publish at

USC. The first shot would be the cover girl from UCLA as she appeared on *Campus Magazine*; then we would dissolve to her live in the studio. We would do an interview with the star UCLA basketball player, Don Barksdale, who was featured in the sports section of the magazine. There were some comedy articles about campus life in the issue. We would rewrite them, so we could put some humorous skits in the show. We went over the magazine page by page until we formatted the first broadcast of "Campus Magazine."

About 20 USC students who worked with the radio station or were connected with the magazine got involved in the whirlwind of rehearsals and deadlines to produce the half hour show on April 3, 1947. When the show was over, there was no doubt in my mind that I wanted to get into television.

By late 1947, KTLA had increased its programming schedule to 35 hours a week and the staff was being increased. Gordon Wright remembered his USC magazine friend and called to see if I wanted to take a full time job in television. I started at KTLA on December 1, 1947.

*   *   *

Los Angeles was a different city in 1947. You could buy a brand new Ford for $1,700. The home of your dreams was waiting for you, with no down payment, in the undeveloped San Fernando Valley for $12,000. The interest on your home loan would be 4%. That same home would cost you over $200,000 today.

Thousands of GIs who passed through here on the way to the Pacific during the war liked what they saw and decided to move in. The big population boom was about to change Southern California. We still had a light rail rapid transit system in those years, but fewer people were riding it. Freeways were mostly on the planning boards. But many exciting things were about to happen.

In 1947 we were still five years away from having jet airliners to travel on and 10 years from having color television. It was before videotape, hand calculators, and other miniaturization that has revolutionized our time. It was before the Beatles, Presley and Michael Jackson, before the electronics industry and expensive gasoline. Computers were bulky adding machines, the Dodgers were in Brooklyn and the Giants in New York. Many felt it was only a matter of time before New York Governor Thomas Dewey would become the next President of the United States.

Developers were just starting to build homes in the suburbs, complete with such new household conviences as garbage disposals and air conditioning. Because Los Angeles was earthquake country, no high rise buildings had been built here. It was before heart pacemakers and heart transplants. Passenger trains ran on time. Clark Gable was still king and people went to the movies twice a week.

Some newsreels and news programs appeared on television. One Los Angeles station ran an ad promising film of news events within 48 hours of their happening. The ad further stated, "It scoops even first-run newsreels in movie houses."

This was before live television broadcasts could be transmitted from New York to Los Angeles.

It took almost two years from the time KTLA went on the air before all seven Los Angeles stations were broadcasting commercially. In those days, it was not unusual for most stations to be on only five days a week. Program logs showed notations, "No Saturday programming on KNBH, no Thursday programs on KTTV and no Tuesday broadcasting on KTSL."

This was the world of television when I entered. I took the job just for fun. I thought it would be an interesting interlude until I found a real position.

3.

THE FORTIES:
I BECOME A NEWS ANNOUNCER

I remember the first day I reported to work. I slowly opened the battered door of the old garage that had become a television station. It still looked like an empty garage when I walked in. The weather-beaten, wooden rafters were hung with studio lights. The cavernous building was one big open stage. At the far end, I saw studio curtains hanging from the tall ceiling to the bare wood floor below. I guessed that I would be working back in there.

I enjoyed the idea that anyone could open the front door and walk in. I put my hand on the back of a folding chair just inside the door. Several rows of them were set up for audiences. I looked around at the sets and props stored around the stage area, at the two big lumbering cameras connected to the control room by large cables that snaked across the floor.

I liked the feel of the place. I felt very comfortable standing in the big open garage. It became my second home. I spent more time here than anywhere else. I was originally hired to work for Gordon Wright in production. That was my primary job, but the list of things that had to be done was so long, production soon became just another task.

I would usually start on the routine sheets for the evening broadcast when I arrived in the morning. It was the run-down that gave all the information needed to program the evening telecasts. It listed all the films, slides, commercials, studios, performers and everything else that anyone had to know to put that evening's entertainment on the air.

It was always changing, so I spent a good part of the day checking details and rewriting the routine, which I would mimeograph and distribute to everyone.

There were phone calls, letters to open, visitors to talk to, props to order, errands to run, coffee breaks at Oblath's Restaurant next door and the necessity of keeping my eyes on the changing patterns each day. I would then spend part of the afternoon working with the stage crew helping Jerry Madden get the shows ready for the evening. We usually had one major set each night. All of them were built in the same area. One evening we would bring in bales of hay, scatter straw about the set, and construct a corral fence that had to be sturdy and well-braced for Cottonseed Clark and his western songs for that night.

Lois Andrews needed a living room set for her Hollywood reports. It was easy to put together, just furniture, a rug, some flowers and lamps. Joan Barton required a whole night club for her show. Risers had to be brought in and assembled to create areas of the club at different levels. There were night club chairs, tables, and dinnerware. Carpets had to be laid, wall decorations put in place and railings anchored firmly to the temporary steps. You had to know what you were doing. I was never good at assembling jigsaw puzzles, nor these complicated sets. One day my new boss, Klaus Landsberg, raced onto the set and told Jerry and the other crew members that they had to immediately go with him to Pasadena to solve some big problem that had developed at the Rose Parade.

"Stan, it looks as if this will be up to you," Jerry said, knowing how inept I felt. "Can you handle it?"

"Sure," I answered gamely.

After Jerry left, I stood in the middle of the empty garage with the props all around me and a deadline over my shoulder. There was no plan or pattern. I had helped put the set together three times before and memory was my only guide.

As I juggled the various wooden risers into place, I felt that urge to run away. I couldn't believe that everyone had left me, that I was completely alone. It was what might be euphemistically called, "a learning experience." The main thing I learned: remote broadcasts take precedent over studio shows. The next thing I learned: no matter who you are or what you know, or how little experience you have, you were expected to do everything and you had better do it well.

I put all the building blocks together, only to find I had several pieces left over. But the set did look a little like the night club I remembered, and somehow the show got on the air without criticism.

A few weeks later, I was given my first real chance at being a broadcast newsman. But my television career was almost derailed before it could be put on the tracks. The villain was the old iconoscope camera that evolved from the first television patent filed by the German inventor Paul Nipkow back in 1884.

The control room was busy. An interview program was on the air. The director spoke softly into a small microphone giving the cameramen their cues. All the crew members had headsets. The cameramen moved their bulky cameras to their predetermined spots.

There was a small cluster of engineers around a monitor that had a close up picture of Stan Chambers' face on it. They were perplexed. "Why do they look so funny?" One engineer asked.

"Strange," another added.

"Kissable," chuckled another as he twisted a few control room dials.

Klaus walked out of the control room, opened the door leading to the studio just wide enough to stick his head through the opening. He carefully looked at the young announcer's face.

"Looks okay here," he mumbled.

He stood motionless for a while, then opened the door wide and walked onto the set. He studied the announcer's lips as he went through his interview with members of the Australian polo team. Then, Klaus briskly walked back to the control room and, once again, carefully examined a TV receiver.

"He looks fine on stage, but his lips look like Betty Boop's on the monitor."

"He does have deep indentations at the end of both sides of his mouth," another said as he peered into the monitor.

"These old cameras do strange things, but that is the first time I've ever seen that," said another.

"That's too bad. He wants to be on the air and these interviews would be good for him to do," Klaus said.

"There must be some adjustment or something we could do to correct it," said the engineer twisting the dials.

"We'll have the new image orthicon cameras next month," Klaus said, "They could make a difference."

"Those lips are sure strange looking!" another engineer joined in.

"I'll just have to keep him off the air until then," Klaus sighed. "His voice is too high, anyway, too young sounding. That's the trouble with these young people just out of school. They need more experience."

The new image orthicon cameras were in use by the time I had a chance to do another interview show. They saved me from looking like the cartoon character with the big beautiful lips. The wonders of science developed a camera just in time to give me more life-like lips and a chance for a television career.

But Klaus was still concerned about my high-pitched voice. At one point a few weeks later, the order was that I was not to be used as announcer. It was all right for me to be seen on camera, but I could not be just a voice over the air. So, apart from the way I looked on camera and the way I sounded over a microphone, it was a start.

Keith Hetherington, who was our only regular announcer, knew I wanted to work in the announce booth and he always tried to help me. Often, when a long movie was running and the sign-off time would be after midnight, he would let me take his place, so he could go home early. I did it from time to time, after long hours on the stage crew. It was so late at night, Klaus never seemed to object. Gradually, I worked my way back onto the announcing schedule.

For everyone working at the station in those early days, the end of the normal working day meant you would get ready for the broadcast day. All of the department heads would take off their business jackets, leave on their ties and take on one of the stage crew jobs. Members of the real crew were the cameramen, but the daytime executives would push the dollies, run the mike boom, move the lights, bring in the props and help set up the various scenes. I was always impressed with the way they made the transformation from executives to crew members. They still maintained the authority they carried with them during the daytime operation. But while the shows were on, they were just crew members. Only their ties flagged them as being different.

I enjoyed working on the crew, but I always feared that might be where I would end up. As our staff expanded, the executives were replaced by new employees on the crew. It wasn't long before we had crew members who did nothing but work on stage and put on shows. I was still there working with them part time.

I took a lead from the executives. I not only kept wearing a tie, but I kept my suit coat on. I thought this might remind people that I wanted to be in front of the camera and not behind them. My job during the day required that I dress like the executives, so I just kept the same dress for my part-time chores on the stagecrew.

No matter how dirty the assignment, I always had my dark suit. I could swing a hammer and carry flats, but I always had my suit and tie. My plan evidently worked. I was transferred to the film and slide department.

The new job blended nicely with my production and operations assignments on the daytime schedule and gave me a chance to be on-the-air at night. As I pulled out all the slides for the evening broadcast and put them in order, I reflected that my dark suit was more acceptable in the film and slide room than on the stage. The new job lasted only briefly. Commercials were becoming important to the station and I was moved into the sales department. Paradoxically, as I no longer had crew duties at night, my career as a television announcer blossomed.

When I started in 1947, newscasts were fifteen minutes or less. The studio cameras were the only ones we had. No recording equipment was available. Videotape had yet to be invented. There were no news crews for local film coverage, no editors, news film cameramen, soundmen or reporters.

KTLA's newscaster in those early years was Gilbert Martyn, a respected broadcaster who had been with NBC Network News for many years. He was also the voice of the Paramount Newsreel. Gil was tall, dark and dignified. If you were a casting director, he would be your first choice for a role as a television newscaster. His voice was resonant, powerful and familiar to his audience. He was a polished ad-libber and always made things flow smoothly when he was on the air. He was even receptive to the new changes triggered by commercial television.

Rancho Soups sponsored his nightly news report. Since we were now a commercial station, we considered it a prestigious accomplishment to have a fully sponsored newscast. When the soup commercial was being developed, it seemed logical that Gil Martyn should do it.

News purists would be shocked today if the anchorman stopped reading the news, picked up a spoon, sipped some hot soup, did the commercial and then went back to his news report. Hard as it is to believe, it made good sense to us back in 1948. The soup tasting was a central part of the commercial every night.

Gil had the dramatic flair of the newsreel announcer. Newsreels were still the main source of our visual news. People went to their local movie theaters a couple times a week. The newsreel, with the short subject and the cartoon, was as important to us as the feature film.

The new television news program was a blend of the pictures from news-reels and voices from radio. Yet, it was more than radio with pictures and far more up-to-the-minute than the weekly newsreels people had become accustomed to. We scored music over various news stories just the way the news-reels did. A sound engineer had several acetate records with various record-ings of mood music on his round tables. He selected the appropriate back-ground music for the news stories of floods, wars and light features seen on the broadcasts.

Our only source of newsfilm was Hearst Metrotone News. One of my jobs was to help unravel the film clips of stories. It was always difficult to update a two-day-old piece of film and make it appear timely. Most of the film was silent. The quality of sound stories was very poor. The optical sound strip on news film in those days was difficult to copy. Every time a print was made from it, it lost quality. By the time it got to the West Coast, it was difficult to understand what the person was saying. So we'd use the footage silent and Gil narrated over it.

There were pictures of important people arriving or departing, heads of state making speeches or reviewing troops. There were horse races and beauty contests, hurricanes, flood damage and assorted light features. In those days, newscasts were routine and were not expected to give the station big ratings. We presented the news because it was our duty to our viewers and the Federal Communications Commission. We did not do it to build big audiences.

In the newsroom, there were desks for Jon Rice, Dick Kusink and Gil Martyn, three news wire machines, two typewriters and a few files. There was also an interesting vintage printer that looked as if it belonged in a stockbroker's office, many years ago. One of my jobs was to try to make it work. The news department was responsible for the "sign-on" news each afternoon. KTLA programming always began with a test pattern and background music. To make the static test pattern more visual, KTLA presented a news summary that viewers could read while they listened to the music and got ready for the television programming that night.

News of the day moved across the bottom of the screen in the manner of the famous moving news headlines on the outside of the New York Times building at Times Square.

Here is where the old stockbroker's printer did the trick. I remember ripping the latest United Press news summary off the clattering teletype machine, walking over to the printer's old keyboard with well-worn protective rubber cushions on each key, and typing out the news. The archaic typewriter printed its letters on a narrow ribbon of paper that was rolled up like film. I would then rewind it, place it on two rollers, one to feed, the other to pull it across the bottom of the screen. I would carefully place the ribbon in front of a pre-focused camera and the news of the day would be broadcast into hundreds of homes in Los Angeles. It was a makeshift, homemade procedure, but it worked well most of the time.

Occasionally, it would get stuck and just stop on the screen. At other times the paper would simply break and the silent newscast would unceremoniously end.

When KTLA News expanded into a "Final Edition" broadcast each night at 11:00, I finally got my chance on the air. The broadcast was a close-up of a talking head. There were no teleprompters. We tried to have as much eye contact with the viewer as possible, but we had to look down at our scripts throughout the broadcast. It was quite a challenge for me.

One day we got a teleprompter and I gave it a try. It was a wooden, podium-like unit, about three feet high and eighteen inches wide, on a pedestal in front of the camera shooting the show. The crew used a heavy stage weight to keep the podium secure on the camera's base. A special typewriter with large letters was used to type the script on rolls of teletype paper about the size of rolls of paper towels. The finished script, fifty feet long, would be tightly rolled up and wrapped around the wooden rollers at the bottom of the teleprompter unit. The top would be just under the camera lens. Then, it would be taped to the top roller. The trick was to place the top line as close to the camera lens as possible so that it looked as if the broadcaster were looking right into the camera lens. When I went on the air, a member of the stagecrew would stand next to the camera and carefully pull up the rolled paper as I read from my script. Since it was manually moved up, I always knew there was the danger of the paper jamming, tearing or wrinkling at a bad angle for reading. Or the chance that the operator would get lost and not be able to find the place in the script that I was trying to read. I was terrified, but after the first couple of times I could see it helped create the "eye contact" that is so important in news broadcasting today.

Another early news show I was lucky enough to get on was "Eyewitness." It followed Gil Martyn's news every night and it usually featured live interviews with people involved in the day's news. The difficulty was in getting newsmakers to drive to the studio at night to be interviewed live. Most of them had never heard of the program and a lot of them did not want to talk about their involvement in the news. We would try to get policemen investigating crimes, firemen who had been involved in major fires of that day, lawyers with cases in court, local politicians, city officials and private citizens who happened to be eyewitnesses to events.

It never occurred to me, then, that one day we would have our own cameraman, soundman and reporters shooting newsfilm for our evening newscasts.

*   *   *

By 1948, young GIs just home from the war and their brides began to save enough money to buy one of those new television sets. The new ten-inch screens started showing up in more and more living rooms. When the baby boom hit, television became an intimate part of their lives.

People stopped going to the movies. They ate TV dinners on trays in front of their new sets. It was the baby sitter and the entertainment center. People were moving to Southern California by the hundreds of thousands and more and more of them were making television a big part of their lives.

The first television family on the block probably bought a new set for under $500. It would change old, familiar life styles. Now, the new owners would get to know more neighbors, who would flock over to see the special programs. Serving snack food and cold drinks became a vital part of the TV viewing habit. Dinner schedules were changed so there would be no conflict with favorite shows. Programs were limited at first. There were old movies, many of them British. None of the major studios would release their feature films to television.

There were short subjects that had played in movie houses years before, as well as cartoons, old western features and kinescopes from New York.

As new television stations came on the air, they developed their own local, live programs. The hosts of these shows quickly developed into well known television personalities. Program schedules expanded rapidly.

Hollywood had the performers and entertainers for these local shows and it was easy for them to switch over from movies or radio. No one was paid much in those early days. Many were able to take advantage of these television opportunities because they had other, better paying jobs to fall back on.

We all learned to laugh at the unusual things we learned to live with every day. I was surprised to discover that despite the tremendous heat on the sound stage, there was no air conditioning for the crew and the performers. The only air conditioning at the station was in the control room that housed all of the important electronic equipment that kept the station on the air. You could operate a station with overheated personnel, but not overheated equipment.

I was startled to learn there was only one bathroom at the station for everyone to use. It was only a temporary arrangement with the city to give us a chance to get relocated, but it took a couple of years before we had the luxury of both a men's and ladies' rest room.

Our newsroom was a little bigger than a large closet, at the end of a long hall at the back of the old garage building.

City building and safety officials worried about how people could get out of there in case of a fire. They insisted that a door be installed that would permit employees to escape to the street outside. However, the room wasn't large enough for a regular door. It would take up too much space. Much negotiating with the city occurred. Finally, as a temporary measure, officials permitted us to install a horizontal escape hatch that would be opened only in emergencies. It was a drawer-like hatch about four feet wide and about two feet above the floor, installed in the brick wall. If something happened, it could be unlatched, the door would fall open and you could roll out of the room through the chute, one by one, to the safety of the street outside. Fortunately, no one ever had to use the escape mechanism. It was always interesting to show it to visitors touring the studio and watch the unbelieving expression on their faces when you explained what it was.

People got involved in this new television revolution for many different reasons. Young Bud Stefan, just out of the University of Southern California and a Navy lieutenant during the war, was a good example of one who loved the pressure and took the plunge. You were expected to do many different things at KTLA in those early years. Once Bud worked his way up the ladder to become a staff director, he would sit in the control room on those long nights when old films were playing and interrupt them by putting commercial after commercial on the air. In addition, Bud wrote and directed a weekly musical dramatic show for children and wrote and starred in his own comedy show each week.

After the first season in 1949, Bud's "Yer Ole Buddy" was named the best comedy show on the West Coast in a television magazine fan poll. He came out ahead of Arthur Godfrey, Sid Caesar, Paul Winchell and Morey Amsterdam.

KTLA's Shirley Dinsdale was named the most outstanding performer on television that year. She received the first Emmy ever awarded by the Television Academy. She was the pretty college student who might have lived next door. She was the children's favorite baby sitter and everyone liked her. Shirley was a ventriloquist and Judy Splinters was her puppet. But to the children watching television, Judy was a living doll. They were two of television's biggest stars in the early years. They created magic chemistry when they were on the air. Children were enthralled. This was their program and Judy Splinters was their favorite.

KTLA's Mike Stokey, the star of "Pantomime Quiz," also received one of the first Emmys that year. A third person to receive an award that night in 1949 was Klaus Landsberg, manager of KTLA. He could be called the Renaissance man of television and is probably the person whose career captures, most accurately, the pioneering spirit of the early days of television.

Landsberg was a one-man show. Although his main focus was on electronic developments and television transmissions, he ran the programming side as well. In those years of being left alone and being completely independent, he learned everything about running and programming a station.

Less than a month after the station became commercial, there was a tremendous explosion in downtown Los Angeles. A huge blast at an electroplating company on Pico Boulevard leveled many buildings. Engineer Landsberg proved what a newsman he was. He managed to get his large, bulky cameras out of the studio onto a truck and set up a signal from the explosion site. The cameras showed the devastation. Dick Lane and Keith Hetherington interviewed the victims and rescue workers and the station broadcast live the instantaneous news report. Little did we realize that the face of TV news had changed then and there.

A hard driving perfectionist, Landsberg had an enormous capacity for creative work. He demanded the best from his staff and would not settle for less. What he did with television, in the few years from the time it became commercial in 1947 to that fall in 1956 when he died of cancer at the age of 40, has become legendary.

He had a knack for knowing what people wanted to see. He called Los Angeles the biggest hometown in the country and he programmed the station to play to that audience. As the number of people owning television sets grew, his KTLA became the television station of choice for the vast majority.

Landsberg showed his understanding of his audience in 1949 when he dispatched a live television crew to the scene of a dramatic rescue attempt. His decision charted the course that television news would follow.

4.

THE WEEKEND TIME STOOD STILL

In April 1949 I was the emcee of a luncheon at the Biltmore Hotel in downtown Los Angeles. I sat next to the chairperson at the head table and spoke to about a thousand women of B'nai B'rith at this annual celebration in the elegant ballroom. I had finished lunch, given my speech, and had just introduced the featured entertainer for the affair. He had a magnificent baritone voice and held the audience captive. No other sound came from the crowded Biltmore Bowl, just his deep, booming voice that created an awesome mood of enjoyment.

Then the phone began to ring. I couldn't believe it: right in the middle of his song the solitary telephone at the maitre d's table was ringing. No one was near it so it rang for a long time. The head table was at the far end of the room and I sat there listening to it for an embarrassingly long time. The singer was experienced and he never let on that he heard it.

I watched the head waiter finally pick up the phone, look around, put the receiver on his table and then start walking along the side wall of the huge Biltmore Bowl. He appeared to be coming in my direction at the head table. I kept thinking how embarrassing it will be for the person who has to get up and answer that phone.

I watched over my shoulder as he walked behind the other guests seated at the table. He stopped right behind me and said, "It's for you."

I felt the eyes of everyone as I followed him back through the crowd. Then, the song ended and the guests started applauding. That gave me some cover as I walked through the tables with a warm blush on my face.

It was my mother. I felt a surge of emotion when I realized my mother had called me at a time like this. How could she do this to me?

I just said, "Hello," and listened.

"Have you heard about the little girl who fell in the well? The station is sending a remote crew there to televise it. You are to meet them out there." I could tell from the tone of her voice she was excited she found me.

I rushed back to the head table and explained to the luncheon chairman that I had been called by the station to cover a news story in San Marino. She had heard earlier about the little girl falling into the well and was gracious about my leaving. "How are you going to get out there ?" She asked. "I don't know," I answered. "I'll have to make some phone calls. I have to get out there right away."

She turned to her husband sitting next to her, "Can you drive Stan out there?"

In a matter of moments, the two of us were on our way out of the room.

She took over my emcee duties. I could see her picking up the microphone. "Stan Chambers has just been called by the station to cover an emergency news story. Let's wish him well and thank him for being with us today."

The audience gave me a round of applause as I left the Biltmore Bowl for San Marino.

I could make out our two KTLA remote trucks in the middle of a vacant field as we drove around a corner to the rescue site before us. I slammed the car door shut, stepped out into the hot afternoon sun and ran up the dusty, tire-tracked trail leading to the cluster of emergency vehicles.

I approached a circle of men standing around an open hole. It was quite steep. A man huddled deep inside at the bottom as small clumps of dirt and rock from the freshly dug earthen sides pelted him.

It seemed quite dangerous to me; this was a huge excavation about 30 to 40 feet wide and very deep. The man at the bottom was cutting a hole in the side of a pipe protruding from the center.

About a hundred feet beyond I saw our cameramen pulling cables and getting ready to go on the air. Just beyond, next to the television transmission truck, was reporter Bill Welsh.

I ran the rest of the way.

"Just in time, Stan," Bill greeted me. "We'll be going on in about ten minutes."

"What's the story?" I asked.

"This little girl fell into that abandoned water well last night and they have been trying to dig her out ever since."

"Is she alive?"

"Yes. Her mother could hear her crying in the well right after she fell in."

Klaus Landsberg stepped out of the truck with cameraman Jimmy Cassin who was carrying earphones and a microphone.

"You made good time, Stan," Klaus greeted me. "This might be a long one." He barely stopped; too busy making sure that everything was ready to for the broadcast. He hurried off with Jimmy for a last minute check of the cameras beyond.

Bill walked me back to the excavation. "They started working last night digging the hole. It got deeper and deeper, the sides began to slide and dirt kept pouring down on the guys working at the bottom. There is no shoring or anything to protect the men down there." He pointed to the well-casing in the center. "Little Kathy, she's not even four years old and she is stuck somewhere inside of that."

I had a sickening feeling in my stomach.

Bill and I were putting on our headphones and walking into camera position ready to go on the air.

"I'll try to line up some interviews while you go on," I said to Bill as we reached the cameras sitting on tripods in the dusty field.

Cameraman Eddie Reznick waved us back to the truck.

Klaus stood with one foot on the running board and called out, "We're all ready."

Bill and I stopped next to the television transmitting unit with the big letters KTLA on its side.

Klaus jumped up into the truck and sat in the director's chair in front of the control panel with its television monitors. "You have everything you need on the story?" he asked. Bill and I put our heads inside the unit and watched the pictures on the television sets in front of us.

Klaus continued to talk as he peered into the television pictures. "They tried digging that big hole to get to her. That didn't work. They are trying to cut open a window in the side of the well-pipe to see if they can spot the little girl. After that, they're going to stop digging. I'll have these monitors in front of me to see what is going on and I'll tell you over the earphones what the camera is showing and you just describe it."

Bill and I went on the air about the time O.A. Kelley finished cutting into the well pipe with his blow torch. He was able to peer through the window and look down into the dark well below. He yelled to the workers on top, "I think I can see something that looks like a dress, but it is too far down there to be certain. But that's about it. I can't see the little girl."

The sides of the huge opening kept on slipping. Dirt was pouring down in steady streams on Kelley as he kept on working.

"Hey, will you guys stop moving around up there? That loose dirt is going to bury me," he shouted up.

"Let's get out of there, Kelley," someone yelled, "I'm afraid the whole thing might go. Come on up."

It was apparent this phase of the rescue attempt had to be stopped. Faced with the probability of a major cave-in, the plan to reach Kathy through the side of the pipe was abandoned.

Although progress was slow, Bill and I had many things to talk about. Bill would take the mike for a while and I would walk through the crowd of rescue workers trying to find out what new developments were taking place. Then I would take over the announcing and Bill would look for the latest information. It worked well and gave each of us a chance to gather material for our next on-camera session. Everything was constantly evolving. There was always a new problem and several possible solutions to narrate. The story moved slowly, but dramatically, with the distant possibility that Kathy Fiscus could be rescued within a few hours.

Bill and I tried to keep an optimistic tone in our reports. I remember saying over and over again, "Kathy's mother heard her crying in the well right after she fell in. Her rescuers believed that she was unconscious, oblivious to what was going on."

I remember Klaus' shots of firemen turning a crank on a small pump that was forcing air down the pipe to the little girl. I talked about it so much, that when it later was shown on the air, I remained silent and let the picture speak for itself.

When we saw Raymond Hill, an engineer and close friend of the Fiscus family, coming in to take charge of the rescue operation, there was a flurry of activity.

I remember getting a brief account from one of the workers about what was to happen, then saw the plan go into action. A huge earth drilling machine dug a new deep hole, its corkscrew burrowing deep into the ground, pulling up layers of loose dirt, depositing it on the surface, then a huge casing was driven into the earth.

As the circular drill dug into the ground and gouged up dirt, the long steel casing was driven deeper and deeper. It was a big steel pipe. The powerful machines would pile drive it with such force, the earth would shudder and shake each time it made impact.

I recall standing in the dust and dirt, feeling the ground rumble and listening to one of the engineers outlining the plan. "We're going to hammer that casing about a hundred feet into the ground to a point below where Kathy is trapped. We have to get out all of the dirt inside the casing, then go down to the bottom and cut a vertical tunnel across, shore it up with timbers, and try to dig across to the well pipe where we can get her.

It was a brave and dangerous plan. However, it meant that it would be a long time before they could reach Kathy. I broadcast for hours as the huge hammering machine pounded the casing slowly into the ground. Then, the earth drilling machine would be inserted into the casing. Its turning, corkscrew drill would dig deep, pulling up more dirt, making it easier for the pile driver to slam the casing deeper. The operation went on and on.

The news of the rescue attempt was picked up by the wire services and transmitted to major cities all over the country. It became an international incident. Newspapers in Stockholm, London and Australia held the presses for news of Kathy. Radio stations kept bringing the viewers up to date on late developments. Switchboards at newspaper offices and radio stations all over the country were jammed with calls from the moment the child's plight became known.

In Chicago, they said it brought the greatest number of phone calls to the city's newspapers since the end of World War II. The *Dallas News* said it got a "jillion" calls. An operator on the *Salt Lake Tribune* switchboard was quoted as saying, "I haven't seen anything like this since I've been an operator. Even tiny children, almost too young to talk, are calling for news about Kathy."

In Minneapolis, the *Tribune* operator said, "Many callers apparently can't get to sleep until they find out the latest about the little girl."

The switchboard operator for the *Pittsburgh Post-Gazette* said one man told her, "I hope you don't mind if I keep calling you throughout the night. I'm the father of three little ones, and this story about poor Kathy really hit me."

Here in Los Angeles, circus thin men and contortionists were volunteering to be lowered into the hole upside down to try to get her out. The opening was only fourteen inches, but they believed they could go down the pipe, reach her and pull her back up. Plumbers, sandhogs, specialty miners and others with varying experience volunteered to go down head first to get her out.

This was one of the first times a television station cut into a film it was broadcasting, cancelled it and went to the scene of a breaking news story. The "long form" of television news coverage was evolving here in this open field in San Marino.

Although Bill and I didn't know it then, the word that KTLA was telecasting the rescue effort swept the city. Thousands turned their sets on and became involved in the drama unfolding before their eyes.

The actor Don DeFore was in his Beverly Hills home planning to study a script, when he turned on the set to see what was on. His television set stayed on all weekend long, his script was never opened.

J.A. Zeeman, who owned a large chain of men's clothing stores, had finished work for the day and had listened to radio reports about the rescue while he was driving home. When he walked into the house, the television set was showing pictures from the rescue site. He started watching and stayed in front of his set for most of the night and the next day.

Berman Schwartz of Paramount Pictures' legal department had a long weekend planned, but he didn't get to anything on his schedule. Myrtle Chizum and her husband had one of the first television sets in their Sherman Oaks neighborhood. They started watching the telecast Saturday night with some friends who were over for dinner. Neighbors, who had heard of the telecast, began dropping in to visit the Chizums and watch the developments. It wasn't long until their television room was overflowing into the other rooms in the house.

They were part of the hundreds of thousands who became so emotionally involved for more than 27 hours, who watched reverently, silently and prayerfully as the dramatic fight to save Kathy progressed.

I remember holding the microphone in hand, watching the large crowd holding a vigil, talking about time and a city standing still while the rescue effort continued. Several thousands had gathered on an adjacent vacant lot. The field had been enclosed by a chain link fence for many years, so there was no problem with crowd control. People pressed close to the fence as possible, watched the operation and hoped to get word of what progress was being made.

I recall saying this was not the usual curious crowd attracted by fires and accidents. This is a somber gathering of people, oblivious to time, watching the banging pile driver send the steel casing deeper into the ground.

Popular actor Scott Brady was on a date with actress Judy Clark that night. They had been to several spots on the Sunset Strip earlier. Every time they turned on their car radio, there was another report on the effort to reach Kathy Fiscus. They couldn't get her out of their minds. When they heard of the large crowd gathering at the site, they decided to drive to San Marino and join it. I vividly remember talking to them in the crowd that night.

Although many thousands were caught up in the action, what they watched on their television set was not very dramatic. At the center of their 10 inch screen stood a large derrick-like piece of heavy equipment illuminated by banks of bright lights. It would pound on the top of the metal casing being driven slowly into the ground. Bill and I would talk about the countless problems facing the rescuers.

The huge cylinder refuses to budge as the pile driver hammers away. A volunteer in a harness steps to the top of the casing, balances himself on the top and is slowly lowered to the bottom of the casing. He discovers why it won't move. The casing has hit a rock formation. The volunteer chips away at the boulders with a small pick. The casing cannot be lowered farther until the rocks are removed.

Now two men are standing atop the casing, protruding about fifteen feet above the ground. Buckets of rocks and dirt are being hauled up and dumped on the surface. The two men catch the buckets, grab them and empty them in front of the rig, then send them back down for more.

This is the heart of the rescue effort for hours on end. The scene repeats itself over and over.

Yet viewers watched every moment throughout the night. Mrs. W.C. Young of Los Angeles called the station early Sunday morning to report that 191 buckets of dirt had been hauled up by the rescue crew.

Bright klieg lights from the movie studios ring the rescue area and make it seem like daylight. Off in the shadows, firemen continually turn a hand pump that sends warm air into the tiny well opening and down to Kathy Fiscus. The pump is hand-turned by many volunteers, but it never stops. There is always a continual flow of air into the well.

Off to the sides are many others who have taken part in the rescue attempt. I described them, resting on cots, sipping coffee and waiting for the moment when they can actively help again.

Surrounding the center of activity are the steel arms of a half dozen cranes, derricks and other heavy equipment brought to the scene at no charge, a visible reminder of how the city was doing everything to rescue the little girl. The heavy equipment rushed here was valued at over a half million dollars. My voice revealed concern when I mentioned the troubling fact that no one is supposed to remain down there longer than twenty minutes, but Bill Yancy was down in the hot and cramped casing for more than two hours.

Klaus Landsberg agreed to drop a microphone on a cable into the opening so the volunteers on top could hear the men working below. It also gave our viewers a powerful narration of what was happening at every moment. I remember the sound of a pick cutting into rock, and the scraping of the bucket against the side of the casing as it made endless trips up and down.

Bill Yancy often sang in an off key voice to keep his spirits up while he tried to break through the layers of rock that halted the pounding of the casing into the ground.

Bill Welsh and I discussed the endless effort over the air. We speculated about how long it was possible for Bill Yancy to stay down there and keep working. We kept trading off the mike; one would take it for about ten or fifteen minutes or until one had said about all we could, then, almost out of words, one would pass it on to the other. However, at no time did we have the feeling we were merely filling airtime. There was always an immediate challenge to be overcome. When that was resolved, countless other problems arose to take its place.

One of the most dramatic moments came when Bill Yancy asked to be hauled to the top after his more than two hours on the bottom. Word rippled through the crowd that Bill was coming up. There was a stir of excitement as his head and body came up through the tube. He stepped off the rickety bucket onto the top of the casing.

Thousands broke into spontaneous cheers as he was helped to the ground. I talked over the applause of the crowd, describing how Yancy was completely covered with dirt and perspiration as he was being wrapped in blankets and helped to the first aid areas where several cots were set up. He dropped onto a cot, his eyes closed tightly.

Herb Harple was the next sandhog to go below. He climbed up on the casing, got his bearings and reached for the cable that held the bucket, stood for a moment at the top, then balanced himself on the tilting bucket for a moment. The crowd gave him a loud cheer. He was slowly lowered and took over the tough job that Yancy had begun.

His pick hammers the rocks, bit by bit as they are chopped into small pieces and scooped into the bucket that is hauled up and down throughout the long night.

Herb murmurs an occasional "hell" or "damn" when something goes wrong almost 100 feet underground. He mumbles frequently to himself, but the words over the microphone are hardly audible. He stays down far longer than the twenty minute time limit, chopping away at the rocky earth.

Bill Yancy gets up from his cot and starts to walk around. He talks to other workers in the first aid area, sips a cup of coffee and appears ready to go back down. We are able to string our microphone and camera cable over the cluttered field to where he is standing and interview him. He gives us a vivid description of what he had to face in that tiny space below and how he was able to work in it.

I remember holding the microphone close to my mouth and trying to remain calm when I heard Harple shouting from the casing. I could distinctly hear him over the microphone that Landsberg placed in the shaft, "I've hit water, it's seeping in on all sides. Pull me up."

What had been routine for several hours suddenly becomes tense. Could the water pour in so fast that it could trap Herb? There is much scurrying and shouting around the top of the casing as the bucket is slowly pulled up. "That's far enough," shouts the voice on the microphone, "Let me check this water level."

You can imagine the impact that conversation, some one hundred feet below the ground, had on the viewers at home. What had been so routine, now becomes possibly life threatening. Everyone listens carefully to that microphone that KTLA dropped down to the work area at the bottom hours ago.

"I think this will be all right. It is just oozing in...Plenty of mud...but we'll just have to haul it out." Herb's voice from the bottom was almost casual now.

A new enemy for the sandhogs below. Throughout the night, sloppy mud is hauled up in the same bucket that carried the earth and broken rocks earlier.

When Herb Harple is brought up, he receives a loud ovation from the crowd. Tommy Francis, race car driver and former miner, takes his turn at the back-breaking job. Next it is O.A. Kelley's turn to go back down. He hadn't been in a shaft since he retired from mining years ago, but his old training serves him well tonight.

Whitey Blickensderfer follows the others. He had to be pulled up right after being lowered. The mud and water level was rising too fast. He is covered with mud up to his thighs. He holds a brief meeting at the top, then descends deep into the tube again.

I try talking to all of the rescuers after they come up and get their observations on how things were going down there. Herb Herple, Tommy Francis, Bill Yancy, O.A. Kelley, Whitey Blickensderfer and all the others become folk heroes over night. Each one of them gives us a vivid description of what it is like down there and what odds they are facing.

Throughout the long ordeal, the lonesome bucket continues to haul up more sloppy mud and water from the depths. There is little new to talk about. Bill and I feel very much alone. Klaus is still talking to us over our earphones, but so little is happening it is hard to imagine that anyone could be watching.

I remember sitting in a pick-up truck just before dawn, the windows rolled up to keep me warm. A small opening at the top of the driver's window allowed the microphone cable to squeeze through. I kept on talking about what was happening and what we thought would be happening next. I remember looking at the mike resting on my lap and wondering if anyone could be out there listening to what I was saying at this time of the morning.

As Sunday morning dawns, they are making some progress. The mud has largely been scraped away and they are able to go deeper into the ground. They cut, hammer, pick, drain and dig their way down to the level where they believe the little girl is trapped.

By early morning, the sandhogs had dug a small tunnel below the casing. Lumber was being sent down in the bucket. The men below, now working in pairs, were shoring up the vertical tunnel. They were digging across to the well shaft where Kathy was imprisoned. The end might be near.

Sunday morning was bright and sunny. Many people who had gone to bed while the drama continued during the night turned their sets back on and were caught up in the rescue effort once again. Few people went anywhere that Sunday morning. Again, when they did, the question was always asked, "Have they reached her yet?" Special prayers were offered for Kathy at church services.

The small group of sandhogs working 100 feet in the ground had become famous. The mud-splattered volunteers were talked about everywhere.

Many people and their guests slept on the floor in front of their sets. Neighbors and friends had watched on couches and chairs all night long. As the morning hours passed, more and more people tuned in their sets and remained there for the rest of the day.

Sunday morning I had a feeling they might reach her at any time. I figured it could be an hour or two away, but I believed the climax was getting closer. I believed most people were fairly certain she would be found alive.

The bright April morning grows into a hot sticky Sunday afternoon. Progress is still slow. Humming drills screech over the microphone as the rescuers continue their long hours at the bottom. By late Sunday afternoon there is a feeling that something important has to happen soon. The sandhogs below have built their tunnel to the well where Kathy is trapped. They have all the shoring lumber they need with them. They have spent hours strengthening the shaft where they were working and it is obvious that they are cutting into the well pipe, when the screeching drills was picked up by our microphone deep in the casing.

The crowd, now hot and sticky in the afternoon sun, still cheers each miner when he is brought to the surface, and shouts encouragement to the next volunteer to go back down.

About six o'clock, I find it much harder to get information about what is happening. Frayed nerves begin to tell. Officials are grim and some are testy. For the first time, the microphone in the casing is turned off. It is our last official contact with the men working below. No reason is given, but it quickens fears that things have turned for the worse.

Kathy's parents were nearby during the entire ordeal, their home a short distance away. We made no effort to invade their privacy during the long hours. They watched in silence.

In a bitter twist of irony, Mr. Fiscus had just returned from testifying at hearings in Sacramento about legislation that would require the cementing and covering of all open wells. He was an official of a water company, the same one that had sunk this water well over 40 years ago. It was the open well that claimed Kathy.

Throughout the day numerous conferences take place among the officials. Bill and I are finding it more difficult to get word on what progress is being made. We just keep on talking about what we are seeing. We are no longer allowed to speak to the men who return to the surface.

As darkness covers the scene, Dr. Robert McCullock, the family physician, is strapped into a parachute harness. His face is grim and he appears uncertain about what he is getting into. He holds the parachute lines tightly with both hands as he is lowered down to the crews working on the bottom.

He is down there for only minutes, then he is slowly pulled back up to the surface.

Bill waves me over and hands me the microphone. I watched him walk away from the scene. I later learned that Los Angeles County Sheriff Eugene Biscaluz, who was in charge of much of the operation, asked Bill if he would go to the Fiscus home and tell them that Kathy has been found dead.

Klaus tells me over my earphone there is to be an important announcement next to the rescue site and moves a camera into position. I looked a short distance away and spot a small crowd of solemn faced rescue workers walking towards the camera. In the middle of the cluster of men is another family physician, Dr. A. Hansen. He stops in front of the camera, picks up a microphone that had been used as a public address amplifier and speaks to the crowd. "Ladies and Gentlemen, Kathy is dead and has been dead for a long time. The family wishes to thank one and all for your heroic efforts to try to save our child..."

Tired, dirty, beaten men cry. Sandhogs with 40 and 50 hours of constant work behind them weep openly with bitter tears. Rescuers stand silently, heads bowed, unwilling to accept the news. The crowd of thousands is stunned. Viewers at home feel the pain of sorrow. Many say it is like losing one of our own. The city has become so involved in the rescue effort there are signs of sadness everywhere, with no way to express the loss.

It would be several hours before they bring up Kathy's body, but the broadcast is over. There is no reason to stay. The volunteers had tried to beat time and save a little girl, but failed.

Bill and I had been on the air for twenty-seven and a half hours of continuous broadcasting. Viewers watched the entire drama unfold and suffered the poignant moment when they were told she was dead. The only solace was the fact that she probably died shortly after she fell into the well and did not suffer long in her prison.

It was especially difficult for the men who had tried so hard to save her. They had given their all for a little girl they never knew but now would never forget.

*　　*　　*

In January of 1994 I opened a crumbling scrapbook on the top shelf of a dusty attic closet, filled with old letters, yellowed newspaper clippings, some telegrams and pictures. Many had been pasted to the loose pages of the scrapbook my mother had put together after the telecast of 45 years ago. Turning the pages, being careful not to damage the paper any more, brought back the vivid memories of that tragic weekend when an army of volunteers tried to rescue 3 year-old Kathy Fiscus.

Historians in 1994 agree that the Kathy Fiscus telecast marked the beginning of the long form of television news coverage. It has long been recognized as the first important news event of the commercial television era.

Television in Los Angeles that spring of 1949 was something you heard about at the office or saw in the window of an appliance store. However, many people were becoming the first on their block to own a new ten-inch set. It was still a novelty and owners showed off their new sets with pride.

Klaus Landsberg's decision to televise the rescue attempt brought the new medium of television to the Southern California general public for the first time. It opened the window of the world to many viewers.

This old scrapbook has some of the letters I received after the marathon broadcast. They show the impact the telecast made on the viewers those many years ago.

Stewart Stern of Los Angeles wrote of the Kathy Fiscus telecast, "...We had been to a party. We sat on the floor in our tuxedos and watched you through the night and into the next night. Until last night, the television set was no more a threat to serenity than any other bit of furniture in the living room. Now you have utterly destroyed this safety forever...you and the epic of which you have been a part of this weekend have made us know what television is for. You have made many of us know that we belong to the world. Through your own dignity and your recognition of the dignity of others, you have given us a flash of people at their best, as we remember them in the battle, or as I've just seen them at Negev outposts in Israel. Many of us had seen you with your polite faces and amiable voices, but none of us had known you until the voices lost their amiability and the polite faces were beginning to sprout beards, along with our own. You will never be forgotten by those of us who saw you there."

I opened a folded newspaper clipping of Owen Callin's column in the *Los Angeles Herald*. It said he was a captive of the binding emotion holding him to the screen. He wrote, "One of the greatest advancements in Los Angeles television occurred over the weekend when the possibility of covering major news events was demonstrated with convincing thoroughness. We doubt if there is a television set in the area which wasn't at some time during Saturday and Sunday tuned to that San Marino pasture where little Kathy Fiscus fell to her death."

I picked up another sheet of newspaper, yellowed with time. It was an article by Bob Stock in the *Sherman Oaks Sun*. "In this reporter's opinion, KTLA's coverage of this event was one of the greatest reporting jobs in the history of television... certainly the greatest in the Southern California viewing area."

There were several others on crumbling paper. The *Fontana Herald and News* wrote, "Television grew up in a hurry last week. The masterly reporting of the tragedy of little Kathy Fiscus, who fell to her death in an abandoned well, and the subsequent rescue was so graphically detailed by KTLA, as to beggar description."

An editorial in another local paper summed up the human involvement that everyone felt. "We were all a part of the rescue attempt, because we were there experiencing it, as the drama unfolded on television."

"It is a curious, sad and magnificent world we live in. A little girl falls down a well in California and the news sweeps across oceans waking untold millions to eager, anxious sympathy. Men work doggedly for 52 hours, baffled, almost exhausted and in increasing physical danger, to free her. There is no talk of work hours, rates of compensation, bargaining agencies, or safety conditions. They just dig on relentlessly while thousands of miles away come offers of help, suggestions and prayers. Kathy's tiny wail has been heard around the world. It speaks for the small victims of war, of famine, of man's inhumanity to man, in Greece, in India, in Berlin and Shanghai, in Harlem and Cairo. And dull though men's imagination may be, San Marino shows us once more, they have in them the ability to respond magnificently."

Daily Variety, in a special editorial by Editor Arthur Unger, said, "The greatest job for the development, progress and advancement of television was done by the crew of KTLA, who for more than 24 hours televised the attempt to rescue alive Kathy Fiscus. Klaus Landsberg and his boys will never realize the important feat they accomplished for the advancement of television by the spot news reporting and visualization they did."

As I thumbed through letters, clippings and crumbling newspapers, I realized how widespread the praise and approval was. The public and the press commended the station for making television history. The emotional effect on the community was staggering. It seemed as if all Los Angeles stopped to watch the drama unfold. A hard-boiled city poured out its tears and silent prayers as brave men worked in the dark tunnels trying to rescue her.

Not only was the telecast a major stepping stone in television history, but it dramatically altered my life. I had been at KTLA for almost 14 months and had been seen on many different programs, but I was unknown to almost everyone outside the small band of loyal KTLA viewers. Dick Lane, Bill Welsh, Gil Martyn and Dorothy Gardiner were the personalities everyone knew. I was just another face who appeared on the screen with great frequency. You would see me from time to time, on news and magazine programs, remote telecasts, cooking shows, community parades, commercials and on program previews. I was the original "utility infielder."

I was on camera every night at sign-on to tell viewers what was in store for them that evening on Channel Five. I would talk for three to four minutes, giving highlights of the program schedule. I would follow the half hour of test pattern and recorded music that opened the station's broadcast evening. The test pattern gave viewers an opportunity to tune their set properly for the evening programs. This was before sets were automatically tuned as they are today.

You could get your best picture by twisting the various dials to make the test pattern as sharp and clear as possible. Once your picture was tuned in, you were ready for an evening of television entertainment. If you didn't finish by the time the test pattern was over, you could still could do it while I was on the air and not miss a program.

I resumed my regular television assignments after the Kathy Fiscus telecast. I received a lot of mail and phone calls over the next few weeks. One telephone call intrigued me. It was from a friend from school, Marie McLoughlin. She had graduated from USC and married her college sweetheart, who had been a bomber pilot during the war. He was just getting started in the business world. They lived on an Oxnard ranch in Ventura County.

Marie invited me over to her house for dinner to meet her husband, Bob Thomas, and told me her sister Beverly would be there.

Beverly McLoughlin was a first-grade teacher at St. Paul's School in Westwood. She had attended USC and recently had graduated from Marymount

College in Tarrytown, New York. I later learned that she had recently broken up with her boyfriend and spent last weekend at the ranch to get moral support from her family.

Beverly and Marie's mother, Mary McLoughlin Maxwell, had spent most of Sunday morning watching the telecast from San Marino.

Marie walked into the room balancing two cups of coffee. She handed one to her mother and sat down beside her.

"Marie, look at that nice fellow on television. He is so concerned, so emotionally involved with the rescue. He must be a wonderful person."

Marie was watching the rescue for the first time and was surprised to see that she knew the fellow on television.

More conversation about the television reporter occurred that weekend. Then came the phone call from Marie.

Beverly and I met the following week at Marie's house in Hollywood. It was one of those meetings that you can't describe. Everything was perfect. They talk of love at first sight, but I never believed it was possible. How could two strangers know they were made for each other? There was never a doubt in my mind. All I had to do was convince her.

Beverly's quiet, regal quality was captivating. Her face had a beautiful glow. Her eyes seemed to be always smiling. She had the softest, most delightful voice I had ever heard.

I can vividly remember meeting and shaking her hands. She wore a blue knit dress. We talked for a while in the middle of the room. From the very start, we were comfortable with each other and wanted to be together.

We went out every night after I finished working at the station. Beverly soon acclimated herself to the strange hours of a television announcer.

We decided just a few weeks after we met that we should get married right away. We were a couple in love and it stayed that way until she died six years ago on February 4, 1989.

We were married at Our Lady of The Lake Church in Lake Arrowhead on May 21, 1949.

Not only did the Kathy Fiscus telecast result in my meeting Beverly, it also radically changed my professional life. The favorable reaction was so great that I became a mini-celebrity. It was a different breed of celebrity, one who was a television news reporter. My status was different from the well-known newsman or radio announcer. It was a new category many others would soon join. It was my good fortune to be one of the first there.

Prior to the telecast, television celebrities were mostly entertainers. All of a sudden, I was in that category because I was a television newsman. I got the credit although it was television that really made everything happen. The viewers were discovering the powerful dimension of television news for the first time and that catapulted me into this new breed of celebrity. I did not deserve it, but because I was there in the beginning I became quite well known.

Bill Welsh and I were praised for our reports and it was something that has remained with us over the years. That telecast has been indelibly marked on our careers.

Although my fame was fleeting, as it usually is, I enjoyed the bright splashes it put on my life. I was emotionally uplifted by the new status and recognition. I felt that finally I was a full-fledged member of Klaus' team.

I was in the news department from the start at KTLA. I had my basic training and paid my dues. But at what point does a television personality become a television newsman?

I believe it happened because of the combination of all of these things and all of the on-the-air work that I did over the years. There is no greater learning experience than doing something over and over again. The fact that I was on the air a hundred times made it that much easier the next hundred times. The real-life exposure to the traps and attractions of live television molded me into an experienced performer who was reasonably at home in a wide variety of challenges.

My transformation from performer to reporter was gradual. I was, somehow, able to take advantage of the luck, the timing and the opportunities that came my way, that made it a reality.

I never had to be an actor. I was able to be myself every time I went on the air. This gave me great experience, because the secret of being a good television reporter is to always be yourself. All the live broadcasts were invaluable training.

The transition was not smooth and I took many detours before I got where I was going. There were no such things as television news reporters in those days. There were news broadcasters and news announcers, but reporters were yet to come. Yet news was where my heart was and every time there was a slight turn in that direction I tried to take advantage of it.

KTLA was small enough to give me a chance and large enough to make room for me. I was able to take advantage of opportunities that came along. I was always around and available. That doesn't mean that everything went my way. It was a bumpy road over the years.

I took the blows and battled my way back to where I wanted to be. There were times when I didn't fit into a specific situation, and wasn't surprised at being left out. That didn't mean I wouldn't be used the next time, either. There is a time for everything. I guess my mother's phone call proved that. She called at the right time, and I answered. My life was changed forever.

5.

THE FIFTIES:
INTO THE CITY NIGHT AND FROSTY FROLICS

One of the programs I really wanted to do was "City At Night," another of Klaus Landsberg's revolutionary ideas. He took his television cameras out of the studio to interesting events happening in Los Angeles at night. He would transport viewers to places they had heard about but never seen. They might have lived in Los Angeles all their lives, but never visited the See's facility where they were making all kinds of chocolate candy. They might drive by a huge automobile plant often, but never had seen the assembly line at work and new cars as they rolled off the end.

When "City At Night" started, Keith Hetherington and Dorothy Gardiner were given the assignment. I was disappointed, but not for long. Too much else was going on.

Keith and Dorothy took viewers all over the city on "City At Night." One week they would be with live cameras in a busy post office as hundreds of employees handled millions of letters each night. The next week, the cameras could be at a bottling plant filming drinks being canned, rolled out and packaged. Next week they would be visiting the Griffith Park Observatory, peering through telescopes and examining the unusual exhibits. Another time, they would take you to a newspaper plant as the presses rolled and the latest edition was printed, cut, trimmed and bundled for early morning delivery.

Radio never did a thing like this. Motion pictures were stories and this type of presentation found little acceptance there. Perhaps industrial films were similar, but "City At Night" had that special dimension. It was live and anything could happen. The audience always related to the unusual circumstances that Keith and Dorothy often found themselves in. Of course, "City At Night" was on the air before there was such a thing as videotape, so it had genuine spontaneity and the possibility of many surprises. When things went wrong, there was no escape. You had to work your way out of them. Cables got stuck around pillars, cameras had to be lifted and tilted to get through some doorways, or moved fast to reach the next shot that was needed. Some people being interviewed talked too long and had to be diplomatically cut off. Others answered questions with a yes or a no, leaving Keith or Dorothy with a short interview as they tried to ad lib their way through the factory. Sometimes the assembly line shut down in the middle of the live shot and the moving, visual element of the program evaporated before their eyes. There were no excuses; they had to keep on talking until it was fixed. The great appeal of "City At Night" was that you were locked into showing what was actually going on at that moment. You had to handle all of the interruptions, technical problems and limitations that beset you while on the air. The cameras showed you what was going on and they gave viewers a look at their city in a way they had never experienced before.

The subject matter was limitless. Cruise ships ready to leave the harbor, military training exercises, a beauty college or a barber's school, passengers arriving at Union Station, the Police Department's communications center, an aerospace plant, a last, nostalgic look at the Hollywood Hotel before it was to be demolished, or backstage at the circus as performers got ready for their Los Angeles run.

Each week brought something new and different. Klaus insisted that the location of "City At Night" be kept a secret. He believed that a show that could go anywhere and surprise anyone would have much more impact, if no one knew where it would be on any given night. Often, even the crew members didn't know where they were going until after they left the studio.

Cecil Smith, the dean of television columnists in Los Angeles, tells of the time he was sitting with all the other reporters in the city room of the *Los Angeles Times*, when he saw this big light at one end of the room and watched a camera move in and start a telecast. He said he had no idea what was going on, until he realized it was "City At Night."

Ken Graue later followed Dorothy and Keith as hosts of the show. He was a well liked staff announcer who did newscasts, worked with Dorothy Gardiner on "Handy Hints" and appeared on many other programs. He served in the Marines during the war and was a lieutenant in the Marine Reserves while at KTLA. Ken worked in radio for several years in Hawaii and his close friend in college, Bud Stefan, got him the job at the station.

Ken's father-in-law was a ham radio operator. I remember the night at his home, when Bud talked to Ken over the shortwave radio. He told him to pack up his bags and fly home, the KTLA job was waiting for him. Like the rest of us, Ken appeared on countless programs, but was probably best known for his role on "City At Night," which he hosted for years.

Ken was almost a victim of the "secrecy mandate" of "City At Night." He was busy with other assignments at the station one Wednesday night, so it was decided that he would go by himself. Klaus and the "City At Night" crew had left for the secret site. When Ken was ready to go, he wasn't able to find out the address. Since it was a secret location, no one at the station knew where it was, and those who did know were on their way in the remote trucks. There were no beepers or car radios in those days. There was no way to get in touch with the crew in the field until they arrived and made contact with the station. Ken was delayed for an anxious hour, but managed to get out there in time.

* * *

I finally got my wish and was assigned to "City At Night" some years later. I co-hosted with Ken when Klaus decided to broadcast the show from two different locations each night.

One night I was to do a live broadcast from the San Gabriel Mission, the oldest church in Southern California. Usually, I did the second segment of "City At Night," but this night I was schedule to open the show and Ken would follow with his live segment from the Los Angeles Civic Center.

"City At Night" was on the air an hour after another program I did, so I had plenty of time to finish the broadcast, get into the car and drive to the remote location where my part of "City At Night" would originate.

I finished my show and started the drive to the Mission Church in San Grabriel. Somehow, I missed my turn-off street in San Gabriel and kept on driving. I went on for twenty minutes or so before I realized my mistake.

I wheeled around, raced back, found the street and parked outside the Mission. When I went in, Father Michael Montoya, the pastor of the church, was on the air, taking viewers on a tour of the museum. He started the broadcast without me and most viewers of "City At Night" thought it was the way it was supposed to be. As soon as I got my breath back, I joined him on the telecast and everything went smoothly.

The ad lib quality of "City At Night" made it especially appealing. In these days when everything is on videotape, it is hard to imagine how involved viewers can get when you are live and something goes wrong.

I remember the "City At Night" broadcast in March, 1950, when Beverly and I were expecting our first baby. We were at her parents ranch at Oxnard in Ventura County. They were on a trip and we were there by ourselves waiting for the moment when we would have to race to the hospital. We were watching "City At Night" that evening, counting contractions and expecting to leave at any moment.

The program dealt with Fire Station 27 in Hollywood, one of the biggest and best in the city. It had all of the new fire equipment and the show was going to give us an inside look at the latest in fire fighting hardware and a chance to see how firemen spend their lives at the station.

The program had all of the elements of a good visual show. However, moments after "City At Night" went on the air, the alarm went off, the firemen jumped into their turn out gear, raced through the station and climbed on their fire engines. Everything and everybody went pouring out of the station.

Only one chief and Dorothy and Keith were left. Their visual show disappeared in front of them. They did a remarkably good job in the big empty fire station. They filled out the hour, showing the fire equipment that was left and talking about the new fire engines that were out there on the scene fighting a local fire.

Beverly and I never saw the end of the telecast. Stan Junior was born the next morning.

What a sweeping change in our lifestyle after that first year of our marriage. Beverly was the perfect mother: giving, kind, understanding, patient, knowledgeable and completely loving. She made everything so easy for little Stan and me.

We moved to Santa Monica Canyon, then to a house on the beach and finally lived the rest of our beach days at 56 Malibu Colony Drive—perfect for our growing family. Malibu was considered out in the country in those days, miles from everything. It was a small beach community with only a hint of its famous past. There were still stories of the movie stars who lived in the Colony before the war and some were still there, but for us it was a quiet, private and totally enjoyable.

Few people lived in the Colony during the off season. No more than a dozen or so families were there year-round. We had the place to ourselves. We would take long walks along the beach, drag our toes in the water, watch the surf crash into the bulkheads in front of our house and thoroughly enjoy the privacy of beach life during the winter. It was a special time of our life.

I still had my busy KTLA schedule. I left early in the morning, and enjoyed my drive along the coast next to the endless blue sea and white waves breaking on the beaches. On the other side of the highway were bluffs and rolling green hills with a few scattered homes.

I would not get back to Malibu until seven or eight at night. But it was worth it. Bev and I were completely happy.

Our daughter Beverly was born in September 1951, our next son, David, in 1953 and Nancy in 1955. We were a happy beach family. We rarely left Malibu, except for work, visits to our families over the holidays, and the trips to the Lying-In Hospital in Oxnard where our babies were born.

Everything seemed to fit in place. Everything was so logical. It seemed we had the answers to everything. I believe most young people just starting out felt that way. We all had a similar feeling about life at that time, a happiness and sense of fulfillment in those post World War II years. Our marriages and our jobs blended so well.

*   *   *

During the 1950s, there seemed to be a national consensus about how things were and how they should be. We were a different people then. Many great changes were brewing in our society, but few were aware of them or realized what they meant. It was a more simple decade, more family oriented, more traditional than the eras that followed.

We soon grew accustomed to the excitement of change in the 50s. More than a million people moved to Los Angeles and the exploding growth meant opportunities for almost everyone. Everything was new and different. Even the term subdivision was new to us in the 1950s. After so many years of wartime housing shortages, Californians went to work to ease the situation. The housing industry exploded and men and jobs were matched by the thousands.

Tracts opened in unlikely areas that were nothing but open fields. Places that had been little more than a gas station and a country store became cities. The entire land was laced with freeway construction and outlying areas were brought closer together by the new, long ribbons of concrete. People moved to distant small towns that soon grew into cities like Lakewood, West Covina and Tarzana.

As the slumbering villages awoke to the 1950s, older residents sold their orchards for housing tracts and their vacant fields for shopping centers. New families were moving in everywhere.

Los Angeles County was growing so fast it had to build a new school and 14 miles of new roads every 16 days. There had to be new sewers, water supplies, and new cities for the more than a million people who would move to Los Angeles during that explosive decade.

The new freeway system enabled the head of the household to move his family out of the city to a dream home in the suburbs. His wife found all of the conveniences of downtown shopping right in her own neighborhood. Major retail chains opened stores in new shopping centers in these suburbs. The new families bought refrigerators, air conditioners and second cars. They built backyard patios, and made weekend stops at the new hardware store in the shopping center that sold the tools and home supplies that helped the amateur repairman keep his home in shape.

They bought on easy credit the inexpensive chrome breakfast tables and vinyl covered chairs. They had new formica-top kitchens, plastic utensils and a variety of unique, newly invented household items.

Of course, their new car had those stylish tail fins, power steering and an automatic shift. Everything was bought on time at very low interest. There were backyard barbecues with the neighbors and little league baseball games with the kids. Times were good and would get better.

However, many of the children growing up in this environment were not too sure about how fulfilling it was.

In the midst of these times of apparent contentment, the consensus gradually started unraveling. It is interesting to note that few television news broadcasts reflected these awakening forces.

A good example of our consensus in the 50s was the popular music of those early years. It belonged to everyone. There were certain bands or performers you especially liked, others you did not care for, even some you hated, but it was all popular music and everyone accepted it as such.

There was such a consensus about the music world that the "Lucky Strike Hit Parade" was one of the most popular programs on radio and television. It presented the top 10 songs of the week. The program was contemporary and very successful. It appealed to all segments of the viewing audience, young and old alike.

It was such an accepted fact that Klaus Landsberg believed that popular music was one of the major ways that television could entertain its viewers. He created many musical programs that appealed to this wide audience that spanned the generations.

Years later popular music began to break into separate worlds. With the advent of Elvis Presley, the Beatles and the entry of early rock and roll, musical tastes changed and marked a turning point that fractured popular music.

But all of this came later, after the consensus shattered. In the early 50s, music was music and television was where you enjoyed it the most.

In thousands of separate homes with funny looking antennas sticking up like flag poles on their roofs, viewers were glued to their television sets. Programs were geared to those ex-GIs who had good jobs, took out big loans and enjoyed the good life with their young families. And because of the newness of television it was also geared to the neighbors and their growing families who were moving into the new house next door. Television was something everyone in the family could agree on. They all watched and mostly liked what they saw.

*   *   *

In early morning hours, the old cavernous wooden Polar Palace ice rink was a strange and lonely place. A soft gray fog hung over patches of the vast stretch of empty ice. The cold temperatures and moisture of the night brewed this ice rink mixture. It looked like an eerie movie set where special effects technicians had poured smoking dry ice to create a mysterious foggy mood. The hazy cloud cover drifted into strange patterns as it was ruffled by the whirling motion of a solitary skater or was tumbled by new air currents when the front door swung open.

The ice-made fog would not last for long as the early morning skaters arrived. As they straggled in to take their private lessons, the slashes of their skates and the sounds of their solitary voices echoed throughout the vast, empty rink. I looked up to the dark, barn-like roof and down to the white ice below.

A thundering pipe organ filled the big, high ceilinged, wooden arena with bright marches and popular skating music. Even the timbers seemed to shake as hundreds of determined skaters rumbled around the rink, caught the spirit of the moment, rushing, dancing and skating as if the party would never end.

This morning crowd was quite different. They were advanced skaters getting their training and practice on the uncluttered ice before the hour when the rink opened and the circling herd of skaters returned.

Once a week, however, all the skaters were the stars of "Frosty Frolics." The live ice show quickly became one of the most watched television programs in Los Angeles during the early 1950s. Most of the performers featured on the show were veterans of the popular traveling ice shows that criss-crossed the country. Shows like "Ice Follies" and "Ice Capades" were on the road most of the time. By appearing on "Frosty Frolics," skaters could continue their careers, but cut down on the traveling. It gave them a chance to settle down in Los Angeles and make their way in the business world. The young women, who often married other skaters, took time out to have their babies and then returned to part-time skating when they were ready.

It was an ideal situation for all involved and every Wednesday was "opening night" on Channel Five. "Frosty Frolics " went on the air in June, 1951. It was the fourth most watched television show in Los Angeles by mid-August, and became a permanent fixture on KTLA's entertainment schedule for over four years.

By mid-September, it was offered for syndication on kinescope coast to coast on Paramount Transcription. On October 3, 1951 it went live over the ABC Network. It was one of first local Los Angeles programs to be seen via microwave relay to the East Coast. This was at the very beginning of national television. The microwave from Los Angeles to New York had just been completed and "Frosty Frolics" was one of the first to be shown.

Despite its popular and artistic accomplishments, its coast to coast network days were numbered. Its sponsor went bankrupt after only four network broadcasts. The kinescopes continued, but the live, splashy network run ended unceremoniously when the vitamin sponsor bankrolling the airtime went under. Sponsor cancellations were a frequent fact of life in those early days and although they happened often, they were never easy to accept.

"Frosty Frolics" continued its popularity despite its network defeat. It was a big success here because it was live and fun. It was a happening and the viewers were a part of it. If a skater fell, he had no choice but to get up and continue his routine. If a set tipped over or a prop broke, there were no retakes. Every skater knew he had to do what he could to make the best out of any embarrassing situation.

On almost every show, there was that uncertain something that could and usually did happen. In fact the skaters began including slips in their routines, to get audience reaction.

During the morning hours of the day of the broadcast, each skater would rehearse his own routine. He often had his music on a reel-to-reel audio tape recorder, and would stake out a section of the ice to practice the jumps, moves and other special techniques necessary for the program that night.

Later in the day, an informal rehearsal would be held for timing and positioning. Then it would be off to wardrobe, make up and the show itself.

"Frosty Frolics" was presented at the Alpine Hotel, somewhere in the green forests of a beautiful mountain retreat. However, everything came from the prop department at Paramount Studios. Fake trees and real plants, tables, chairs, red carpeting for a walkway on the ice, cloth flats that were used to make the side of the hotel and banisters for the dining area were all hauled over to the Polar Palace in the afternoon as the stage crew created their Alpine Hotel.

The flimsy, cardboard stone walls were sprayed with a paint gun by an artistic genius, Sherman Laudermilk. He would bend, twist and cut cardboard, spray it with fast drying paint and create real-life settings that you could not tell from the real thing.

Laudermilk's crew would set up and build verandas, walks, gardens and a small pine tree forest around a setting that was an outdoor restaurant. The tables bordered the ice stage where the show came to life.

This was a complicated, live stage production. The crew wore ice skates, the props were brought in on sleds or pushed across the smooth ice surface by skating stage hands.

Several members of the crew had been hired because they had been professional hockey players. The others were novices who learned to skate in record time.

KTLA would get countless calls from viewers wanting to know where the Alpine Hotel was located and if they could make reservations for dinner, or perhaps spend a weekend. It was difficult for the switchboard operator to make them understand that the Alpine Hotel had to be taken down and returned to Paramount Studios after the show was over.

Those in the audience at the Polar Palace sat on wooden bleachers normally used by the paying ice skaters at the public sessions. It was always a great treat to be selected from the audience and led to the dinner tables that ringed the ice. About two dozen of the lucky ones would be escorted each night from the audience area, across the slippery ice, to the tables on the veranda.

Those at ringside tables were now a part of the cast and they felt the tension that builds as the countdown to airtime got down to the last few minutes. It is one thing to be in a big arena sitting on the sidelines waiting for the show to start. It is another to be center stage, looking into the cameras, facing the stage crew on ice as they make their final moves. Your palms go moist as you wait for the magic cue and the show goes on. There is pressure, suspense, nervousness and even stage fright as the show begins. Then it fades and becomes part of the entertainment.

The show is the thing, but getting ready for it is what makes it work. Since KTLA was owned by Paramount Pictures, we had access to the vast prop and wardrobe department on the studio lot. These were the vital ingredients necessary to make the show a success.

"Frosty Frolics," actually begins in an old warehouse where history was hung up to dry. Uniforms from the old soldiers' home, here. Over there, sheiks of the Sahara stashed their flowing robes. And there, elegant attire from the court of Louis XIV.

The room is a harvest of vintage clothes on plain pipes, in narrow aisles, with the smell of mothballs and leather. Costume treasures of all kinds hanging from bare racks three and four levels high. I am surrounded as I slowly walk down a crowded aisle with garments brushing my shoulders from both sides.

Each garment, no matter how important looking, nor how lavishly designed, is crushed together on the pipe. They look like brightly colored rags waiting to be stored in some dusty attic. Yet some others look as if they were coats in a mansion's cloak room waiting for their owners to retrieve them, after the ball is over.

Paramount's wardrobe has almost every possible costume. They are the legacy of the thousands of motion pictures filmed on the lot over the years. In the past, when you were making a high budget film, you did not worry about how much costumes were going to cost. The designs were selected, the drawings approved and the orders turned in.

If you needed a wardrobe for twenty Russian counts of 1905, ten German naval officers, seven English ladies-in-waiting and street wear for one hundred Parisian pedestrians, this was the place. The designers and dressmakers would go to work and their costumes would be finished and ready for fitting far ahead of the shooting schedule for the new film.

When the motion picture was complete, the costumes would be stored and hung in this great warehouse for use in later films. This was a precious gold mine for the skaters of "Frosty Frolics." I remember them walking down the narrow, cluttered aisles and talking of routines for which a certain costume would be just perfect. Or they would hunt for that one outfit that would be ideal for this week's show. The variety was almost limitless and the skaters took advantage of all they could to enhance their acts.

When the novelty of the Alpine Hotel cafe began to fade, Klaus changed the format to take advantage of the rich collection that the studio had to offer.

Art Director Sherman Laudermilk, who loved creating the sets for the various productions of "Frosty Frolics," kept a close watch on what was new and available on the studio lot.

"Props just got in a Morrocan Village. It's beautiful and just ideal for us," he told the production meeting.

"I was thinking more of a Hansel and Gretel theme for next week," Klaus answered.

About a dozen of those involved in next week's show were sitting in the living room of Klaus Landsberg's home in the Hollywood Hills, overlooking the city below. Many were sitting on the floor. They had notebooks, folders, music tapes and clipboards.

This was an informal session. Bits and pieces of next week's program would slowly come together.

Klaus Landsberg, creator, producer and director of "Frosty Frolics," ran the production meetings. No detail was too small for his attention. He did everything because he knew he could do it better than anyone else.

The meetings always took second place to the ringing telephone. Joanne Boogar, Klaus' secretary, would try to tame the ringing as much as possible, but each call was usually important enough to be brought to his attention.

Joanne covered the mouthpiece. "It's Harry Maynard. You called him earlier when he was at a client's office."

He took the phone. "Harry, did you sell him anything?" He had a half smile on his face and listened.

"Well, maybe a third of 'Spade Cooley.' That's going to be available soon. Dick Lane can do their commercial, but it will cost them extra," he added.

"Harry," he changed the subject, "I didn't like that commercial on 'Bandstand Revue' last night. It ran too long...way over. It's bad for the show. Give them a call and tell them either to do it right or get off the show."

There was a pause on the other end of the line.

"Harry, you don't want sponsors like that ruining the show, do you?"

He listened, then said, "Of course not. You tell them I didn't like it ...and that it had better not happen again next week."

He then turned to Sherman Laudermilk. "Do you think the Morrocan set is better than those thatched huts we used on the Hans Christian Andersen show? We could use the same ones, just change the forest around them."

He had abruptly ended his sales call and was back in the middle of the production meeting, at the exact point where the phone call had interrupted.

"I was thinking the Morrocan set was new. It is something we have never done before," Sherman answered.

Everyone else got their notebooks and clip boards ready to jot down the details of next week's show.

"Joanne, get me Ted. That picture just doesn't look like it should." He squinted at the ten inch black and white television set with its sound down, at the other side of the room. He stared at the old movie intently and put his hand out for the phone.

Charles Theodore, who everyone called Ted, was the station's chief engineer. He was a Stanford graduate, an electronic wizard and had been with Klaus from the beginning of KTLA.

"Ted, I've been looking at it for 15 minutes and the picture just doesn't have it." He paused a moment. "I know it is an old movie print, but look again. Call Ray at Mount Wilson and have him fix it." Sherman Laudermilk was looking at the television picture. "Looks good to me," he said to himself.

Manny Strand's face looked a little strained as he glanced at his watch. He was the director of the Tyrolean band on the show. It was strictly a part-time affair. He had other bands and engagements and he could see the time to get to his evening's appearance fading away. He would have to leave for the Beverly Wilshire Hotel soon, but he knew how upset Klaus would get when he tried to leave early.

"Manny, I certainly liked the medley you did for Mae Edwards and the Schramms last week." Klaus seemed to sense Manny's uneasiness. Manny flushed a little, "Thank you Klaus. I was thinking of something like that for Joan and Buff McCusker next week."

"Will it be in Morroco or the Black Forest?" Klaus half smiled. "Joan and Buff have a couple ideas about their routine I know they want to talk to you about it," Manny answered.

"Let's go with Hansel and Gretel," Klaus abruptly decided. "Sherm, those thatched roof cottages are okay, but make them look different. I want a lot of trees all over. Give me some skating room through the trees...I've got a chase sequence that could be good." Penny Joyce smiled at Klaus as he turned to her.

"Penny will be Gretel, Bob Kaspar is Hansel and Bob Turk is the wolf." He paused and looked at Roy Schramm, "Roy, you and April will be the woodsman and his wife." He turned to Buff McCusker. "Buff, you and Joanie will be woodsmen, too. Work out your routines. I want all of you chasing Bob Turk through the forest. There will be plenty of room through the trees. Sherm, make those cottages strong. I want a lot of banging on the doors. Manny, can you get the music together for everyone?"

"I didn't know there were wolves and woodsmen in the Hansel and Gretel story," said Joanie McCusker as she walked down the stairs from Klaus' house to the street below.

"I don't know if there were either," Bob Turk answered. But there will be some next Wednesday on the show."

I was the host and emcee on "Frosty Frolics." I usually wore a gray Eisenhower-style jacket with a bright scarf. Both came from Paramount's wardrobe. Usually I wore my regular suit pants and put on skates.

I always put in my regular day in the Sales Department and when things quieted down there, I would walk the two blocks to the Polar Palace and go over my lines for the evening's show.

The format called for me to introduce each number as if I were introducing them to the audience sitting at the tables on the ice at the Alpine Hotel. I had my place on the ice amid the gardens of the Alpine, next to the polka band directed by Manny Strand. Klaus liked to keep everything fast and brief. I would make my introductions short, just long enough for the stage crew to make the necessary changes for the next number. Once they were ready, Klaus would give me the cue through the stage manager and I would quickly end my ad-lib introduction.

Since we were addressing our remarks to the live audience, viewers at home had the feeling that they were watching a performance given for those at the Alpine Hotel. It somehow made everything seem more real.

Since I was the only non-skater on the program, Klaus developed a piece of business for me. At the end of the broadcast, I would leave my garden set and skate to center ice the best I could. Then, as I was making my closing announcement, I would somehow slip and fall down on the ice. That would be the cue for the full cast of skaters to come on camera and skate in a big, free-wheeling circle around me. I would just sit there and wave while the skaters whirled to the music and the applause of the audience. It became a trademark of the show. There I was, perplexed and sitting on the wet ice, waving at the viewers. The others would skate exciting, fast action circles around me as the orchestra played our theme, "Sleigh Ride," in a bright, stirring arrangement.

That led to one of my embarrassing moments. The first broadcast of "Frosty Frolics" that went coast to coast ended a couple of minutes early. Since network timing was precise, I had to sit there in the middle of the ice, in cold wet slacks getting wetter all the time, and wave. I had to wave to that national television audience for at least a couple of minutes, as the smiling, laughing and skating cast made circle after circle around me. You can only smile so long and you can only wave so long, before you begin to feel completely ridiculous. That is exactly how I felt for those long minutes.

Later on, we tried to make my end of the show routines a little more unusual. I jumped off a jeep one night, made a perfect landing and skated a few feet to the applause of the crowd. Then I fell as I stopped to take a bow. I tried turns, whirls and different movements to show how my skating was improving, but somehow I fell every night.

The landings got harder and harder, and wetter and wetter, and they had another undesirable side effect. I would usually hit my knee when I fell. I started scraping holes in my suit pants. Those would be the same pants I might wear on sales calls for the station later in the week. Each torn knee meant my already limited street wardrobe was down one suit and I decided no longer to wear street pants on the show.

Looking back, I believe "Frosty Frolics" was the most entertaining show that Klaus developed. Few would be so daring at that time to rent a rink, put together such a large cast, create new stories and know the entire production would come together at airtime. Klaus had confidence in what he did and he knew the show would come off.

6.

ATOM BOMB AND AN EARTHQUAKE

Gale force winds were whipping around my old Lincoln. It offered protection from the blustering cold gales, but the car shook and swayed as it was plummeted through the night.

I was half asleep in the front seat. The irregular rocking of the car kept waking me up. Beverly was asleep in the back. She had an overcoat over her as a blanket and a folded jacket as a pillow.

It was the summer of 1951. We had driven to Point Loma late that night to be with the crew when the preparations for the telecast started in the morning. Point Loma is a high, beautiful hill overlooking San Diego Harbor. Klaus had selected this spot for a relay transmission truck. The plans called for our mobile unit to be on the dock where the ships would tie up. The signal would be sent up here and then relayed back to our main transmitter on Mount Wilson for the broadcast.

San Diego is well over a hundred miles from Los Angeles and it required accurate engineering to transmit a signal over such a distance. Nothing like this had ever been done before in Southern California. This was the telecast we promised our viewers more than a year ago when we showed the Marines going aboard the ships that were to take them to the war in Korea. Today, they were coming home. The war was winding down and the boys were heading back.

KTLA set up its own microwave network to bring their arrival in San Diego to the viewers in Los Angeles. In 1951, it was a daring engineering feat to try something as complicated as this.

So many things could go wrong, and even though the equipment was set up on a temporary basis far from maintenance facilities, Klaus felt we had to do this telecast.

The somber faces and long lines of men going aboard ships that we showed back in the summer of 1950 would be replaced by the bursting excitement and expectation of their arrival home today. It had been a bitter war, far more brutal than we had expected when they left.

When Klaus heard the ships were returning to San Diego instead of heading home for Los Angeles, he vowed to put up his own television microwave link to cover the arrival. He held a series of long sessions with Charles Theodore and John Silva, his chief engineers. Original plans were to set up several locations on mountain peaks where the signal could be relayed over shorter distances. As they got into the details of the effort, they discovered that a single relay station could do the trick—this windy peak on Point Loma. The theory had been worked out. Now at this early morning hour, they were trying to complete the effort and get the signal back to Los Angeles. Everyone was confident it would work, and it did. Engineers, flushed with their victory, were napping in their trucks and cars.

Beverly and I drove down to the harbor a little after daybreak to get ready for the telecast. Beverly left me at the Navy dock and took the ferryboat over to Coronado to our rooms at the Hotel Del Coronado. She would watch the arrival on television. We were going to take a few days off from work after the broadcast.

The bunting was up in red, white and blue. A huge "Welcome Home" banner waved in the breeze. The Navy band had arrived in buses and instruments were being unloaded and tested as the musicians stepped off the bus onto the dock area. Hundreds of family members were there early and their numbers grew as the time for the arrival approached. There was a feeling of jubilation as the crowd grew and waited for the three ships coming home from Korea.

The Navy officials were very cooperative. They even offered us a chance to go aboard one of the ships before it entered the harbor. There was no way we could get a camera aboard, but Klaus took them up on their invitation. He gave remote engineer John Polich a sound transmitter to haul out on a pilot boat and take aboard the troop ship. The unit was the size of a large suitcase, and heavy and bulky. John Polich just put it under his arm and climbed the ladder in the choppy seas from the small boat to the deck of the ship with hundreds of happy Marines cheering him on. KTLA talked to the combat veterans on the troop ship while cameras on the dock showed the faces of the waiting families.

It was an emotional telecast. Bands played the bright marches, tears of joy filled the eyes of those on the dock. This was the moment they had waited for, everyone waving and cheering. The atmosphere was inspirational, gushing, sentimental and thrilling. The beautiful bride with her emotional smile, her glowing face with tear-stained cheeks and the bewildered expression of the tiny child she held, blended to create an expression of happiness never to be forgotten. Her picture was one example of the contagious, soul-stirring love that permeated the homecoming.

This broadcast was further proof of Klaus Landsberg's understanding of the television audience. He let them share in the great emotional moments of the time. He involved them in the spectacle and let them experience the moment as it was happening. The telecast reflected the feelings of an entire nation as the war neared its end.

Viewer comment was vocal, positive and so enthusiastic that Klaus scheduled another similar telecast a few months later. It, too, showed that the cameras are there only to record what is happening. Little could be done to make those long moments of waiting seem shorter. The viewer at home had to wait it out with Navy wives and children, anxiously waiting for their husbands and fathers returning home from the waters off Korea.

Dick Lane and I were surrounded by thousands as we stood under a hot November sun on a crowded Navy dock, scanning the horizon just beyond the breakwater. We wanted to be among the first to spot the cruisers, *Helena* and *Toledo*, when they came into view. Their long wartime Korean tour was over and they were coming home for good. We had seen the Marines return from war earlier, now the men of the Navy were almost back home.

KTLA went on the air at 11:30 this Wednesday morning and it would be a full three hours before the welcome home party was over and the telecast would go off the air.

Mothers chased toddlers, older sisters held baby brothers with their bottles and grandmothers tried to straighten out pretty new dresses and bonnets on their five-year-old grandchildren. There was much squealing and laughter, some crying and tears, and a growing tenseness and excitement as the moment neared. The little ones had no idea what was happening, but they enjoyed running around the pier and playing with new friends. Some mothers held babies born after their husbands had left for war. Others pushed strollers, baby buggies and carts.

Much small talk went on among those standing next to each other. They talked of children, of letters from their husbands and the things their babies were now doing that they couldn't do when their fathers were here before. They tried to mask the surging emotion of expectation that enveloped them.

The ships had left Long Beach last July and had been in action off Korea for many months. But, today, tears of joy had replaced those of sorrow. There was little Dick Lane and I needed to say over the air. Pictures told the story. The cameras panned the crowd and caught the suspense, the excitement, the raw emotion that could not be hidden. We provided just enough commentary to tie things together as we waited for the ships.

Klaus did not believe scripts were necessary for telecasts of this kind. He wanted the cameras to tell the story. They followed the action as the event unfolded before the viewers' eyes.

The moment the superstructures of the cruisers were spotted outside the breakwater, murmurs of recognition turned into electrifying cheers. Hands pointed, tears flowed down cheeks, smiles and laughs camouflaged the unbearable rapture within. The Navy band played and the expectation became bigger than life.

As this was a true-to-life adventure, told in real time, there was no way to speed up the arrival of the ships. They moved slowly past the breakwater, into the harbor and even more slowly to the dock at Pier B and their loved ones.

Klaus kept telling us to take our time talking. We didn't have to fill, just let the faces of the families, the music of the band and the scene at the pier tell the story. Their faces show what is happening. They are transmitting to our audience the reality of what is taking place. The long delays are agonizing, but they showed the suspense and impatience demonstrated by those on the pier. The cameras focus on the wives and mothers. They show the squirming, tired children. Cameras with their long lenses show the crew members standing at attention on the decks of the cruisers as they near the dock. People at home see the men long before those here spot their loved ones. Those watching at home are engulfed in the same emotional experience those on the dock are enduring. The television camera transcends the moment and makes everyone a participant. The boys are coming home and you are there with them.

Many of the shots are too personal to comment on. They show the individual statement of love. The young bride's face, seeing her husband only a hundred yards away, says so much more than the human voice could. The viewers react to what they see, without excessive description from the announcers.

Klaus believed this was television at its best; the unfolding of great drama in which people were caught up in emotion.

Bob Hull, television critic for the old *Los Angeles Mirror,* praised KTLA for its coverage of the arrival of the cruisers. He wrote, "The KTLA personnel handling the assignment are to be complimented. There were moments when Dick Lane and Stan Chambers on the microphones could have been maudlin in their commentary, but they were smart enough to let the viewers' own emotion react to what they saw, without giving any verbal prompting."

Emotion continued to build as the cruisers were secured dockside and the troops disembarked into the arms of their wives, children and families. The joy of the moment filled the television screens. Each reunion told the same story; the war is over and we are together again.

The extra efforts that went into these broadcasts helped build the KTLA tradition. The pattern had been set. When Klaus decided that something was of vital importance and had to be televised, there was nothing that would stop him from getting it on the air. Programming would be thrown out, all commercials cancelled and the station would concentrate on the big story that had to be televised.

The microwave link set up for the San Diego broadcast could be duplicated almost anywhere. Now, even long distances could not interfere with the station's coverage and the stage was set for other ambitious engineering efforts.

* * *

These were great years of experimentation for KTLA and 1951 was one of the best.It was a time when things were happening and a tradition was being born. KTLA continued to be different.

Viewers had Channel 5 locked in on their television sets and were watching the station in big numbers. In January, KTLA programs took nine of the top fifteen spots on all the rating services. In March, seven of the top 10 most-watched programs were on KTLA and in August all of the top eight shows were on KTLA.

A series of atom bomb tests were scheduled for the Nevada desert in 1951. Theses events were top secret and there was little a television station could do to show them. But Klaus Landsberg decided he would try anyway.

Television is best when it shows pictures, but what do you do when it is impossible to show them? You might do what Klaus Landsberg did when he covered this story.

Experts predicted that the light from the test blast in the Nevada desert could be seen all over the West for several hundred miles. Klaus decided to go live with a telecast in the early morning hours. There was no way of getting close to the bomb test site. It was off limits and restricted. However, because of the widespread interest and concern about the tests, Klaus was determined to cover it. The viewer would see only one thing: the light in the sky when the bomb exploded. Landsberg believed viewers would want to see it.

Gil Martyn was sent to Las Vegas for an audio report of what he saw. Dick Lane went to Mount Wilson with the only cameras to cover the blast. The picture of the detonation would be taken hundreds of miles from the explosion site.. It was an early-morning telecast. When the bright light exploded in the dark eastern sky, it lasted for just an instant, but viewers knew they were the first to see a live atomic blast on television.

Dick Lane and Gil Martyn were on the air for about an hour talking about the bomb and what the viewers would see. They brought us right up to the countdown and the blast in the early morning hours in February 1951. A transcription of that coverage was donated to the Atomic Energy Commission.

When the rating surveys came out, they showed that over 30,000 viewers were up and watching that 5 a.m. broadcast. In 1951 that was a substantial audience. Landsberg was right again.

In 1952, because of growing interest in the tests, the Atomic Energy

Commission decided to permit live television coverage from the Nevada Proving Grounds.

The project looked doomed right from the start. Network officials said they were not going to cover it because it would be almost impossible to get cameras to the bomb test site. Phone company officials had completed their surveys and determined it would cost more than $60,000 to set up a relay link to transmit live picture more than 250 miles from the desert to Los Angeles. They also said they did not have enough time to construct the microwave system before the scheduled blast.

Klaus Landsberg was astounded that the networks would pass up covering this historic event. He offered to take over the project and put up his own microwave network to assure the coverage would take place. He planned to place television transmitting equipment on desolate mountain peaks between KTLA's transmitter on Mount Wilson and the test site at Camp Mercury in the Nevada desert outside of Las Vegas. He had less than a month to do it.

Not much equipment was available. All of it was large and bulky and there was almost no way to get it to the mountain tops to set up the communications link.

Landsberg spent hours over maps selecting peaks that might be used as transmission sites to relay the signal. He worked closely with Ray Moore, Charles Theodore, John Silva, John Polich, Hec Heighton and others on his KTLA crew to gather everything he needed for the broadcast. Klaus and Ray Moore flew to Las Vegas to check out possible sites first hand. The survey showed he had a good chance of pulling it off, with one exception. There was an unmarked, inaccessible mountain in the middle of the Nevada desert, a key relay site necessary to make his plan work. Unless he could get his bulky equipment to the top of it, he could not meet the deadline.

Landsberg returned to Los Angeles to take care of some pressing problems at the station. He was doing all of this surveying and exploring on the weekend, so it would not interfere with the regular operation of the station.

He had a major disappointment on his next trip to Nevada. A survey flight over the desert had to be cancelled because of heavy winds. His plan was to fly over the route of the proposed link and have a visual sighting of all the points, to make sure they were the right locations. He was stumped when he returned to the office Monday morning. There seemed no way he could get his gear up to the 6,500-foot level on the uncharted mountain. His attempt to televise the test was getting wide publicity and everyone was rooting for him, but he had almost reached a dead end.

The only way to get the equipment to the top would be to copter it in, but who had helicopters that could carry that much weight and fly that high? Klaus' answer was the Marines...the Marines...El Toro Marine Base. He phoned the commanding officer, told him of his problem and asked it they would be interested in tackling such an innovative operation, something Marine copters had never tried before.

The Marine chain of command started working. The answer was yes. Landsberg was jubilant. Now, his television link had a good chance of being completed. He pulled out all the stops, put the station on the back burner and took his crew to the Nevada desert.

Valley Wells, a small community near Mount X, became his operations base. All the gear necessary for the relay system was hauled up there from Los Angeles. The Marines flew up two big helicopters and landed them on the flat, dusty desert at Valley Wells.

Landsberg was optimistic although the job ahead was difficult. This became one of those television firsts, one never tried before. By the time all of the gear was gathered at the base camp, Landsberg was faced with the challenge of flying something like 12,000 pounds of equipment to the mountain peak. In 1952, Marine helicopters had never flown higher than 5,000 feet. Now, they had to carry all that weight to a 6,500-foot peak in an unpredictable desert atmosphere that creates tricky flying conditions for pilots.

The copters took off with their heavy loads, easily climbed beyond the 5,000-foot level, and successfully air-lifted the sensitive gear to the mountain peak. On successive flights, all four KTLA crew members, with their parachutes strapped around them, were also flown up and deposited next to their gear on the top of the wind-swept mountain.

On one of the flights, the big, eight-foot transmitting dish had to be tied on with ropes and carried outside the copter. There was no way they could get it inside.

Landsberg worked around the clock with his crew to get the system operating. Mount X was the critical point, because it was set to link up with Mount San Antonio in Southern California 140 miles away. He had another link at the 9,000-foot level of Mount Charleston about 40 miles from the blast site.

His crews were spread out at different transmitting sites. They knew they were stuck there until the telecast was over. It was windy and freezing cold at night, with gale force wind and blistering temperatures during the day. John Polich, Hec Heighton, Jimmy Cassin, Ed Reznick and Robin Clark set up camp sites on the mountains and worked almost every minute to try to get their part of the link operational.

They used familiar tricks like flashing lights on a regular basis at night to try to establish visual sightings between their transmitter sites on Mountain X, Stone Mountain and Mount Charleston.

A sandstorm swept over the desert. The tiny grains of sand could easily put their equipment out of commission. A blizzard over the mountains made life miserable for the crew up there. Permanent damage might be done to the relay equipment. Everything was happening to disrupt the operation, but Klaus felt he had the system established and it would work. He ordered the rest of the crew to leave Los Angeles and get ready for the A-Bomb test.

Klaus kept the link operational and ran it 24 hours a day until the blast test. There was always at least one engineer on duty and awake at each location babying the equipment on the desolate mountain peaks. A young cameraman, Robin Clark, was stationed on remote Mount Charleston, 40 miles from the atom bomb test site. A craggy, desert hill covered by boulders and sagebrush was the designated viewing site for reporters and dignitaries invited for the test. It was only about 10 miles from "ground zero" where the bomb would be exploded. This is where our cameras would capture scenes of the historic event.

Grant Holcomb and Fred Henry were the announcers for the broadcast on April 22, 1952. Landsberg set up the engineering side, but the networks provided the pool program coverage televised to the nation.

Robin's Mount Charleston camera position was to show the mushroom cloud from a distance and to give viewers an overview of the vast desert scene as the test preparations continued. It was also a back-up position in case anything went wrong.

That morning, reporters Holcomb and Henry were on the air from "News Nob" broadcasting the event nationwide. All eyes were on the sky looking for the Air Force bomber that would fly over the desert site and drop its load on the target.

Robin, 40 miles away, could just barely see the giant plane. Bright desert skies can fool you. It was so clear, Robin decided to see if he could see the bomb falling on the target.

Just before the zero hour, a power failure occurred at "News Nob" and the cameras went dead. Klaus screamed and yelled at his crew, "What happened? Where's the picture? Somebody out there fix it!"

Several engineers rushed from the makeshift control center to the desert floor to look at equipment, cables, cameras— anything that might need fixing in the next 10 seconds.

Robin, on the backup camera, watched what he thought was the drop plane. Because of the power failure, he had no communication with anyone, but he carefully tracked the target. At the precise time of the scheduled drop, he pulled back to a long shot and centered on the area he thought the blast would be in. He actually felt he saw the bomb dropping.

Robin had the only picture that reached the transmitting link. The awesome blast exploded in the desert sky, right in the center of Robin's camera, 40 miles away. Moments later, the power failure was corrected, the primary cameras came back on the line and the coverage continued. Most people watching thought that Landsberg had cut to the long-shot camera to show how the atomic blast dwarfed everything around.

Thirty years after the bomb test Robin told me his story. He is now a successful motion-picture producer, but still looks back on that awesome moment when he saved the telecast of the first atom bomb blast in the Nevada desert.

Another little known fact was that one of the big Marine helicopters that helped put the network together had trouble landing on a mountain peak. It bounced, fell on its side and was a total loss. No one was hurt by the spinning blades, but all of the gear the copter hauled up had to be hand-carried down the mountain by the KTLA engineers who had put the whole effort together.

The telecast was historic in every respect. KTLA was showered with accolades, awards, commendations and nationwide industry respect. The AEC had another test the following week and KTLA was granted permission to televise it from Mount Charleston where Robin and his camera were stationed. This was an all-KTLA telecast. Gil Martyn and I were the reporters for the broadcast. Gil did most of the work, but it was a moving experience for me to be part of such a momentous television event.

In another postscript, since the relay link from Las Vegas to Los Angeles was in place, I flew back up again with the KTLA crews the following weekend to broadcast, live from downtown Las Vegas, the annual Helldorado Parade.

Landsberg, the showman, always believed in taking advantage of situations. If the link was up and working, why not do another live special from out of state and show that KTLA was there?

*   *   *

Our beachfront home in the Malibu Colony was built on short stilts. When Santa Ana winds blew out of the canyons behind us, the house would almost shake. The raging force rattled windows, overturned patio furniture and battered the house with such fury, you often wondered if it would survive.

The wind was nothing compared to the battering the house took from an earthquake that hit July 15,1952. It jumped on its stilts, rolled and shook and sounded as if it would split apart. The roar of the quake jarred us from a deep sleep. The creaking and cracking built like a crescendo. The brief moments of the quake seemed like an eternity. Each additional roll of the house seemed to be the final one that would tear it apart.

Beverly and I tried to get to the children's rooms, but it was as if we were walking on the deck of a storm-stricken ship. We tried to go one way, but the force of the earthquake sent us tilting another. When we finally reached them, they were still half asleep. They then remained surprisingly calm in the arms of their mom and dad. The quake measured 7.8 on the Richter scale.

This was the first major quake I had felt since the March 10,1933, Long Beach magnitude-6.3 earthquake that killed many people and did widespread damage to Southern California.

When the force was spent, Beverly and I carried the children from one room to another to see how much damage had been done to our beach house. There was none. The wood construction bent with the shattering quake and survived everything.

But it was the start of a memorable day for me. There was surprisingly little damage done in metropolitan Los Angeles. It took a little time, but word began to reach our newsroom that there had been fatalities and considerable damage to the little town of Tehachapi, not far from Bakersfield. As more information filtered in, we discovered that Bakersfield itself had suffered major damage.

KTLA quickly geared up for coverage of the disaster. A map check of the mountain town of Tehachapi showed that it would be almost impossible to televise out of there, though it was obvious this was where the story was.

We had never tried to get a television signal from anywhere in that area and there were many reasons why it might not be possible. The success of the atom bomb coverage from Nevada less than three months before, and all of the problems that were overcome to make that possible, spurred us on to try to get cameras there.

Gil Martyn and I were sent with the crew to downtown Tehachapi to try to bring our viewers live coverage. It was more than 150 miles away with mountains everywhere to make the job difficult.

The telephone company was on this emergency from the start. Based on their permanent installations, there was a good chance they could provide us with a link to Los Angeles. Klaus made contact with them and ordered the loop. Officials didn't know if they could deliver. Klaus believed the important thing was to be the first to make the request. Some of the other stations were now covering news like KTLA. The atom-blast telecast made a lot of television executives realize the importance of live coverage.

While our units drove to Tehachapi, all the stations were trying to secure phone lines from the earthquake zone to Los Angeles. An impasse quickly developed. Phone company officials decided they could set up a television transmitting line to Los Angeles, but only one. All of the stations wanted it. KTLA had been first to order and by rights should be the one to get it.

There was considerable negotiation back and forth, but it was up to Klaus to make the offer that he would share it with the others. A compromise was reached so that each station would get its share of time on the broadcast link from the earthquake site. However, they were not on the air until after KTLA. Channel Five had equipment there early and when the phone company opened up the line, we were first again from the scene of a major news story.

Most of the damage was downtown in the old 1910-style buildings. Made of unreinforced concrete, they were not able to withstand the shattering forces. Many were toppled by the quake. Several persons were killed in the brick and rubble that crushed their apartments and stores.

Other Los Angeles stations arrived on the scene and televised live reports out of the stricken city.

We stayed there for a couple of days. We showed the damage, the clean-up and talked to those involved. This was a very important telecast because it brought to the public's attention a fact that had been forgotten by many—Southern California is earthquake country. We had not had a major quake for almost 20 years, but now everyone realized that we were vulnerable and could be hit at any time.

One experience in Tehachapi I will never forget. I was on the air reporting from the quake-damaged section of the city, when I felt a deep rumble and powerful movement under my feet. It was a large aftershock. I was not just a reporter now, I was living through the uncertainty that hovers over everyone in the midst of a grumbling, rolling, jarring quake. It surprised me. I had trouble keeping my balance but I knew I had to keep on talking and describing how this latest tremor felt. I have no idea what I said, but I was greatly relieved when the shaking stopped and I went back into only being a reporter instead of a participant.

That night we slept under the trees in a nearby park. Cots and blankets were set up for the relief workers and others who might need help. A religious group from Box Canyon in Chatsworth arrived with clothing, food and beds for everyone. They wore the long, flowing robes of medieval times and looked like ancient monks tending their flock.

I remember lying on my cot that night looking at the black sky and bright stars and enjoying being a television news reporter.

I found a satisfying fulfillment being in the center of things when events like this happen. It is a great privilege to be a source of information that helps people cope in troubled times.

We can stop the rumors, dispel the fears, give the viewers the facts, and keep them up-to-date on the changing news of the moment. I slept well that night under the stars.

*   *   *

I covered my first Presidential election in November 1948. By 1952, election returns would be covered live on television coast-to-coast for the first time. The networks had just begun to make big inroads on KTLA's stranglehold on the Los Angeles market. Election coverage was bound to get a big audience as local viewers experienced the excitement that live national elections generate.

There are times when a station manager knows he cannot beat the competition at its own game, so he tries to regroup by counter programming. He looks at the competition's strengths and weaknesses. He then determines what he can do best under the circumstances.

Klaus refused to sit back and let his audience slip away. He counter-programmed election night with a vengence. He was a close observer of the political scene and, although he liked and admired Adlai Stevenson, he didn't think he had a chance against a popular general. He figured Eisenhower would walk away with the voting and, for all practical considerations, it would be over early Tuesday evening.

This was before exit polls, projections and other scientific tools that permit the networks to call the results of an election far in advance of the actual vote count.

Ina Ray Hutton and her all-woman orchestra was KTLA's big rated show on Tuesday nights. Klaus knew she would do well, but worried about how much the network coverage might cut into her audience. There was no way that his news staff could compete with the live election returns broadcast from all over the country. The coverage on the networks would go on for hours and the sheer size of it would capture the biggest share of the audience.

He had his news reporters, Gil Martyn, Jay Elliot, Tom Hatton, Ken Graue and me, prepare for short cut-ins throughout the night. There would be no continuous coverage, just quick updates that would show who was leading and how the election was going.

He expanded the "Ina Ray Hutton" show to two full hours and called it "Election Jamboree." There was much on-the-air promotion of KTLA's election night coverage. It featured entertainment, the excitement of an election party, good music and all the election returns.

Ina Ray had been a successful performer for many years. Her band was an entertaining contrast to all the male bands of the era. She got attention whenever she played. The members of her band were beautiful. They dressed in formal gowns and were excellent performers and talented musicians. It was unusual to see women playing saxophones, trombones and clarinets in those days, so she had a big following.

There was a rule at the station that men did not appear on the "Ina Ray Hutton" show. The election night jamboree would mark the first time that men had been allowed on the stage with Ina Ray. We reporters gave election returns that night, while Ina Ray Hutton provided the music and entertainment.

The election turned out the way Klaus predicted. General Eisenhower jumped out to a big lead and there was never a contest. For all practical purposes, it was over early in the evening, but the networks continued full coverage throughout the night. There were the national races, the governors in each state and local contests all over the country that had to be covered.

Ina Ray Hutton started the evening off by getting mixed up on some of the returns that she was giving on the air. The audience enjoyed it. We gave brief updates on the latest returns throughout the program.

That night, "Election Jamboree" was mostly music and entertainment, with scattered election returns. The viewers apparently approved. The television program ratings showed the largest audience was getting its election returns on KTLA that night watching the "Ike and Ina" combination on "Election Jamboree," beating all the network and local stations.

7.

NEW YEAR'S EVE:
STAGE FRIGHT, AND GUN PLAY ON LIVE TV

The frantic, bellowing chorus of hundreds was pressed into the intersection of Hollywood and Vine at this magic moment when Old Man Time trips on his scythe and passes into oblivion—midnight, New Year's Eve.

I was shouting greetings into the microphone, unable to hear the words above the tumultuous din. People surged back and forth in the emotional cauldron as they blew horns, rang bells, waved silly hats and lost themselves in the chaos of the moment.

As the roar made it completely impossible to talk, I just listened and enjoyed it. It was my regular assignment on New Year's Eve, a live telecast from Hollywood and Vine. I turned my head to protect my eardrums from a lethal horn blaring inches away and ducked under a new barrage of confetti that flew into the crowd from close range. Because I was on the air, most of the revelers felt their enthusiasm should be aimed at me. After five or six staggering minutes, the roar dipped in volume and we finished our New Year's broadcast.

I weaved through the crowd to my car and as I slowly pulled out into the traffic, I mentally outlined the time schedule for the next few hours. I would be home and asleep by 1:00. I would get up before 5:00 and be in Pasadena in the pre-parade area by 6:00. Our telecast would start at 7:00 and we would be broadcasting until noon. I gave up any idea of going to the Rose Bowl game, feeling I would be lucky just to be awake by kickoff time.

Sidewalks still were filled with stragglers with their paper hats and blaring horns, but the edge was off the noisemaking. I drove down Vine Street and enjoyed the experience of being out on New Year's Eve, without being a part of it. I was a spectator.

Turning the lights out on the car, I slipped into the driveway of our house, switched off the ignition and moved to a silent stop in front of the garage, hoping not to awake the household. Beverly met me at the door with a kiss.

"What are you doing up at this hour?" I chided.

She took me by the arm and walked me into the den. "The show seemed like a lot of fun. How many people were up there?" Beverly asked.

"More than I could count."

"Would you like a drink?"

"I better not. Maybe some coffee," I answered as I picked up the paper and sat down at the table.

"Good, the water's on." She smiled, kissed me again and walked into the kitchen.

I asked how everyone was.

"Not too good. Jimmy and Johnny have been sick a couple of times tonight. I've just changed the sheets on their beds," she answered as she reached for the jar of instant coffee.

"How about the older ones?"

"A little better, but that flu takes a lot out of them."

"And the baby?"

"Restless, she keeps waking up."

"Do you think any of them will go to the parade with me in the morning?"

"I feel terrible about it, but I'm afraid if I let them go, we'll have colds around here until summer." Beverly poured me a cup and placed some cookies before me.

I nodded and looked up as I heard a cough from the bedroom off the back porch. Beverly poured herself a cup and sat next to me.

"Poor Lupe, she's had a real case of the flu, also. She's been up a half dozen times." Lupe Flores was a pregnant teenager from St. Anne's Hospital staying at our house while waiting for her baby to be born. "She's talked to her doctor twice already. She's afraid the baby might come tonight."

"I didn't think that she was due for a couple of weeks."

"Three," Beverly said as she went to the porch to check on Lupe. She seemed to be walking much better. Last week, she reached over to pick up the paper, something snapped in her back and she couldn't straighten up for days.

I turned pages of the paper, not really seeing anything but the pictures of a few of the Rose Parade floats as they were being readied for the parade in the morning.

"I think she'll be all right," Beverly said as she returned from Lupe's room. "Poor thing."

"Let's take our coffees upstairs," I suggested.

"What time are you setting the clock?" she asked as we started up the stairs.

"About five. I'm just going to dress and run so don't you dare wake up," I kidded.

"Joan called about the party. She was really upset we weren't there."

"You mean we have a houseful of flu, a friend who is about to have a baby and the fact I had to work didn't satisfy her?" I asked.

"You know Joan. She felt if there was any way we could get there, we should have made it," Beverly said. At the top of the stairs she picked up a doll and two unmatched shoes off the floor.

"Who's that?" I asked as a small cry started in one of the back bedrooms.

"I think it's John again. You go ahead." Beverly put the collection of dolls and shoes on a table and went to Johnny's room. I put my wallet and comb on the dresser in my room, then the credential ribbons for tomorrow, a pen, two pencils and a booklet describing the parade, two handkerchiefs and a parking pass in a stack in front of the mirror.

I examined the assortment and added a little container of make-up from the drawer. I looked over the collection and computed that I'd be ready to head out to work in the morning quicker if all of these items were ready to go tonight.

The lights were out when Beverly returned from John's room. She opened a dresser drawer and started to look for something. I turned over and said, "Can I help, dear?"

"No, just looking for the hot water bottle. I think poor Johnny has an ear ache." She found it and threw me a kiss in the dark. "You get some sleep, you only have a couple of more hours."

That was the last I remembered until I heard a knock on our door. It startled me, because the children never bother with such formalities. It was Lupe calling for Beverly. I half listened to their conversation and was asleep again before I knew what it was about.

Baby Margaret Mary cried next. Her crib is on my side of the room. It's usually quite easy to get up, reach into the crib, find her bottle and let her get back to sleep in no time at all. In fact, I'm usually asleep while I am doing it. However, she is getting quite big now and moves about in her crib. This means she can lose that bottle in many different ways. Tonight, she was at her best. It was not under her pillow, blanket or either of her arms. I ran the borders of the crib, feeling and looking and hoping, but no bottle. Even when down on my knees the bottle was nowhere to be found. Some might wonder how this investigation can be conducted in the darkness. A street light glows through the window and gives just enough illumination to see highlights of things in the dark. A white bottle is usually easy to find. But not tonight, however, and it looked as if I might have to turn on some lights after all. This compounds the danger of waking the baby completely and, even worse, waking myself. It had to be done. I turned on the switch in the bathroom and a sliver of light was enough to reveal the bottle—stuck between the mattress and the crib, neither on the floor nor in the bed, but halfway down. The baby welcomed the bottle without opening an eye, turned over and fell back to sleep.

I let a few stray concerns about the parade tomorrow clutter my mind for a few minutes, but soon fell asleep.

The next thing I remember was Beverly leaning over me. "Sorry, darling, but where are the keys to the car?"

I looked up startled. Beverly was dressed and obviously in a hurry.

"Lupe's doctor wants her to go to the hospital. He thinks she might deliver tonight," she explained.

"Should I take her?" I asked.

"No, you have the parade in the morning. I'll be back soon." She kissed me and was gone.

I still had time for a few hours of sleep before getting up for the parade.

You have to be lucky and be loved to succeed in this business. I got my sleep, Beverly was back with the car in time for me to leave and Lupe had her little boy that morning.

*　　*　　*

A television studio is a wondrous place to enter. You know something important is inside because of all the precautions they have taken to keep you out. Often, there is a "Closed Set, No Admittance" sign on the worn exterior. A ringing bell and flashing red light startle those about to enter when the really important action takes place inside.

The ponderous doors bar you like a badgeless policeman. You have to wrestle with the pressure weighted handles to finally push the unwieldy door open. It is usually dark on the other side. The action is often hidden by hanging cloth backdrops or portions of stored sets.

You have a tendency to whisper as you enter the darkness, not knowing what kind of welcome to expect. Our old studios always have the musty smells of splinter-prone walls and hot, burning, studio lights. Often you whiff an electrical odor, as if a short circuit lurks somewhere in the winding cables and connections that are wrapped around the hanging vertical pipes and draped from power sources overhead.

The interior is barn-like in size and appearance. It is rough hewn, a storage center, a random collection of electronic equipment, cloth and plastic sets, props, set pieces and bric-a-brac for other television shows. Countless coiled, black cables lie motionless on the wooden floors like sleeping snakes. Overhead, rows of crisscrossed pipes with a mixture of hanging studio lights with small doors, adjusted to get the right light at the right spot on stage.

The working set is always the center of attraction. Cameras, lights and crews are circled about the stage. This is the showcase. Everything else is there to make this work. No detail is too small. Lighting directors check shadows and glares while shouting changes to their aides overhead. Soundmen recheck their microphones for placement and sound reproduction. Make-up persons scan the monitors to make sure they have done everything they can to enhance the appearance of the performers. Cue sheets are studied by the cast and crew. Props and sets are closely examined to make sure everything is in the right place. The engineering staff is constantly making last minute tests to be sure the cameras, monitors and special effects are ready for the show.

Sometimes those great soundstages are filled with adventure and defeat, like the time I did a commercial on the "Lawrence Welk Show."

I had been the announcer for years and did four live commercials every week. I would usually get my script the night before and start memorizing it in spare time during my regular daily sales schedule. I would not really get down to the business of full-time memorization until late Friday afternoon, the day of the show.

An alley ran off the side of the station. I would walk out there with my script presenting the strange sight of a man holding a piece of paper, walking up and down the alleyway, talking to himself.

I don't know how I did it. That day it would be next to impossible for me to memorize several complete commercials. The program was televised from the great old Aragon Ballroom on Lick Pier in Ocean Park. "The Lawrence Welk Show" continued to be one of the most popular programs on the air. Viewers got to know me very well during those years I was on it. There was always a family feeling and for those many years I was one of the family. However, I rarely got to see any of the other members of the cast in person because they were appearing at Ocean Park and I was announcing from our KTLA studios.

We had limited facilities at KTLA then. When we had to use a car in a commercial, we would block off the street in front of the station and do it there. Bronson Avenue was a one block street that ended in front of the old main gate at Paramount Studios.

On one side of the street was the rear end of the Western Costume building. A small bar, the Playboy, stood at the corner and next to it, a men's shop. On the other side, a gas station, a parking lot, an alley, the KTLA studios and Oblath's Restaurant. In the early and late evening, little traffic passed through there and we could work around the few cars that did pass by. So, when a Dodge commercial called for new cars, our stage crew would dress the street with flats on the sidewalk in front of the Western Costume building. They would set up lighting on the sidewalk in front of KTLA, put some potted plants up and roll out a big red carpet. The commercial was ready for air.

Stage crew members always waited until the last minute to put out the carpet, so no cars would be running over it. The greenery and other items used to dress the set were held back until just before airtime. Usually we would finish the full commercial without any cars pulling up. But, sometimes there would be one or two drivers patiently sitting there until the commercial ended.

When we put up extra props and expanded our sets for certain presentations, we occasionally got in trouble. We had a gusty wind knock over some prop trees and buckle a set just before air time. The director just shot around the damage and I just changed a few words from my memorized commercial.

The producer for Dodge, John Gaunt, did not like cue cards or teleprompters, so everything I did was memorized. The long hours walking in the alley helped me get my lines down pretty well, but I would always be going over them with my script in my hand, right up to airtime. When I finally got my cue and the red light went on, something would always happen inside to make the lines go together and the commercial memorized. I was in familiar surroundings, working with good friends and in a comfortable atmosphere, even though it looked frantic to outsiders, and unreal to motorists who sat in their cars and watched the commercial going on in the center of the street.

However, on a new soundstage, adventure and defeat were spelled out for me. I had none of these security blankets to fall back on. Dodge had such great success with the "Lawrence Welk Show" in Los Angeles that they put it on coast to coast. Although it was a wonderful move for the Welk organization, it was a major loss for KTLA. We had discovered Welk and developed the program over the years to where it was one of the most popular on the air. Now we lost it. When Welk started his long career over the ABC network, Klaus started a search for his musical replacement.

I was asked to be a part of one of the commercials at KABC shortly after the Welk show started on the network. Where I had done four separate commercials at KTLA, I was only part of one at KABC. But, that single commercial was to take all day long to rehearse and was presented before a live audience.

It was almost like a party for me that day. I got to meet all the Welk regulars. We got along as if we had been working face to face over the years. We were talking like old school chums who hadn't seen each other since last semester.

"How did Klaus Landsberg take the move?" Larry Hooper asked. "I'll bet he's furious."

"It was a blow, but if Welk is going to go to a network show, there was no way it could stay on KTLA," I replied.

"How's Johnny Polich and John Silva? We miss the crew," said Myron Floren. Everyone wanted to catch up on what was happening at KTLA. The day got off to a great start.

The commercial was an elaborate and elegant production, live in front of the Welk audience. I wore a tuxedo and was to walk down an imposing staircase, looking at a magnificent 1956 Dodge, center stage and bathed in colorful lights. I had no lines. It would be simple for me. Lou Crosby, the regular Dodge announcer on the show would read the commercial off camera.

My day focused on that commercial. What had appeared to me at first to be so simple began to worry me. This wasn't the Lawrence Welk program that was familiar to me.

The show was now a major production. There were sets after sets, several production numbers, a huge audience and a whole new environment I was not used to. As I sat in the makeup chair I was really quite uneasy about the whole thing. I carried on light conversation with everyone and tried to look casual, but I wasn't very successful. I was nervous, clammy, and had a first class dose of stage fright.

The feeling baffled me. I had been on hundreds of shows. I had appeared before countless live audiences, but I never had this sense of foreboding. My mouth was dry. It was fortunate that I had no lines. My breathing was forced. I really wanted to get up, thank the producer, say I was sorry, and go home.

The commercial was half way into the show. I had a small waiting area at the top of the staircase. I stood there dreading my moment on stage. I could hear the audience, but not see them. I could hear the orchestra, but not see it. I began to feel dizzy as I stood there. My heart pounded so loud, I was sure the audience could hear it over the music.

I was disoriented. I wondered if I would remember my cue or fall down the stairs. I was frantic. Moments wore on, the tension mounted and I was almost paralyzed as I waited for the cue. I used all the old tricks to calm myself.

"Being nervous means you will give a fine performance."

"Breathe deeply, let the air out slowly."

"Remember, they are all your friends out there. They are behind you."

"This is fun, exciting. You're lucky to be here."

But nothing worked.

The music stopped, Lou Crosby started his narration about the new Dodge. He said my cue words. I froze for only a moment then I walked on stage, almost on cue.

I stepped briskly and moved down the staircase, looking at the car. I was only half way there. All I had to do was to open the door, turn the key and drive slowly off. Everything still swirled around me.

Somehow, I managed to get all the way down the stairs. I stopped, looked at the car; out of the side of my eye, I could see the live camera get into position. I walked over to the door.

"What if the key isn't in the ignition?" I panicked. The door opened smoothly. I sat down behind the wheel. The key was there. I turned it and the engine started perfectly. I was almost home free.

I put my foot on the clutch and let it up slowly. The car bucked. It was to go smoothly off the stage, but the clutch made it buck. The car jumped a second time. The smooth ride off stage became a series of halting starts before it finally smoothed out and took me into oblivion behind the curtains. I was completely defeated. I had hoped no one had seen what had happened. I wouldn't let myself believe that this was a network show and my driving exhibition had just been seen by people in every state in the union. Instead of being a suave, sophisticated owner of a new Dodge, I looked like someone flunking his first driving test.

I never went back for more live commercials and resolved never to allow myself to get into such a desperate situation on stage ever again. This was a moment of agony I created myself, but when you are on live you are vulnerable to situations you can't completely control, but still have to try to handle. It happened to me again on "Hollywood Opportunity."

*   *   *

Despite the humiliating experience of the Dodge commercial, I still like the "feel" of being backstage. The old mustiness of the rough, barren walls and the faded, maroon curtains, adds spice to the frenzied excitement of getting ready for a show. It is especially true when a lot of amateurs are involved.

"Hollywood Opportunity" was KTLA's weekly talent show. Hopefuls from all over Los Angeles auditioned for the broadcast and the best were selected. Every Thursday evening was the "curtain call" as performers paced back and forth, softly hummed their songs and silently went through their routines.

Ballet dancers were stretching their legs, jugglers polishing timing and techniques, tap dancers limbering up for their routines and ballroom dancers swirling amidst the backstage props and clutter.

Harry Babbitt, popular singing star best known for his duets with Ginny Simms in the Kay Kaiser Orchestra, was the emcee. Harry was friendly and always supportive to those amateurs making their first television appearance.

As the commercial announcer on the program, I usually carried a bottle of White Rock Black Cherry with me. It was a new soft drink that made a big splash on the market and I was pleased with my part in making it a success. Television was still new enough that we were involved in the campaigns of our sponsors and took special pride when sales soared.

I would walk around the back-wall area mumbling my memorized commercial, using the bottle as a prop, practicing the way I would hold it on the air. I would recite my lines over and over, and I never seemed to reach a point where I could confidently tell myself that I knew it perfectly.

The muted sounds of the musical tests on violins and trumpets assured me that all the others were just as nervous as I was. The tension was contagious. By airtime, the pounding heartbeats and intoxicating exhilaration rolled through each performer like distant drumrolls. It only subsided when their individual numbers ended.

During much of the program, I would watch the show from the wings. I was always there during the numbers before my commercials. I would hang on to the prickly ropes that opened and closed the curtains, making sure I kept out of the way of the harried stage manager who ushered the performers on and off with great dispatch. I enjoyed being part of the charged atmosphere, seeing so many performers waiting to do their best.

Some were silent and motionless. Others barely held back the sparked electricity inside. Many became transformed instantly as they stepped from the shadows backstage to the brilliant lights on stage. A new radiance exploded from deep inside as if a klieg light illuminated them with sparkle and smiles the moment they stepped on stage.

In those days, we rarely used contestants who did monologues. Usually they were dull and hurt the pace of the program. But this night, I was watching a tall, wavy-haired performer rehearsing a monologue. I didn't pay too much attention to him, but I applauded as Harry introduced him as he took the stage.

It was a dramatic, stiff presentation, with a lot of shouting and frustration being expressed. He told how he was an actor and how he couldn't get anyone to listen to him. It was a monologue about going from place to place and getting nothing but rejection. This ego bruising business had finally caught up with him. He took a dramatic pause. It was too long. It broke the pace of his presentation. He reached into his coat and sneered at the audience.

He pulled out a gun. An audible gasp rose from those in the theatre.

"What's he doing?" Director Jack Parker screamed as he saw the gun on the monitor in front of him.

"It must be part of his routine," his assistant director tried to assure him.

"He didn't do that at the audition," Jack shouted back.

"Walter, be careful I don't know what he's going to do," he whispered into his mike to Walter Vukoye, who was one of his cameramen on the floor.

"Let's play it cool," Walter whispered back over his mike.

I was standing in the wings about 15 feet away. Everyone sensed something was wrong and was about to happen. I thought about running out on stage and grabbing the gun.

He continued his monologue, waving the gun as he increased the intensity of his speech. He was almost shouting now. He appeared ready to crack.

All of us clustered off stage silently.

"We can drop the curtain," one of the stagehands suggested.

"He might fire through it. The bullets could tear through the curtain and go into the audience," I answered.

"Or he could turn and try to hit us," the stage manager cautioned.

Walter Vukoye's camera was the closest to the gunman. "Walter, just stay still, let's not do anything that might trigger him," Jack Parker cautioned from the director's booth.

The audience was deathly still. They did not know what to believe. This was a monologue given by an actor. But was that gun he waved at them real?

I wanted to do something, but nothing that made any sense, except to wait and hope nothing would happen. Everyone on the crew seemed to reach the same decision. We did nothing. We watched, listened, and stared at him, as he continued his tirade.

His voice became softer, his mood calmer, his delivery more deliberate.

"There comes a time, when we have done all we can, when it isn't worth trying any more." His voice became a whisper. "There comes a time when you realize it is the end."

He put the gun to his stomach, a shot rang out, he fell. The audience shuddered. He was motionless on the floor of the stage. It seemed like an eternity. No one moved toward the stage. Then, he moved, got up and brushed himself off. Some in the audience gave him a nervous applause. He bowed and walked off, with his realistic-looking toy pistol in his hand.

Evidently, he had planned it all as a way of getting those agents to notice him. He had rewritten his monologue to include the gun, the shot and the fall.

Jack Parker cued the commercial that was scheduled on film and faded to black. I don't recall much of what was said afterwards. We were all too much in a state of shock to do anything. I don't remember anyone talking to the man, scolding, complimenting, or even acknowledging him. I just remember my feeling of helplessness watching him stand fifteen feet from me, waving the gun at the television cameras and the audience.

Jack Parker was still chalk-white as he came out of the control room after the telecast. Although he was in an acute state of shock, he somehow finished directing the rest of the show as if nothing had happened.

It was a humbling experience for me because I did nothing, although I always consoled myself by saying there was nothing that could be done. Besides, it did have a happy ending.

8.

KTLA AND KLAUS LANDSBERG:
THE FIRST IN THE WEST

Rear wheels were spinning in the soft sand. Each time the driver tried to free the truck, it would burrow deeper. Now it was buried up to its hubcaps. Beachgoers, watching the hilarious attempt to get the television remote truck out of the sand, were laughing and jeering. The KTLA Telemobile had driven off the paved road and started across the beach to the tide line where a Navy landing barge was waiting. Once it began to slow down, it stalled and got firmly stuck in the sand.

The crew used boards and rocks and even coils of cables to try to give the truck enough traction to dig itself out. Finally, the four KTLA crew members got out and tried to push it free.

The swimmers laughed loudly, until a big guy shouted out, "Let's give them a hand."

Three or four joined in, trying to rock it forward. Then another half dozen took positions behind the truck and started to shove. Another dozen joined in and rocked the big remote truck free and pushed it across the soft sand. The crew of the Navy barge even slung a line around it and used a special rigging from a powered hoist to pull it to the wet sand. The crowd cheered and pushed the truck to the surf line where the open ramp of the landing barge was waiting.

An aircraft carrier, the *Valley Forge*, was anchored off the Santa Monica Pier this Fourth of July, 1953. The Navy and the City of Santa Monica had planned a big fireworks celebration. Later in the evening, thousands would jam the park on the palisades overlooking the ocean to watch the fireworks and thousands more would watch from the beachfront.

It wasn't often a carrier anchored off Santa Monica and everyone involved wanted to make this occasion as festive as possible.

When Klaus heard about the holiday plans, he decided to do a live show from aboard the carrier. The Navy liked the idea and KTLA was getting royal treatment from the Navy brass. The broadcast would concentrate on the fireworks, but Klaus wanted to show whatever he could about life on a Navy carrier.

There were many invited guests that night. Shore boats tied up to the fishing dock of the pier, picked up the visitors and took them out to the decorated ship.

I remember the great ride out. The salt spray was invigorating as the small craft bounced over the white caps to the towering carrier. Bill Welsh and I were the reporters on the telecast. I even wore my Navy Reserve ensign uniform.

While preparations were being made, a Navy helicopter came in for a landing on the deck. Klaus was always trying to improve the visual possibilities of a telecast like this. Remember, there was no video tape at this time. You only could show what was going on at the moment. With so many variables, there was little chance of pre-planning too many of the events. Since Klaus was so flexible he had a chance here to try something he had thought about for a long time.

"Commander, what about sending a camera up in the helicopter?"

"I don't know. We have never done it," the officer answered. "Is it possible? I thought those cameras were too big for a chopper." He paused, then turned to Landsberg. "What about the cable?"

"I could feed a lot of cable to the camera, if the helicopter went up slowly. It could go higher than the bridge of the carrier. It would give us a great shot of the action."

"I don't know," he hesitated.

"Who can we check with?" Klaus asked.

Klaus explained his plan to the Captain. He, in turn, talked to his executive officer, then to the helicopter pilot. Everyone liked the idea and felt it would be an interesting experiment.

The pilot had a few questions about weight and size and how the cable would be raised into the helicopter, but he had no hesitation about trying it. In record time, the test was agreed upon.

Ed Reznick, our cameraman, was surprised how easily he was able to squeeze the big camera into the bubble of the helicopter. He decided to keep it on his lap and shoot through the open door.

The holiday broadcast went smoothly: the fireworks, the interview with the skipper and the guests visiting the flight decks went off without a hitch. But the highlight of the evening was the live picture from the helicopter as it rose to about fifty feet above the deck of the mighty carrier. This summer of 1953 was the first time that a live picture was ever televised from a helicopter in flight. It was quite a sight in the darkening sky, hovering over the flight deck with fifty feet of cable hanging out the side door and another hundred feet or so coiled on the deck below.

It made a great impression on Klaus. The flight test was really only a stunt to make the telecast more interesting. However, a helicopter would make a magnificent flying television station. But how could he get rid of the dangling cable?

Klaus passed the dream onto one of his chief engineers. John Silva put a helicopter into the air with a miniature camera, make-shift transmitting equipment and a complete broadcasting studio on board. What a challenge! And he succeeded ten years before anyone else in the industry. Because of his foresight, KTLA was flying its copter before police and fire departments even considered the possibility of having their own. Once again, in the Landsberg tradition, KTLA scooped the nation.

But just when everything was going so right, it all turned out so wrong.

*   *   *

Ed Hunt was spinning off film from one reel to another. The first half of the evening movie was over and he was rewinding it, so it could be shipped to San Francisco tomorrow morning. Stations bicycle films around the country, to keep their print costs down.

Ed stood in front of the editing table turning the rewind handle at a rapid rate; then he would disengage it and let the reel spin freely until it began to lose momentum. He put his masked hand on top of the whirling metallic reel to check its speed so that the film strip would stay taut. There is nothing worse than to give it too much slack. In seconds, it can fly up and out into a tangled mess and roll all over the floor. Many a good print has been ruined that way. Ed Hunt was always careful to protect his film.

The phone on the wall behind him rang. He stopped rewinding and picked it up.

"Who edited this film I'm watching?" It was Klaus Landsberg.

"The one on the air now?" Ed asked.

"It makes no sense. There is no continuity," the voice on the phone continued. "Who edited it?"

"I did," Ed admitted with an apologetic tone.

"Ed Hunt, you are a good editor, what happened here?"

"I don't know Klaus, I..."

"Don't let it happen again. You know how to edit. You must have continuity. You must have continuity."

"Yes, Klaus."

Ed was very upset. He is always a perfectionist, takes pride in his work and it hurt to have Klaus criticize him when he knew the picture was edited properly.

The next morning, Ed got a call from Joanne Boogar, Klaus' secretary.

"Ed, I just wanted to tell you not to worry about Klaus' phone call last night. He was heavily medicated when he was watching the film. He would fall asleep, wake up and go back to sleep. He hardly saw any of it."

"I understand," Ed answered.

"Klaus is just trying to keep things going smoothly although he can't get to the station," Joanne added reassuringly.

Klaus Landsberg's cancer had become serious and it was evident he would not last much longer. He had been very sick for much of 1956 and as summer wore on, he had to spend much more time away from his beloved KTLA. In spite of his condition, he still operated the station. He watched the air picture closely, had Joanne answer phone calls, read all of the daily reports and planned ahead for future shows.

I had worked especially closely with Klaus during the last year and more and more of the station's operation was on my back. I had allowed each department head to take more responsibility and things were going along well. When anything special had to be done, Klaus would ask Bob Mohr, our sales manager, or me to do it.

It was a difficult time. Klaus was loosening the reins ever so slowly. He knew he could count on Bob and me. Klaus was asking us to do more things outside of our sales responsibilities. We had to walk a fine line. We didn't want Klaus to think we were going ahead without his approval, but we knew we had to act on certain problems just to keep the station going. It was a difficult and emotional time for all of us and we all tried to live with it.

John Polich, a director and engineer who was very close to Klaus, had talked to Barney Clougherty, owner of the Farmer John Meat Packing Company, about buying time on KTLA. He had known the Clougherty brothers since his days as a star athlete at Loyola University.

Dick Sinclair, a radio personality had presented a new show to the Cloughertys. It was "Polka Parade," a musical costume show with plenty of old-world charm and music, the kind of show that appealed to many ethnic groups.

John Polich convinced Barney that he should put it on KTLA. Although Klaus was very sick, he insisted that John bring Barney up to his Hollywood Hills home and talk about the show. I was invited to join them for lunch.

Klaus had lost much weight. This was the first time I had seen him in about two weeks. He was cheerful and up for the occasion. He wore a bathrobe and seemed quite frail, but he was determined to be a good host.

The two of them were on the same wavelength and liked each other from the start. Both were strong individualists who had been able to build very successful businesses. The deal was set. It was the last sale Klaus made.

Barney Clougherty kept "Polka Parade" on KTLA for over fifteen years. Whenever any problems would come up, he would always refer to the meeting with "the Dutchman" and tell the new people what Klaus had promised and why he believed him and kept the show on the station for so long.

That luncheon meeting at his house was the last time I saw Klaus. He was optimistic and looking forward to the future. He was determined not to let cancer beat him. I almost believed he would win.

In the fall of 1956 I had just finished the first part of our "Fisherman's Fiesta" telecast. My next assignment was to help announce the parade of the floral-decorated boats as they came down the main channel of the harbor. This was like a Rose Parade, only the floats were the colorfully decorated fishing boats with family and friends aboard. A big crowd waited on the pier to watch the colorful event. This was an annual telecast and Klaus always directed it. However, John Silva was doing it this year because of Klaus' illness.

It took me a few minutes to get to the dockside location where our mobile units were. When I walked into the control room before the beginning of the boat parade, I could tell something was wrong. John Silva had just been told that Klaus had died. We did the broadcast that Sunday morning knowing that he was gone.

It was almost impossible to think of KTLA without Klaus. He was its driving force, inspiration, leader and the person who made everything work. He was one of the few great men I had ever met.

He had done so much in a short time. What he had started would continue, but things would change and his dreams would never be.

He left a legacy many of us shared. Doing the impossible became commonplace for us, and striving to be the best became our second nature. And while he was here, how great those years were! It all began on that sound stage on the Paramount lot.

* * *

The arched main entrance to Paramount Pictures, with its graceful wrought iron gate, double pillars on both sides and ornate, classical cement work above, is famous around the world as a symbol of Hollywood. Visitors often drive by just to look at it and perhaps glimpse some movie star crossing the street to Oblath's Restaurant for a bite to eat.

No one gets through the gate unless he is an employee or has business at the studio. In summer 1942, it was a very busy place. The war was on and the studio was making pictures as fast as sound stages could be cleared.

"Hi, Bill, how are you this morning?" waved a tall man in a cowboy outfit as he walked through the gate.

Bill, the veteran guard, smiled back and motioned him through. "Fine, Harry, beautiful day, isn't it?"

A parade of people passed through the main gate. Each one had a morning greeting from Bill Foster at his guard station.

Everyone seemed to be in a hurry through the gate as they moved, actors in costumes and crew members in their work clothes.

Once on the Paramount lot, the make-believe world moved at a lively, brisk pace. Many were riding bicycles. Stagehands rolled bulky sets on dollies to some distant location. One man was carrying several helmets in wicker baskets as he walked out the prop room door.

Wardrobe people were pushing racks to their assigned sets. Actors in their costumes walked back and forth balancing cups of coffee or studying their scripts for the next scenes. It wasn't unusual to see a Bobby from London talking to a Japanese soldier from Bataan in the front of a stage door.

Dick Lane was walking to the sound stage where his latest film was being made, when he passed the studio's old still gallery. He looked through the open door, but was startled to see the still gallery wasn't there anymore. The camera stands, backdrops, lighting and other gear used to take portraits of the stars were gone. Dick stopped for a moment and looked at the new equipment that had replaced them.

"What do you have in here?" Dick asked as he peeked inside.

"Some television equipment," was the reply.

"You mean television works? I thought that was something for the future."

"Well, you're right. We are just putting it together for our experimental station," Klaus Landsberg answered with a slight German accent to his voice.

"I'm Dick Lane. I'm working on the stage next to you."

"I recognized you from all your films, Dick. I'm Klaus Landsberg and this is my station." He pointed to a scattered assembly of unopened boxes, work benches and electronic equipment in the old studio.

Klaus Landsberg and Dick Lane became good friends over the coming months. Dick often dropped by to see what progress was being made.

"Remember, when you are ready to do some programs, I'd like to help out," Dick would tell Klaus.

"I've some ideas where you would fit perfectly," Klaus told Dick.

Those ideas became realities in September 1942 when Landsberg started transmitting several programs on his experimental television station. One show starred Dick Lane as master of ceremonies. Dick was one of the first to be on W6XYZ. He was the host of "Hits and Bits," a musical talent show that originated in the same still photography gallery where he first met Klaus Landsberg.

Klaus built a small control room in one section of the stage with a portable console. He had one camera set up where film and slides could be projected directly into it.

Two other Dumont Iconoscope cameras stood on stage ready for live broadcasts. Klaus had two engineers at the television transmitter on Mount Wilson. The total workforce of the station was six, including the new emcee,

Dick Lane, who was hired to do the first show.

"Hits and Bits" and other public service shows were televised over the experimental station during the war years. Most were simple productions that dealt with civil defense, wartime news and entertainment broadcasts.

The station remained in the still gallery on the Paramount lot until 1946 when it outgrew the small stage and moved to an empty garage across the street from the studio. W6XYZ shared the old building with Oblath's Restaurant.

Dick Lane enjoyed working in the new spacious, if rough, quarters. The open garage left much to be desired, but it became the new home of W6XYZ.

"How is Danny McShane doing, Dick?" Klaus asked one afternoon when Dick walked into the garage to say hello.

"Won again last night," Dick beamed.

Danny McShane was a professional wrestler and Dick was his manager. Dick always had a wide variety of interests going for him. Acting and television were just two of them.

"How do you think wrestling would do on television?" Klaus asked. "Do you think the general public would go for it?"

"I don't know," Dick replied. "It appeals to a special group."

"It would be easy to televise. We could do it right here."

"Here? Why, you'd need an arena like the Hollywood Legion or the Olympic Auditorium," Dick answered.

"We could start here, see how it goes, then if it's doing well, move in to one of those places," Klaus said.

"Count me in."

Dick Lane was soon announcing wrestling matches from the garage studios. Dick could create instant excitement. His enthusiasm and colorful descriptions helped build wrestling into the first big new sport on television. The matches outgrew the garage and were moved to the Olympic Auditorium in downtown Los Angeles. Attendance surged and wrestling became a new television sport that appealed to a surprisingly large audience.

Wrestling was good programming for W6XYZ because it was inexpensive to produce and it filled up a lot of air time. Dick added so much excitement and interest that the matches seemed to appeal to everyone. Fans cheered the good guys and booed the bad ones. Viewers enjoyed the combat, the one-on-one battles, the pseudo-heroics and the colorful characters who became wrestling stars. Gorgeous George, Barone Leone, Lord Blears and a host of others vied with Dick Lane as to who would be the most recognizable television star.

Viewers got to know Dick Lane early in television and they liked what they saw. Dick had style, flair and believability. Everyone knew him from his movie work. People liked the idea that a movie star was on television all the time. He was a great talker. He liked people and had a friendly word for everyone. He was just the same off screen as he was on television. He continued his movie work and expanded his television appearances as the medium grew. Before long he was on the air several nights a week and, despite the competition from the wrestlers, became Los Angeles television's first real star.

When KTLA inaugurated commercial television in the West, Dick Lane was the announcer, but the host was Bob Hope. His opening line: "This distinguished audience is on hand to witness the production of the most ambitious television program yet undertaken....This is Hollywood's first all-star program." Dick Lane ushered in the commercial era of television in January 1947.

*   *   *

Today KTLA operates out of a sprawling 10-acre site that used to be Warner Brothers in Hollywood. Historical milestones are all around it. It's only a few blocks from "Gower Gulch" where many of the earliest movies in Hollywood were made.

In 1927 the first talking feature film was shot here. Al Jolson made the "Jazz Singer" on stage six. The film was a revolutionary development in the history of motion pictures. The silver screen began to talk and the movies were changed forever.

That same year, a little more than a mile from the station, in his home laboratory on New Hampshire Street, television pioneer Philo Farnsworth made a breakthrough: he devised one of the first practical electronic television systems that transmitted pictures from one point to another.

He refined an experiment that Paul Nipkow, a German scientist, had introduced in 1884. Nipkow's scanning device was a mechanically rotated disk. His invention probably marked the beginning of television. It wasn't until the 1920s that further progress on television's spinning disk was made. In 1922 in England, there was a public demonstration of the miracle of television. The Scottish inventor, John Logie Beard, who had experimented with Nipkow's spinning disk for years, used bicycle sprockets, tin cans and lenses to create images. The Russian scientists Boris Rosing and Vladimir Zworykin were also refining the early experiments of Nipkow. All three came up with improved scanning systems independently that became the basis of modern television. In 1927, Farnsworth developed his inventions to such an extent that television became a practical reality.

Only 20 years after Al Jolson sang "Mammy" in the "Jazz Singer" and Farnsworth made his breakthrough, the screen went through another sweeping change. This time the silver screen moved out of the movie theatre and into the home; commercial television became a reality. Some called it radio with pictures, or motion pictures in the living room, but in 1947, television was here.

Most people did not even know it existed. There were few sets to buy; those who had them were hobbyists who made their receivers from television kits. Television for most people was still a long way off.

At the time, movie makers considered television to be something like a toy, an interesting concept that might be fun to play with someday. Since Paramount Pictures had hired the young German scientist to head up its experimental station, Landsberg was the only one who knew anything about television. Studio officials left him alone to operate the station. Landsberg was a refugee from Hitler's Germany. He was on the engineering team that televised the Olympic Games in Berlin in 1936 and was an engineer with NBC on its history-making telecasts from the New York World's Fair in 1939 that marked the start of television broadcasting in the United States.

In Germany, young Landsberg developed a navigational system using electronic sound. His experiments were in the scientific areas that led to the radar and sonar discoveries during World War II. When his requests for patents on some of his inventions were classified as military secrets by the Nazis, he knew it was time to leave Germany. He arrived in the United States hand-carrying his inventions and turned them over to U.S. authorities.

He joined television pioneer Allen B. Dumont and took part in many of his early television experimental projects. Paramount Pictures was an investor in Dumont's laboratory efforts and when they announced plans to build a television station in Los Angeles, Landsberg was named as general manager.

He built the station's transmitter himself, with hard-to-get spare parts that he was able to find even though the war was on. It was the most powerful transmitter ever built at that time. He placed it on a perfect site for transmission, the 6,000 -foot peak of Mount Wilson. It provided television coverage to most of Southern California. All of the other stations eventually followed his lead and set up shop on Mount Wilson.

Of course television didn't just jump into the commercial age. In Los Angeles, it dates back to December 1931 when experimental station W6XAO went on the air. There were five receiving sets in the city at that time. It was operated by Don Lee Broadcasting and its first transmitter was in the building of a car dealership downtown.

Harry Lubke was the pioneering general manager of W6XAO. He charted the way for KTLA and all the others to follow. When the transmitter was moved to Mount Lee in Hollywood, the signal improved. Now, more people with sets in distant parts of the city could receive the picture. Mount Lee is located above the famed Hollywood sign that can be seen for miles around. The move greatly improved the station's television signal, but the elevation was not high enough to transmit effectively throughout Southern California.

The Depression years were a difficult time for the new medium. Most people could not afford to buy a television set and few were even aware that experimental television was on the air. The outbreak of World War II closed the books on any hope that television would progress.

When the war ended and the effects of the Depression waned, the launching pad was set for television to take off. It became the first new industry to emerge in the post-war years.

I remember visiting the Packard Bell television offices on Wilshire Boulevard and seeing Sales Manager Don Johnson. He gave me a special price on a new 10-inch console model. I paid him $400 in small bills that I had saved for this big purchase. I also bought a large glass bubble for $20. It was used to magnify the 10-inch screen into a size that was truly wondrous. At least we thought so then.

The only problem was that you had to sit exactly in front of the set to get the benefit of the magnification. If you were off to either side you would get too much distortion. But new viewers like me bought those bubbles by the thousands in those early television years.

Klaus had the advantage of the sharp, clear picture transmitted by KTLA and his ability to develop popular live programs. Much of his programming format was based on the wide appeal of popular music. It was universal entertainment and he capitalized on it.

Klaus dipped back to the past on Monday night. He created a television version of an old-fashioned minstrel show. Dick Lane pasted on sideburns, dressed as an old Mississippi riverboat captain and emceed "Dixie Showboat."

Tuesday night's musical extravaganza featured Ina Ray Hutton and her orchestra. The hour-long show was a musical variety with guest acts and many specialty numbers featuring the various women in the orchestra.

Thursday night was amateur night on KTLA. Auditions were held every week and the best performers were booked to appear on "Hollywood Opportunity."

Friday night continued the music tradition on KTLA. "Harry Owens and his Royal Hawaiians" presented music of the islands. Owens was known from his years on radio where he played his exotic music from the magic isles. Many say he was the one who made it so popular. His old radio show used to be heard over short wave and the distant, haunting quality of the music made Hawaii one of the original far-away places that everyone wanted to visit. He had a cast of handsome and beautiful Islanders who performed the traditional songs and dances. United Airlines, interested in creating more customers for the island flights, sponsored it.

Each summer, Harry Owens would return to Hawaii and Klaus Landsberg had the problem of filling the hour. Klaus had admired the music of Lawrence Welk for years. The Welk band traveled the country and had a large following in the Midwest, but was never able to become a major entertainment attraction like other big bands that dominated the music scene. Landsberg made a deal with Welk to televise four shows from Ocean Park.

There is a kinescope still available of that fourth program, which would have been the last of the audition period. It shows Lawrence Welk signing off the show, saying how much he enjoyed doing it and how he hoped he would be able to bring the band back on the air someday.

Just as Welk finished, Dick Garton, the KTLA announcer, came on stage and interrupted Welk, telling him that KTLA had received so much enthusiasm from viewers that the program was going to be renewed and that it would remain on the air all summer.

Welk looked surprised, everyone cheered and it was an emotional moment everyone enjoyed. The videotape looked natural enough and Welk appeared happy and pleased. I would imagine, however, that the event was scripted into the program to get the surprise reaction and even more favorable response from viewers. After a few years, Welk went over to the ABC Network under the sponsorship of Dodge and became a fixture on the network for a quarter of a century.

Another Landsberg program featured Betsy Mills, a stunningly attractive woman who played the harp. Her music was elegant, her technique was flawless and her audience acceptance was excellent. She just played the harp. It was an interlude on the air, completely different from all the action and fast paced entertainment that was all over the dial. Everyone you asked liked Betsy Mills. Her program sounded too unusual for many program directors, but not for Klaus. He felt there must be a place for such a classical and soothing experience.

Klaus was not always right. He didn't think Jackie Gleason was funny and predicted he would never make it on television. He also turned down a show featuring Liberace, who went on to become one of the big stars of television.

*   *   *

There were always a lot of new currents generated around Klaus Landsberg. He was always going in many directions and making decisions that affected all of us at the station.

Sherman Laudermilk was a creative art director. He handled several shows at once and never failed to meet a deadline, although he often came close.

Sherman was attending one of Klaus' production meetings and the discussion centered around new programming. Klaus wanted to schedule a western action film every afternoon. The station had a large library of them. Many were not very good, but packaged together they could appeal to a large audience.

Klaus wanted a cowboy to host the program. There would be a little western set, a fence post, bunk house, a wagon wheel or two, a background with open fields painted on it and some children would be invited onto the show each day. By the time the meeting was over, he had decided on everything but who would be the cowboy star.

He went over a list of possible candidates. Hollywood was a perfect place for casting with so many cowboys in town. However, too much time had gone by and Klaus wanted to settle this right away. He looked at Sherman Laudermilk. "Sherm, why don't you go over to wardrobe and get yourself a cowboy outfit. You would be an excellent host."

Sherman was surprised and thought Klaus was kidding.

"You could do this in the afternoon, and it wouldn't interfere with any of your regular art work on other programs." He sat forward and smiled at Sherman, "We can call you Cowboy Slim."

Cowboy Slim became the star of the program. He just added the assignment to his regular work schedule. The program caught on and Cowboy Slim became one of the most popular hosts of children's programs on the air. He was so successful that another local station offered him a similar spot at double the money. He accepted and KTLA lost a great art director and a popular children's personality.

Announcer Tom Hatten was also a cartoonist. Klaus had Tom put on a sailor's cap, set up his drawing easel and host a series of Popeye cartoons. It ran just before the news program, became a big hit and helped build the audience who watched the news program every night.

Frank Herman became an important part of KTLA when he came aboard. He was another host on the block of children's programs debuting on the station. He was a magician, but Klaus wanted to continue a nautical theme so Frank Herman became Skipper Frank and he hosted "Cartoon Carousel" at 5:00 every weekday. These cartoon hosts became great role models for children watching television through those years. Hundreds would show up on weekends when the television hosts made personal appearances at local shopping malls and business centers.

A special relationship grew between those personalities and their audience. They treated the children with respect, a reassuring experience for the young viewer. They took some very positive values away with them. On a day-to-day basis, children's programs were an uplifting experience and made a positive impact on the young viewers. Sheriff John, Engineer Bill, Webster Webfoot, Major Domo and others who entertained the young viewers were household names for years. They were the good guys and they tried to entertain and educate their young audience.

They were ideal role models. Their father-figure images evolved from a natural love of children and from their own feelings that this was the best way to reach the little ones. It worked and it influenced a whole generation.

Whenever I am reminiscing about the old days of television with someone who grew up during those years, they always talk of their favorite children's show and tell me how much it meant to them. They will recite some poem or story that they remembered while watching television in those early years.

It was ironic that the demise of the hosts on childrens' shows was the result of an effort by those who objected to the commercials on the programs. Since the hosts did many commercials, they believed they took an unfair advantage and forced unwanted products on the children. Gradually, the opposition grew and the hosts disappeared from the screen. That exciting era of childrens' shows that so many people remember so fondly came to an early end. The hosts were gone, but the commercials remained.

Klaus felt these family values were important. He made sure they were in his programs. Klaus Landsberg would never allow Santa Claus to do a commercial. He refused commercials that he felt did not meet the station's standards. Mortuaries, undergarments and feminine hygiene were not considered proper subjects. If national commercials arrived on film that did not meet the test, he would notify the advertisers that the station was not able to air their submissions.

When a guest skater on "Frosty Frolics" was ready to go on-the-air in a costume he considered too low cut for television, he raced out and had someone in wardrobe find appropriate lace to make the costume more acceptable.

He programmed KTLA for those who believed in family values and wanted entertainment that they could enjoy and not be embarrassed by.

He was a firm believer in good taste and good judgment. Since most programs were live and anything could happen, he kept a special watch to make sure that what went over the air was in good taste.

It was an era of growth and adventure. Klaus believed that standards, tastes and good judgment were as important as the programs themselves. His judgment was shared by a majority of his viewers.

Klaus was always willing to try something new, but most of all he believed in the news.

If a big news story developed, programs and commercials would be cancelled and he'd see that the event was covered. This made a big impression on viewers. It was a breakthrough, a new adventure. Our coverage engulfed you. It was happening right there on the screen, and you were a part of it. It riveted your attention. It intruded on your life. It upset you. It made a mark on you. That was all due to Klaus Landsberg, who in his short span of years pioneered much of what we consider the best in television today.

9.

THE TELECOPTER:
OUR BEST KEPT SECRET

Today, when helicopters are such an accepted part of television news coverage, it is difficult to imagine that in 1958 pilot-reporter Larry Scheer and cameraman-engineer Harold Morby were flying in the only television transmitting copter in the world.

There were no other helicopters that could carry live electronic cameras and operate as a flying television station. Most of the industry showed little interest in developing the copter. Equipment was too bulky and the cost of developing one that could transmit pictures was too enormous.

In those early years, KTLA's chief engineer John Silva didn't worry about what couldn't be done. He concentrated on what could be done.

Silva's helicopter project was one of the best kept secrets in early television. It was under wraps for a year. His experimental lab was away from the station. He worked in a complete vacuum from the rest of us. He had to use the primitive equipment of his day and somehow develop it into a flying television station. No one knew at the time, but it was another job he did as part of his duties as chief engineer at KTLA.

The first flight of the Telecopter occurred in 1958. After a year of secrecy and rumors, the project was unveiled and many in the industry were stunned to hear that KTLA had a flying television station.

The antenna system was one of the most important parts of the new helicopter. John had answered many of the transmitting problems by dropping the antenna below the landing skids of the copter. It gave him the best possible transmitting position. However, It made it necessary to retract the protruding pole from under the ship before setting down.

On its first test landing at the station, it slowly descended, its antenna still lowered. It came closer and closer to the ground. It was only a few feet from the concrete. As it swooped in for touchdown, the tip of the antenna actually hit the ground, the ship wobbled, it lurched to one side, but the pilot immediately regained control.

If the pilot had not been able to quickly respond on that first approach, the jutting antenna pole could have caused the experimental bird to career off to its side and crash. Instead, it was only a minor inconvenience.

In 1957, General Manager Jim Schulke gave the go-ahead to Silva, who was concerned that if the word got out that we were trying to build one, other network stations with bigger budgets and unlimited equipment could beat us at our own game.

He planned to put it together piecemeal. This way he could use as much existing equipment as possible without tipping his hand.

Silva had been in television from the start with Landsberg. He was an expert on the state of the art and he knew what breakthroughs were around the corner. He knew how to modify existing equipment to make it usable in his flying television station.

He estimated that the copter would have to carry about two thousand pounds of existing electronic equipment to make the project fly. He knew from the start there was no way he could cram all of that gear aboard and still leave the copter flyable.

There were some alternatives. One of the new huge copters that could carry more weight was too expensive. He figured there was no way an independent station could afford such an expense. The size alone, would make it impractical for daily use over populated areas where news stories were likely to take place. He was a realist as well as an engineer and decided to go with what was possible.

The smaller Bell helicopter was the most used model at the time. It would be able to carry a pilot and a passenger, with a payload of about four hundred pounds. However, to meet that four hundred pound limit, the copter could carry only half of its normal fuel supply. This would restrict it from long flights, but it would give the station great coverage over the city.

John then turned to the problem of squeezing 2,000 pounds of equipment into 400 airborne pounds. He worked over existing parts and electronic equipment, redesigning and reshaping. He cut out everything he could. He had an industry pipeline to what changes could be expected in the near future. He banked on those new developments when they meant they could save him hundreds of pounds.

When he found the new items he needed, he made deals with the companies to use their products and give them field testing. New generations of essential items were now being used daily, so that when they were ready for the market, manufacturers could say they had already been thoroughly tested by KTLA.

Silva designed his helicopter at the right time. Dramatic changes were on the horizon. Transistors were making miniaturization possible. He was able to incorporate all the new science into his transmitting gear and cameras.

The space inside the bubble of his copter was too cramped for anything new. John added boxes on top of the landing skids. They carried most of the gear.

He had a big problem in selecting the right antenna for the copter. After experimenting with everything, he selected the General Electric helical antenna, which was made for UHF television stations. However, it was too big for the copter and John reached a dead end.

He broke his secrecy pact to tell GE engineers about his problem. His specifications were studied at the GE plant in Syracuse, New York. They were able to modify the antenna design into a smaller, efficient and workable unit. The actual antenna was put together in the Paramount Studio workshop.

To complete the secrecy of the operation, a Bell helicopter was hauled from the Van Nuys hangar to the Studio City garage of its owner, Dick Hart. The miniaturized equipment was installed here under the guidance of Silva and Hart.

There were constant changes, modifications and complications before the yellow and red Telecopter was finally fitted for its first test flight. Silva had shrunk that original 2,000 pounds of equipment down to 368 pounds when the craft finally received its CAA government approval.

Dick Hart hauled the craft back to Van Nuys Airport and it was ready to be flown. Hart took it on its first test flight July 3, 1958. The flight went beautifully.

The next day, pilot Bob Gilbreath took the Telecopter up. John was his cameraman-engineer. The first pictures were sent over the 368 pounds of equipment that John had crammed into the copter. Silva was shooting out the window and his signal was being transmitted to Mount Wilson. The Telecopter was a reality.

There were lots of developments over the years for the copter. Equipment got better, cameras got smaller and the black and white pictures changed to color. The small Bell was replaced by another model and eventually the Telecopter became a Jet Ranger. The Telecopter became the envy of every news department across the country. It was many years before anyone was able to match it. The copter was there to give KTLA its exclusive edge in covering all the major stories in the years to come.

I recall one of the first news assignments for the new Telecopter. The circus was coming to town and as part of the hoopla promoting the arrival, ten elephants were to parade down Hollywood Boulevard. The copter was sent up to show pictures of the giant beasts marching trunk and tail through the city. However, the story was a scrub. Although there were supposedly 10 elephants down there, the Telecopter couldn't find them.

Our News Director Gil Martyn muttered, "How do you like that, 10 elephants in the middle of Hollywood Boulevard and you can't even find one of them with the Telecopter."

The Telecopter did much better on subsequent stories.

Larry Scheer was that rare combination: a professional broadcaster and an experienced helicopter pilot. It was this combination that made the Telecopter successful.

I was often in the newsroom relaying information to him over the radio while he was broadcasting on-the-air. He would keep talking while he absorbed what I told him. Then he would weave the new facts into his narration as he continued to report the story. Larry could give you a concise sixty-second report or continue reporting for long periods of time depending on the requirements of the news coverage.

He was a superb pilot. He knew just what he had to do in any situation. He was cautious at all times. He always refused to do anything foolhardy or dangerous, but always came back with the story.

The Telecopter flew from 1958 to 1973. For 15 years it covered news over the skies of Los Angeles. Helicopters are an accepted part of television news coverage today, but it took years before other stations started using a copter like the one at KTLA. Even today, none of the latest models have been able to duplicate the live picture quality.

In 1973, KTLA changed its emphasis on news and sold the Telecopter to KNBC, Los Angeles. Larry Scheer left the station to continue flying the Telecopter for KNBC. Larry was later succeeded by Francis Gary Powers, who was the famous U-2 pilot shot down over the Soviet Union in 1960. Powers was convicted of spying for the United States by a Russian court. He served part of his jail term in the Soviet Union before being released and sent back to the United States.

The shooting down of the U-2, and the subsequent denial by President Dwight Eisenhower that the U-2 was flying over the Soviet Union on a spy mission, created severe international tensions between the United States and the Soviet Union. Premier Nikita Khruschev blamed Eisenhower personally for the debacle.

Powers and a KNBC engineer were flying back from covering a brush fire near Santa Barbara when the Telecopter encounted engine trouble and crashed in a field not far from its destination, Van Nuys airport. Both Powers and his passenger were killed in the crash.

10.

THE FRACTURED FIFTIES:
DOWN FROM THE UP SIDE

Pages are turned so often in life. Some bring minor reversals, others can radically change your direction. In September 1958, a big chapter closed for me.

Gordon Wright, my mentor, who had given me my first job in television, died of cancer. He had left the station years before and we had drifted apart. I didn't know how sick he was, so when I heard the news it was a great shock.

Also at this time, Gil Martyn was recovering from a throat cancer operation that ended his on-the-air career.

It had been only two years ago in September that Klaus had died of cancer. Three of my closest friends had been hit by the cruel disease. All had been instrumental in helping me develop a career in television.

Everyone has his story about how he got started in television. It is usually the accidental blend of circumstances that results in an offer. Gordon not only offered me my first job, but he was always a booster of mine and a great friend. I learned much from him. The most important, how to withstand crisis and pressure. He was a master at it and could wade through the most terrifying ones. I copied his style and approach. It worked well for me through many of those invisible, frightening moments that can spring up and haunt you when you least expect them.

Klaus Landsberg offered inspiration and leadership, and showed me how important drive and determination are in reaching your goals. Men like Klaus and Gordon are rare and vital to those getting started in any field.

Gil Martyn helped me to keep that close tie to news that was so important to me. He always gave me support and encouragement. I was still an outsider, but he accepted me as part of his operation.

I was someone in the sales department who was interested in news, rather than a newsman who worked in the field. It was a slight distinction, but it describes my status at the station.

After Klaus died, it was Gil who did so much to help with the funeral arrangements and assist Klaus' family. A short time later, doctors found that Gil had throat cancer. An operation was essential. It impaired Gil's speaking voice and left visible scars that would take time to heal. In the interim, I anchored his 6:30 news broadcast. I did my sales work during the day and then hurried to the newsroom for my on-the-air report that night. That temporary job as a newscaster lasted 15 months. Gil was very helpful during that time. It became apparent as the months wore on that he would not return to his anchor position. He did a few stories after his operation, but he knew that his days as an on-the-air reporter were over. Gil died a few months later. The station held off a long time before announcing that a new anchorman would take Gil's place. They were able to bridge the time by keeping me on the air as Gil's temporary replacement.

I enjoyed the nightly newscast. It was what I had always wanted to do. I felt fortunate that I had the opportunity to do it on KTLA, instead of leaving town and settling in some other city. When the word came out that I was to be taken off the program, I felt a deep loss. I had the chance to make it and I fell short. I was good enough for a temporary replacement, but not good enough to be a permanent newscaster.

I had wanted all my television years to be in news and special events. Once I reached the goal, it hurt to give it up. I was fortunate to have morning and daytime news broadcasts and I was still used on special news events as they happened. Instead of feeling completely dejected and discouraged, I looked at the long-range possibilities and felt this was only a transition to some new opportunity.

At the same time, rumors were floating around that I would have the chance to move out of the sales department and become a full time announcer. This was encouraging, because I had wanted to be on-the-air from the time I started at the station. I did the other jobs because I felt they were essential and had to be done. They were the work. The on-the-air spots were the fun. Somehow the two had to be blended together. As long as I had some chance to be on camera, I was willing to work long and hard on the other jobs.

Still, the rumor made me a little unhappy, because it was forcing me to limit my options. If my on-the-air work didn't pan out, I always had the sales department to fall back on. If sales took a dip, I had my camera work to back it up. It was a good combination, although it required long hours. That was the price you paid for the double opportunity.

I had always remained silent about my personal preference and the new executives at the station didn't know me that well. I liked the high commission check that salesmen earned, but I knew I would be happier if I didn't have to give up my on-the-air work.

From the time I had started more than 10 years ago, I had been at the center of the operation. I did everything and felt the station was my personal obligation. I believed I knew what was best for KTLA and now I was easing out of the mainstream. It was hard to see the center-stage action of the past 10 years slip away as I took over more limited duties in September 1958. Others would run the station. I would be an announcer and reporter and whatever else I was assigned to do.

During the months that followed, I was still doing my daily newscasts and involved in special events that the station covered. It was a new experience to be free of the business side of the operation and I found it easy to adapt.

* * *

The unsettling events in my television career seemed to mirror changes going on all around me. The world view of the 50s that held so many things together for much of the decade had been unraveling gradually and the effects of its disintegration were beginning to show.

In general, most of the boys who returned from World War II made the transformation into civilian life smoothly. In spite of thousands of exceptions, the conventional wisdom of the time applauded the ease the GIs demonstrated when they became civilians and went on to make something of their lives.

This was not the case for many returning from the Korean war. A large sub-group of veterans began to change the atmosphere of the 50s. While most people were getting on with their lives, this new group was developing a fascination for the Bohemian life.

Though largely ignored by most people, they planted seeds of discontent that began to take root. Bohemians were nothing new to the United States. Their literature and life styles lured many to the Left Bank in Paris during the post World War I years. Their ideas influenced more people than their numbers would indicate. The Bohemian life appealed to the new group of rugged individuals who became a part of the Beat Generation.

Many of these Korean war veterans resembled the Vietnam veterans of two decades later. They were not welcomed home with open arms and jingoistic parades. Their war was on a hostile Asian soil and never really ended. There was no victory. It was a stalemate and both sides still glared at each other over the truce line decades later.

Some of them had fought two wars in five years and had become disillusioned with the so-called American dream. They were turned off by the mad dash for prosperity and material things. They hated conformity and were repulsed by those in the mainstream rat race. They wanted to be different and in their personal revolt they set up a new conformity of their own. You could see them on the beaches at Venice, in their new style coffeehouses and in small clusters on college campuses.

They wore butch haircuts, old sweat shirts and khaki pants. Many wore sandals and sprouted beards. It was the symbol of their disdain for the system that had alienated them. They were no longer fighting it. They were merely dropping out.

Their girlfriends wore black leotards and no makeup, except for generous amounts of eyeshadow which gave them their characteristic doe eyed appearance. Their shoulder-length, straight hair style was the beatnik trademark.

They became the in group. They created their own slang that blended elements from jazz musicians and tough teen gangs. They used marijuana, lived in "pads" and made just enough "bread" to live on. Their open life style demanded little from the individual and permitted him to do almost anything.

Like so many new tides that sweep the nation, California felt the impact first. I don't remember doing many stories on the beatniks. After all, interviewing angry young men with butch haircuts and old sweatshirts, who didn't have much to say, wasn't very newsworthy. Those stories were for the feature writers and sociologists.

Jack Kerouac became the prime spokesman for the movement. His book, *On The Road,* caught the spirit of the times and told of his footloose wanderings across the country. San Francisco was in the first wave of the movement. City Lights bookstore, owned by Lawrence Ferlinghetti, became the mecca for the new life style and a place where the new literary movement gained momentum. Kenneth Rexroth read Beat poetry over the radio. His iconoclastic verse blasted the system and echoed the contempt of the young converts who were fed up with it.

Allen Ginsberg was the the Beat generation's poet. His lines exploded with cutting humor that showed how devastating laughter can be. Everything was fair game. The Beats shot hard and cut deep with their barbs. These acid attacks on society should have told the ex-servicemen in suburbia and the rest of the country that something had gone wrong in the land. However, little reaction appeared and the movement remained an undercurrent. Clusters of people in coffeehouses and along the beaches, reading their poetry and telling their jokes, was hardly a harbinger that things were changing.

The tough guys of the streets, like the gang members in "Westside Story," began to evolve into heroes. The sullen loner, James Dean, made a few movies and became a cult hero to young people. When he died in a high-speed car accident, he epitomized the empty boredom that plagued so many during the changing 50s.

The Beats grew older but had set a pattern for the next generation of restless young people who had their own grievances with society. They, too, just wanted to drop out.

California was hit by the next wave as the Hippie era spread across America and fueled campus disorders that were so devastating in the next decade. Popular music caught the changing tides of the 50s. Chubby Checkers did a dance called the "Twist." Bill Haley and the Comets sang "Rock Around the Clock" and Elvis Presley crashed onto the music scene. The tidal wave rolled on and the contemporary music world would never be the same.

Elvis wrestled his electric guitar, shouted, screamed, trembled, did the bumps and grinds and shimmied his way for millions. Ed Sullivan's effort to tone down Elvis' television debut by showing him only from the waist up failed to turn the tide. By the mid-50s he was the biggest innovator in music. He opened the dam and the new music poured out all over the nation, loud, impossible, grating to some, but very profitable.

The new dominators of the music business were the very young buyers. Records of the older stars didn't interest them. New names replaced Jo Stafford, Teresa Brewer, Kay Starr, The Four Lads and Tony Bennett.

Frankie Avalon, Fabian, the Everly Brothers, Bobby Darin and Ricky Nelson rose to the top of the charts. New stars were everywhere. Dick Clark's "American Bandstand" became a daily hit on television and kept teenagers up on the new music and who was the current in group.

The serviceman, home from World War II, and now a little older, didn't care for the new sounds. He shrugged his shoulders, asked his daughter to turn down her record player and gave her $10 to buy more albums. Somewhere along the line, things had changed and turned out differently than he expected.

Few of our news broadcasts reflected many of these rumbling changes. Things, for the most part, stayed on an even keel. However, at a time when the world seemed almost controllable, a big gash ripped open its stability.

The civil rights movement began and its message swept the country. "We Shall Overcome" became a call heard in every state. There is a time for everything and the time was now for civil rights.

The resistance to the Vietnam War was growing. Then undercurrents that had been flowing through society broke to the surface. A social revolution changed the patterns of the country. Hippies dropped out and ridiculed what the establishment was doing. They appeared in large numbers with their new creed on the streets of Haight-Ashbury in San Francisco and the Sunset Strip in Los Angeles.

Their ranks fueled demonstrations, flooded the free speech areas on campuses and heralded the efforts to take to the streets and thumb their noses at what had been. "Never trust anyone over thirty" became the war cry.

Anti-Vietnam War fervor violently disrupted campuses across the nation. Riots burst out in Chicago, Miami, and Berkeley. The disenchanted took to the streets and the fabric of the nation was torn apart. Hostility flared openly and resentment, ridicule, and rage were everywhere. The decade was one of turmoil and suffering.

General unrest throughout the land tilted the status quo and drastically altered our national consensus in the mid-60s. The forces unleashed began to rumble and gather momentum changing forever the way we were.

Remember, however, that life in the 50s was untouched by these forces. It was before the deluge. It continued to be a time of hope, optimism and prosperity.

In the 1990s, there's a gentle yearning for those distant days of the 50s. The era that was described as the "bland leading the bland" and what was called the "do-nothing presidency of Eisenhower," looks a lot better to us now. There is even a national nostalgia for the good old days of the 50s. Rather than shun it, we are trying to relive some of those good times.

A good example of how we have changed since then was a documentary I did in the early 60s. The social eruptions that would shake the nation had not yet taken their toll. The students on the broadcast had been raised in the traditions of the 1950s.

We decided to produce an hour special about what students worried about in their day-to-day life in high school.

We sent our huge mobile units out to a youth camp at Malibu for an all-day conference of student leaders. We wanted to find out what were the big problems on campus. These were the best and the brightest. They were student body officers from schools all over the city taking part in seminars to discuss problems facing their friends on campus. School officials hoped by having these free and easy open discussions, they might find some answers to these problems.

Students were separated into small groups from all over the city. They relaxed under the magnificent oaks, amid the scent of sage and dry brush, under a clear blue Malibu sky, and talked freely.

There wasn't a single complaint about drugs or gangs, or hand guns on campus, or fights or assaults on teachers. That doesn't mean those things didn't happen in schools, but that the students did not consider them to be major problems.

When our broadcast went on the air, the big issues were minor. We listened as student leaders talked about the problems of keeping the campus clean, about devising ways to cut down on talking in the classrooms, how to get better behavior in the hallways, what should be done about smoking on campus and the problem of some students who wore clothes that were too extreme for school.

That's not bad when you consider today's high school discussions would deal with drugs, alcohol, teen pregnancies, gang warfare, assault on teachers and campus fights and robberies. Things have changed.

It is no wonder that today there is a great nostalgia for the 1950s. That era now represents a time when life was comfortable, simple, when there were answers and not just questions, when family values were the same for the entire community. People today look back and dream of those better days, although I doubt that the teenagers growing up then thought things were so good.

Now the 50s seem to offer comfort and consolation to us more than a generation away. We were a more pleasant country in the 50s.

Some complain that there is no certainty today, that everything is unpredictable. That might be why there is a longing for those days of "Leave It To Beaver," "Ozzie and Harriet" and the coziness of some of those family television shows.

"Father Knows Best" was an accepted fact. Who would ever think that Robert Young could make a mistake as a father? He never did. If he were on the air today, he would be psychoanalyzed, second guessed and ridiculed for offering pat answers to complicated problems. Yet it worked for that generation.

The fathers of those 50s teenagers were the ones who came back from the war and encouraged their families to enjoy the limitless optimism that permeated the decade. That feeling was translated into the early television shows.

Other signs show those times are having a revival. Malted milkshakes have made a comeback, although you will have to pay a 1990s price for your malt of the 50s. However, you can still get three scoops of ice cream with whipped cream and a cherry on the top.

Many of 50s diners are the in thing. Old tunes, old magazine ads and old coke glasses are the rage. They represent something more than the past. There is a strong yearning for that age of seeming simplicity.

Convertibles are back. Detroit banished the convertible so popular in the 1950s, halfway through the 70s. The open car was the rage of the 50s when it was fun to drive and no one worried about the problems of the world.

Look at the reruns of Jackie Gleason and Art Carney on the "Honeymooners." They are seen on more than 100 stations across the country. The series was one of the most popular in the 50s and its slapstick style of humor seems very fresh today.

"The Beverly Hillbillies" and "The Andy Griffith Show" are on television in more than 100 markets as well. It is because they capture the spirit of the 50s, a time of the old values and the old humor that makes the viewer comfortable whether he is a teenager or an adult.

Social tides that were to sweep away the old were gathering force as the 50s gave way to the 60s. Clete Roberts was the reporter who would bridge this storm for the station. He was well known and brought a faithful audience with him when he moved to KTLA. He quickly established himself as the station's anchorman and became one of the most watched newsmen on the air.

* * *

Clete Roberts modernized KTLA news. He was best known as a foreign correspondent reporting from world-wide trouble spots. Clete developed his own network of cameramen in major cities around the world. They would send him film whenever breaking news stories occurred in their countries. Although he anchored the evening newscast, he was always getting ready for another trip to an important news story in a far-off location.

His foreign correspondent image was reinforced every night when his newscast opened with film of Clete in his trenchcoat, passport in hand, stepping off an airplane. He was the perfect example of what viewers thought a foreign correspondent should be. His image enhanced the station's news coverage reputation and it helped build an immediate audience for his newscast.

Clete was always the perfect gentlemen, insightful, bright and knowledgeable. He handled pressure with a reassuring ease and confidence. He liked black knit ties and red-checked shirts. He enjoyed good food, good wines and the independence of being a newsman who could pack up and be on a plane on a moment's notice.

His life was news, but he had many avocations. He was interested in everything, but especially aviation. He built his own planes, refurbished many and flew them on a whim. It was his relaxation. His hangar at the Santa Paula Airport was his getaway. He loved being around his antique aircraft. He was always working on them, keeping them in the best condition.

He loved Mexico. His idea of a perfect weekend was to fly his open seater down the coast to Baja, land on the beach and enjoy the sun and sand and the beauty of the sea.

Clete was like a poet who saw beauty in classic cars, exotic locations and his old bicycle, which he rode on the beach bikepaths of Santa Monica and Venice.

Clete used his cameras to show what was going on in the world. He took you where things were happening. It was during Clete's years at KTLA that the picture took over. His nightly commentaries dealt with international news. He had an amazing working knowledge of the world scene. He was able to communicate complicated international problems with ease. He had observed many of them firsthand and was able to draw from personal experiences using his vast film library to authenticate his comments.

He was just as effective on the local scene. When a breaking story developed, Clete Roberts knew how to get the most from the live camera. He had the ability to make viewers feel that they were intimately involved in the story. When a devastating fire hit the mountains of Bel Air in 1961, Clete

Roberts, with his team of reporters, presented one of the most powerful and dramatic telecasts ever seen.

The marathon coverage of the fire's unbelievable devastation was the telecast that first brought the visual powers of the KTLA Telecopter to millions of viewers in Los Angeles and across the country. The copter was in the air and Clete was on the ground where the flames were consuming homes on both sides of the street. Clete was there on camera next to the roaring, blazing fire that was destroying the luxurious homes that lined Roscomare in Bel Air. The live cameras dramatically caught the devastation as the houses went up in flames. Clete was always in the middle of it, making it possible for viewers to share the emotional experience with him. He was a powerful figure on the television screen and he made those watching feel that they were there, on those wind-whipped, winding streets in Bel Air as the firestorm swept through the hillside community.

During the long broadcast, the new helicopter camera depicted the magnitude of the fire. It graphically marked its wild, erratic path as rolling, red balls of flames devoured almost everything on the entire mountain range. It was powerful television and I was fortunate enough to have been one of the reporters working with Clete Roberts and Bill Stout on that telecast.

Clete was asked to take over the entire news operation when he came to KTLA from CBS in 1959. He brought in his own news company to produce the broadcasts. He was the one who hired the first television news film cameramen, soundmen and film editors at KTLA. Prior to Roberts, there were none.

Veteran cameramen Coy Watson, Russ Day and Ed Clarke were first on the new staff. Tom Brannagan was the soundman and film editor, who would go out on stories with the cameramen, then return to the newsroom and edit the film for the newscast that night.

In those early years, we were careful about the amount of film we shot. It was expensive and we were cautious not to go over our budget.

We continued to subscribe to United Press for national and international news film that arrived by mail. However, the important stories would be shipped by plane that arrived a few hours before air time. A messenger would be waiting at the airport to pick up the film and, if we were lucky, would get it back to the studio to meet our deadline.

The real breakthrough in film quality came when Kodak applied a magnetic strip to the side of its film. The sound on the "mag stripe" was excellent and it could be copied many times without any quality loss. This became a major turning point for television news.

Our film was, of course, black and white. It was also negative. When you saw it projected in the editing room, it had a reverse image like the negatives you get back with your Instamatic film from the photo store. It only became positive when it was projected over the air. The film was reversed by electronic means for broadcast. The editor never saw the positive image. He did all of his editing while looking at negative images in his viewfinder.

Clete Roberts put together a small but effective news operation. His broadcast soon became one of the highest-rated news programs on the air. It ran thirty minutes and featured a sports segment with the former All American football star from Michigan, Tom Harmon, one of the best known television sportscasters in those years. Clete also had a special segment with reporter Pat Michaels and later Tom Franklin. The combination worked very well and "The Big Three" dominated the news.

When I went to the Soviet Union in 1959, Clete loaned me his Bell and Howell Camera. I shot about 2,500 feet of black and white film and made a documentary on Moscow. It was shown over KTLA when Premier Khruschev visited Los Angeles that fall. The station received a George Peabody award for its extended coverage of Khruschev's historic trip to Los Angeles.

When the *Daily Mirror*, owned by the *Los Angeles Times*, folded in 1960, Clete believed television news should step in and take up the slack. He assigned me to anchor a morning newscast. Larry Tighe, Julian Wolinsky and I produced the half-hour show each morning, five days a week, for more than a year.

After the newscast each morning, I would become the staff announcer and do several five-minute newscasts throughout the day.

While KTLA was riding high, Sam Zelman and other newsmen at Channel 2 were working on a new format that would set the pattern for all news operations. It was called the "Big News" and it featured Jerry Dunphy, Maury Green, Ralph Storey, Saul Halpert and Bill Keane. It was a revolutionary one-hour broadcast, with excellent newsfilm pieces and a wide range of stories. It dominated the local news scene and cut into the big ratings that Clete had built up. The "Big News" dominated Los Angeles news for years.

When Clete Roberts left the station, my daytime newscasts were cut back and I was not included in the station's expanded news operation. I was on the fringe of news once again and not a part of the new emphasis. I learned a long time ago that it was best to roll with the punches and not get discouraged when these things happen. Over the years, I became involved in many non-news activities, but that did not preclude that one day I might again be a very active member of the newsroom operation.

Now, instead of news, I found myself much involved in game shows.

11.

GAME SHOWS AND BACK TO NEWS

Early in the 1960s, KTLA took a big jump on its competitors by airing game shows in prime time. These audience participation programs had been a mainstay of the networks during the daytime hours. Our program director, Bob Quinlan, believed that the time slot from 7:00 to 8:00 was wide open for a station that would try something new. All three of the networks were broadcasting their national news programs from 7:00 to 7:30 and each followed it with a local program at 7:30. There were no major entertainment shows on the air during this hour. This could be a perfect time for some creative counter programming.

Tom Kennedy, Jack Narz, Dennis James, Jack Barry and Mike Stokey, some of the most popular hosts in the business, were among the emcees featured on the new shows. The innovative gamble became a big rating success.

At first, the station televised these new game shows live every night. However, this was the era when videotape was beginning to revolutionize the industry. Big, new videotape machines began replacing film projectors in master control and soon afterwards the game shows were videotaped. It was quite an undertaking, but the producers were able to take advantage of the cost-effective benefits of videotape. One production crew could videotape three shows in its eight-hour shift. The programs could now be syndicated to other stations around the country.

KTLA was just beginning to use the new videotape equipment when they made me the announcer on some of the game shows. It was a good break for me. It meant a considerable amount of money.

I would work the game shows after my regular announcing shift. It was like having two jobs and two paychecks. During the day, I was a staff announcer and did about a half dozen "Telecopter News" broadcasts. Next, it would be time to go over to another stage on the lot and do my stint as a game show announcer.

My duties were quite simple. I would be the off-camera voice at the start of the show. I would announce the prizes the contestants were trying to win. However, I soon realized that my most important job was trying to keep the studio audience happy.

It wasn't easy to gather an audience for the shows. The station hired someone who specialized in collecting people. She would bring them to KTLA, let them stand in line for a while, then deliver them to the studio when we were ready to tape the program.

It was easy to handle the audience on the live shows. I would welcome them, make them feel at home, tell a few standard jokes and introduce them to the host of the game show.

I had my earphones for cues, a bright light over my script and a microphone stand at the side of the stage. I read my copy when the director cued me. It was a simple formula I followed every night.

Things started to change dramatically when we started videotaping the shows. The new tape machines were always breaking down. That could mean a 10 or 15 minute wait for everyone while the engineers opened up the new machines and tried to trouble-shoot the problem. The cast and crew would just go back stage, go over their scripts, have a cup of coffee and wait until the engineers were ready to go again.

It was a far different story for me. I had a hundred or so people sitting in the audience waiting to be entertained. I usually did my brief routines before the show started and now I was unprepared, caught in the position of having to fill a void while the equipment was being fixed. My main job was to keep them in a pleasant mood. I had to make sure they were relaxed and happy, so that they would be an appreciative audience. I had to keep them that way until the show began again.

No one had bothered to figure out what to do with the audience when the tape machine broke down. It was now happening frequently and I had to do a lot of improvising.

I certainly was no stand-up comedian. I would talk to the audience, explain what was happening, tell them a few stories about the shows and answer their questions. It would work for a while, but not for extended periods of time.

Fortunately, I had recently completed a memory course with memory expert Arthur Borenstein. He taught me several intriguing systems for remembering things, faces and dates. I decided this material might be good in a situation like this. I could use as little or as much as I liked. There was no special continuity that I had to follow. The material was like an accordion: I could squeeze it into a couple of minutes or stretch it out to 20 minutes, then cut it off abruptly as soon as the technical difficulties were corrected. I kept the memory routine in mind, but never used it unless I unexpectedly had to fill a considerable amount of time.

If the videotape machines were working normally, I kept to my regular plan. I always made it a point to be at the door when the audience came in. I would shake hands and welcome them. I got to know many of them on a one-to-one basis before the warm up began. The technique was so successful, we never had to start an official warm up. It really began the moment they entered the theatre. I would ask them where they were from, what their job was and a whole list of personal questions. I always remembered bits of answers from everyone, so I could talk about each individual in the audience in a personal manner.

They seemed to like the idea that I remembered so much about them. There was nothing funny about this. I did nothing special to make them laugh. It was just a personal welcome to make them feel at home. However, it did get them in the right mood for the broadcast.

I always stayed down on the audience floor. I would walk up and down the aisle talking to them. I never went up on stage. I carried on personal conversations, but in a voice where everyone in the theatre could hear me.

The friendly approach worked nicely. Then, just before air time, I would go to the front of the theatre and introduce the host who would come out on stage and make his opening remarks. If things went smoothly, that is all I would do. However, if something went wrong and I had to fill, I would go into my memory routine.

I would tell them I had taken the Arthur Borenstein memory course and how impressed I was that I could retain so much information.

"Now, Jane, John, Paul, Mrs. Webster, Anne, Harry and Rachael," I would walk up the aisle and look at each of them as I talked. "We met before the show, so it is easy to see how I remember all of your names."

I would just keep on talking, "In the memory course, they showed me how I could meet 20, 30, 40 or even more people and remember their names. Want to try me?"

"Sure, bet you can't," voices would drift up from the crowd.

"Let's try. Now everyone in the first row give me your first name when I ask you."

I would start from left to right. Each time I saw the person close-up and heard his name, I would associate it with someone I knew by that name. I tried to make a visual association between the person I knew and the guest sitting in each seat. I had been working very hard on the project and the brief burst of concentration on each individual would give me a strong imprint of his name.

After I had associated all of the names in the first row, I would roll them off to the audience. Then the next row, the next and the next. On a good night

I could remember as many as 50 of the people sitting in the audience. This made a good impression and filled up a lot of time.

Once the problem was licked and the videotape was ready to go, I would end the memory routine and go back to my straight announcing chores.

When the tape equipment broke down again, it was back to the memory game.

Anytime anyone asked me a question, I would always say his name before I answered it. The routine was very successful for many months. No matter how many names I remembered, there were always a few that I could not recall. Usually, it was because I could not create a strong, visual connection with a friend whose name was the same as the one I was trying to remember.

Most people seemed to really enjoy the routine, but they were the ones whose names I remembered. I noticed the others were really hurt when I could not remember theirs. I can understand the feeling: you can remember everyone else, but you can't remember mine. I gradually phased out that memory routine and shifted to less sensitive subjects.

Life magazine was still a weekly in those days and everyone read it. I used another technique that Arthur Borenstein taught us. This was another routine that you could stop immediately, if necessary, or stretch it out as long as you liked.

It was based on a visual memory association between the page number and pictures that were printed on that particular page.

I would always back into my memory routine, not making it look as if I had planned to do it. When the tape machines broke down and it was obvious that there would be another delay in the show, I would tell the audience what was happening, what went wrong and what the engineers were doing to correct the problem. As part of my ad libbing, I would tell them about the memory course I had just taken. Since I had established a good rapport with them, they would usually ask questions about it.

I would bring up the subject of *Life* magazine to set up my memory routine. Then I would go over to my desk and pick up a copy.

I would keep on talking as I thumbed through it and walked back to the front of the theatre, "This is just a technique, I'm no memory genius, but sometimes it works quite well. I do this by associating words with pictures."

I would tear pages out of the magazine and give them to various members of the audience. There were well over a hundred pages in the average issue, so this meant that fifty people would have two pages to try to stump me.

"Who wants to start? Just tell me the number of the page and I'll tell you what is on it."

What the audience didn't know is that I had studied the magazine quite thoroughly. I carefully looked at each page and tried to remember what was printed on that particular page. I remembered as much as I could. On some pages I could recall many items, on others just enough to make it look as if I knew everything that was there. While studying each page, I had associated each one with a visual scene and was able to recount what was there every time someone gave me the number of that page.

It was an impressive demonstration and kept the audience in a good mood during those long periods waiting for the show to start again. Each one would try to stump me, but I usually had the answer for them. I could fill 20 minutes of time just talking about the magazine.

Whenever people came up to me after the show and asked me how I did it, I would show them. They often didn't believe me because the examples seemed foolish and sometimes they thought I was just kidding.

Arthur Borenstein had selected a particular word to represent each number. I learned it so thoroughly, that each time I heard that number, I would associate that word with it instantly. I learned those picture words by rote, like we memorized the multiplication tables in grammar school.

I eventually knew those words as well as I knew the alphabet. Once the words were second nature to me, I started working with them.

I would forget several pages when the audience asked me, but the overall effect was entertaining and it kept the people busy until the program was ready, once again, to begin.

I had several variations for my memory routine. I was able to memorize people's telephone numbers. I would put together a little picture story combining the key words representing the numbers in their telephone number.

Arthur Borenstein taught us many different ways to remember things and I used most of them in the long ad-lib sessions while waiting for the new tape machines to get back in order.

Using the same technique of visual association and storytelling, I would write 50 or so numbers on a blackboard, memorize them, turn my back to the blackboard, face the audience and reel off all of the numbers from memory. I even recited the memorized numbers backwards. It was very effective. It was the same picture association technique I used for phone numbers, only the stories were longer. Once you got your picture story together, with each key word tied in to the key word next to it, you just told your story backwards and you could reel off all of those numbers on the board backward.

Over the period of time I was on those game shows I developed a reputation for having an outstanding memory. I always told everyone that it was just a system and that my memory was no better than theirs, but even though I told them how I did it, they were impressed.

Those were long, busy days for me. My announcing shift would start before eight in the morning. I did my live newscasts and worked in the announcer's booth until about five. I would usually go home for a nap, before going back to the station for the shows.

Sometimes I would wake up in total darkness, not knowing whether I was going to work for my morning news shift, or going back at night for my game shows. We weren't specialized in those days. The main reason that I was doing a half dozen newscasts every day was because I was the staff announcer. I also did the station identifications and the off-camera openings to various scheduled shows.

In those years, KTLA ran movies in the morning. My announcing over-the-air was limited to the sign-on, a few public service announcements, an occasional station break and a rare tag to a film commercial. From 8:00 until 11:30, I would sit and read the newspaper or a book in the announcer's booth waiting for the next announcement.

At one point, I decided I was wasting too much time and decided to do some writing. I brought my portable typewriter and went to work writing a book. I spent a couple of hours on it each day and wrote almost a thousand pages before I put it in a desk at home, where it has been ever since.

By noon, I was getting ready for my newscasts. They were different from any other news programs on the air, because we had stories from the Telecopter on most of them.

The copter was up there to catch any breaking story. But, even if there was no major event taking place, the Telecopter showed scenes and events from all over Los Angeles.

As the reporter on "Telecopter News," many people mistook me for a copter pilot. Larry Scheer, Harold Morby and often Matt Zadroga were the airship crew and I was in our Telecopter only once. I was just the announcer at the studio. Between the reputation of being a pilot on the "Telecopter News" and being a memory expert on the game shows, I was flying under false colors, flattering but untrue.

My easy-going tenure on the game shows ended when a new network producer from New York took over and explained to me that studio announcers had to warm up the audience from the stage, not from the aisles. He said they had to tell jokes and get the audience laughing. He also said he didn't like what I was doing.

It was difficult for me to change, though I tried. Fortunately, by the time he arrived, the tape machines didn't break down as often and it wasn't necessary to have those long memory routines to keep the audience entertained.

As I mentioned, Jack Barry, Tom Kennedy, Jack Narz, Dennis James and Mike Stokey were among the well known personalities hosting those different game shows. All of them had successful careers and moved on to network programs. It wasn't long before I became the senior man on the shows.

In the summer of 1963, I decided that I had to do something about my throat. I was always hoarse and frequently sick. The doctors said that I had to have my tonsils out. I took a week's vacation and went through the painful process of recuperating. My throat became so sore I couldn't even whisper.

While I was still in the hospital, Bill Derman, who produced our biggest

game show, called and asked me to become the host. I couldn't even whisper
a "thank you" on the phone and had Beverly do the talking. He said it had to
be right away, he needed a new host for the next night. I had Beverly thank
him and someone else got the job.

Bill was always a good friend and helped me in many ways. He even
used me as the host on several pilot game shows that never made the air. I was
thankful Bill asked me to take over, but my voice just couldn't handle the
assignment. Later, in 1963, my days with game shows came to an end.

*   *   *

When you are a utility infielder on a baseball team, you can play any
position. The manager likes to have a good back up, in case he needs someone
in an emergency. I had been a utility infielder at KTLA since the early 50s.

I was the announcer who appeared with the *Los Angeles Times* society
editor on one of the big social events of this year, the "Las Floristas Head-
dress Ball." I announced the Rose Parade with the garden and flower editor of
the "Sunday Magazine." I teamed up with a horseracing expert to broadcast
the weekly quarter horse race from Los Alamitos. When Dick Lane was on
vacation, I announced the speedboat races from little known Lake Los Angeles, which is now the huge Marina Del Rey harbor complex. When Larry
Finley was sick, I did his overnight talk show from a Long Beach nightclub,
interviewing celebrities and introducing musical acts until the early hours of
the morning. When Paul Langford was away for a few months, I did his Sunday morning real estate show. It ran for more than an hour and I showed
pictures of new housing developments and discussed the latest news in real
estate.

On occasion, when the hostess of "Romper Room" was sick or late, I
stepped in and did her hour-long show with a dozen or so pre-school children.
I had seen the program enough times to follow the general format. One of my
embarrassing moments happened on "Romper Room."

The teacher always led the children in the Pledge of Allegiance. When it
was time for me to do so, I started saying it, but got mixed up in the middle.
One of the little girls looked up at me, corrected me and led the rest of the
children through the remaining part of the pledge.

During the election campaign of 1964, backers of candidate Barry
Goldwater bought air time on the station for a speech on his behalf by actor
Ronald Reagan. I was the off-screen voice who introduced the program. We
all listened in awe as Reagan spoke glowingly of Goldwater in one of the
most persuasive speeches I had ever heard. I remember distinctly the conversation after it was over. Everyone was congratulating Reagan. Goldwater said
Reagan should consider running for office. He said Reagan would make a

great candidate. It was still several years before he began his political career as Governor of California.

I enjoyed my position as the ultimate utility infielder. It was good to know that our new Program Director Bob Quinlan and his assistant, Loring d'Usseau always turned to me when there was something unusual to do. I liked being a jack of all trades.

A big turning point in my career took place in 1963. Although I was always busy, for the first time in my life I seemed to be drifting. I was concerned about where I was going in television.

I seemed to be moving farther away from the news operation. New people were being brought in, but there did not appear to be a full-time position for me in news. I told myself that by doing all of the daytime newscasts, I was still part of the team.

Bob Quinlan was trying to rebuild the news department. He hired Sam Zelman away from KNXT, the local CBS station. Sam was the power behind KNXT's "Big News" that dominated the local news scene for years.

Sam Zelman had extensive contacts in the news business. He was able to search out and sign people he considered to be the best newscasters around the country. He brought in Joe Benti, who later became a well known CBS anchorman, Tom Snyder, who gained national prominence as a talk show host and newsman, and Bob Arthur, mainstay of the "Ken and Bob Show" on KABC radio in Los Angeles for years. Sam also gave CBS reporter Terry Drinkwater his start in television. Sam already had Bill Stout, another former CBS newsman and probably the most respected reporter in Los Angeles, at the station. Sam put together a strong news team and produced an excellent broadcast. He hired more camera crews and put together a top news staff in a short time.

As the daytime newsman, I worked closely with the newly hired news team. Sara Boynoff was especially great to work with. She was a creative assignment editor, who shared her expertise with me.

It was difficult for me to see this great news operation being built at the station, but not be a part of it.

From the earliest days, I worked with the news department, but I was always the outsider helping out. I did the newscasts whenever there was no one else around to do them. I was assigned to the big, live, special, news events when they happened and felt very much a part of the news operation.

When Gil Martyn was operated on for throat cancer in 1957, I took his place on the 6:30 news for about a year. Others came in and took over, but somehow I hung on. When Clete Roberts joined the station, I was able to help out on stories. For those many years I was in the news, but not an official member. It worried me, and I wondered if it would always be this way.

The only thing certain in this business is change and I wanted to stay with it through the ups and downs. The station was pleased with the Sam

Zelman news operation, a very impressive newscast. The reporters did a great job, and the quality of the broadcast was high.

Bob Arthur was anchorman, Joe Benti was co-anchor and Tom Snyder did sports. Zelman was disappointed that the newscast didn't take a big jump in ratings right from the start. He knew it takes time to build an audience, but he gambled that this new combination of proven professionals would be able to start at the top and stay there. When it did not happen right away, he returned to CBS.

He left on friendly terms. He and Bob Quinlan had worked together at CBS and knew each other well. Bob asked Sam Zelman who he thought should take over the department on a temporary basis.

Sam said, "Stan Chambers."

I became news director on December 1, 1963. Two weeks later I was immersed in my first big story as news director—the collapse of the Baldwin Hills Dam.

12.

THE DAM COLLAPSES

Christmas shopping is always a staggering challenge at the Chambers' house. In 1963, we were buying presents for eight young sons and daughters. One of the important rules is to make sure that each child gets the same amount of toys. Nothing can ruin a Christmas morning more than seeing one of your brothers or sisters getting more than you did.

Beverly and I always paid special attention to that problem by buying a few family presents that everyone enjoyed. A table-top hockey game seemed to appeal to all of the children. We bought a new one every year as kind of a family tradition.

From Christmas morning on until the start of school after New Year's Day, that hockey game was in almost continuous use. It appealed to all ages. It would be bent, broken and plagued by lost parts later in January, but for a few glorious weeks it was the center of attraction for the Chambers' children and their friends.

On a Saturday afternoon in early December, right in the heart of the Christmas buying season, Beverly and I found one on sale at a Thrifty Drug Store near the KTLA studios.

We were standing in the check-out line of holiday shoppers, balancing the huge, boxed game on the counter, when a lady in front of me turned and recognized me.

"You're Stan Chambers of KTLA, aren't you?"

"Yes," I answered. "Pleased to meet you."

She smiled back, then her expression changed to a frown, "What are you doing here? The dam is about to break," she said.

"What dam?" I asked.

"The Baldwin Hills Dam, haven't you heard?"

Those were the days before the pocket beeper and private radios that we now carry most of the time. It was quite possible that the station had tried to call me. We had been Christmas shopping for several hours.

"Thanks, I'll check."

I left Beverly in line and walked over to the bank of phones at the other end of the store.

I was concerned. The lady wasn't making something up, but I didn't even know there was a dam in the Baldwin Hills, and I had lived in Los Angeles all of my life. I dialed the hot line to the KTLA News Department.

"Stan, we've been trying to get you. There's a dam about to go. The Telecopter is already up and we've called in a crew for the Telemobile. Can you get here right away?"

"It'll take me five minutes." I hung up fast and ran back to Beverly who was still standing in line, "Dear, just leave it there. You'll have to come back."

"What is it?" she asked.

"The dam, just like the lady said." I turned to the smiling woman who was standing next to Beverly, "Thank you for the tip." We ran out of the store.

I felt a hot surge roll through my body; my head felt as if I had a fever. I had been news director only two weeks and now I was missing my first big story. I ran to our car.

Fortunately Joel Tator, who directed our newscasts, got the word early. He raced to the station and called out all the crews he could and sent them on the way to the dam site. When I got there, everything was going smoothly. Our helicopter was being prepared for the flight to the dam site and our Telemobile was already nearby, but was having trouble working its way up the winding road past the many street blockades.

Police had decided to evacuate everyone below the dam. KTLA had already broadcast several bulletins telling people to get out. Joel Tator had made arrangements with the program department to cut in on the air as often as necessary. We were running feature films. We would interrupt for a few minutes, give the latest information on conditions at the dam, then return to our programming.

The moment I entered the newsroom, I was quickly wrapped up in the mounting tension. My Christmas shopping adventure became unimportant.

The Baldwin Hills Dam problem had been detected earlier in the day. Some cracks were observed. Water was running out of the dam. However, officials publicly said they would be able to handle the situation. As the day wore on, though, the cracks got bigger and there was real concern the whole thing might collapse.

Terry Drinkwater was the reporter with the Telemobile, our latest model of a self-contained, remote broadcasting unit. It could be rolled on a moment's notice and was performing just the way it was designed.

The crew drove the Telemobile through the police lines and up the crowded streets filled with residents fleeing the hills around the dam. The evacuation made it extremely difficult to get up those narrow winding streets. Although no one on the crew was familiar with Baldwin Hills, friendly police officers and firemen helped them get to a vacant lot on a bluff on the west side of the dam. It was high enough to be above the water, if the dam failed, but close enough to be able to have a panoramic view of everything. Of course, there was the danger that the entire bluff could be washed away, but the crew seemed comfortable at the spot. They set up their transmitting signal and waited to see what might happen.

Terry and his crew were set and ready to go before anything major occurred.

The first problem was getting a crew for the Telecopter. This was Saturday and most people were off duty. Larry Scheer, who had gained considerable fame as KTLA's Telecopter pilot, had resigned to buy his own radio station in Santa Rosa. If there ever was an assignment that demanded Larry's calm, professional reporting style, this was it. Larry had covered countless breaking news stories over the years where he ad-libbed for hours. But Larry was gone.

Harold Morby was Larry's cameraman and engineer. The two of them were unmatched in what they did. They had spent years developing their specialty. This was Harold's day off and he could not be reached despite countless phone calls to his home. His back-up cameraman, Matt Zadroga, also had the day off and could not be found—probably off Christmas shopping like I was.

This was one of our vulnerable spots. We did not do any newscasts over the weekend and gave our crews the days off. When something like this happened, we had to be lucky. Although not prepared, we now had to try to handle this one. It was a classic example of trying to do everything with a small staff. You can take care of the regular stories, but when the unexpected happens, there is a good chance that you can fall flat on your face.

Lou Wolfe, one of our chief engineers who had flown camera in the copter many times, was at home when the phone rang. He raced to the airport to be the flying cameraman in the Telecopter. It became a day he would never forget.

Don Sides was our new copter pilot, hired because he could handle the ship so well and had the potential to develop into a good television reporter.

Both of them had been thrown into the middle of one of the biggest stories of the decade. They somehow got to the airport and were able to fly to Baldwin Hills and circle the dam before anything major happened. Thanks to Joel Tator, I was a lucky news director. We got to the scene on time.

The picture was ominously peaceful. I shared the on-the-air reporting with Don. He was broadcasting from the copter and I was in the studio booth, looking at a screen in front of me that showed the picture transmitted from the Telecopter.

I kept on reporting all of the facts coming into the newsroom. I was talking on the air as the Telecopter showed the pictures of water leaking from the dam. At one point, I was able to get a spokesman from the Department of Water and Power on the telephone. That phone conversation with Bob Lee, press officer for the department was broadcast live to the viewers. They were able to watch the television picture from the copter and listen to the two of us discussing the serious situation developing. We talked about what was happening and what those living in the vicinity of the dam should do as a precaution.

Bob Lee said, "We're trying to reduce the water level to take the pressure off the dam. We're taking out water as fast as we can."

As he spoke, the copter camera showed a close-up of water pouring through the escape system.

"Mr. Lee, is there any imminent danger that the dam will fail?" I asked while watching the live picture from the Telecopter.

He answered immediately, "It has held so far, and we believe it will hold..."

At that moment, a big gaping hole opened in the face of the dam. A circle of concrete in the face of the dam just fell away and water went roaring through. I quickly threw the audio to Don Sides in the copter.

Don picked it up. "Just as the man was talking about it holding, the dam gave way," Don started his narration.

He looked down on the unbelievable scene. The thundering water on a wild rampage gouged a widening hole as the dam broke away. The gushing river roared out with a crushing force, exploding over the catch basin below, down the winding roads, through the narrow streets, wiping out everything in its path.

The live television picture from the Telemobile on the ground next to the raging wall of water was just as awesome. A huge section of the front of the dam disintegrated as the unleashed force of the water kept tearing it away. All of this was taking place live, in front of the KTLA cameras.

All of us at the studio and hundreds of thousands of viewers at home and later millions across the country could not believe what we were seeing. I vividly remember the tumbling flood waters scooping up dozens of automobiles that had been parked in driveways and along the curbs. They looked like half submerged toys being bumped and pushed as the raging torrents catapulted them down the winding streets and threw them against buildings that would be later broken and carried away by the violent force of the turbulent waters.

The wall of water pouring out of the dam demolished and uprooted everything in its path. Houses were ripped apart. They were cracking, breaking up and wrenched from their foundations.

It was so devastating you could not accept the fact that you were watching it live, that it was happening right now in the heart of the city. You challenged the reality of what you were seeing on the screen. This was 1963, and dams do not collapse in the middle of a modern city like Los Angeles.

Dams don't break up and wipe away countless homes. Dams don't collapse on live television. The impact was painful as this seemingly unending event played out on television. We had no idea what happened to the people who lived in the shattered homes on those devastated streets. The fear that there was a great loss of life hung over all of us as we watched the destruction unfold.

I received calls from networks and television stations all over the country asking permission to televise our live pictures of the devastation. All the national television networks picked up the KTLA coverage as the Telecopter overhead and the Telemobile on the ground delivered live pictures that would not be forgotten.

Before all the water drained out of the reservoir, about 80 million gallons inundated the canyons below the dam. The angry mud and water washed out 40,000 tons of debris. More than a hundred homes and apartments were destroyed or badly damaged. There were only a few fatalities. The evacuation had been ordered in time.

Although hundreds had been able to flee before their homes were destroyed, one person was killed on the flatland below the hills. The driver was going through hubcap deep water that covered the entire street. The car, with windows open, continued moving through a flooded intersection. The driver had no way of knowing that workers had dug a huge excavation in the middle of the street. The car ran into the water-filled hole and quickly sank thirty feet to the bottom. The driver drowned.

The Baldwin Hills Dam was never rebuilt. It remained for years an empty brush covered cement hollow, with a large "V" section still cut out of what used to be the face of the reservoir. It eventually became a city park with rolling lawns and trees. All signs of any devastation are now gone, but the memory of that December Saturday remains with everyone who saw the dam collapse.

Reporter Terry Drinkwater did such a remarkable job reporting live from the Telemobile at the scene of the dam he was hired by CBS News shortly afterwards.

Joe Benti, who anchored much of our extended coverage of the disaster, received wide acclaim for his work and later left KTLA for an anchor position with CBS News.

Tom Snyder was another reporter who received praise for his coverage. Tom eventually moved on to NBC News, then to his very successful career as a network television and radio talk show host.

It was a couple of weeks before Beverly and I got back to Thrifty's to buy our hockey game for the family. We bought it Christmas Eve and had it wrapped and under the tree the next morning.

I had become news director just as three of the biggest news stories of the decade happened in America. Within a period of less than a month, I was on-the-air reporting that President John Kennedy had been shot in Dallas, the Baldwin Hills Dam had collapsed and Frank Sinatra Jr. had been kidnapped in Los Angeles. I knew that being a news director was going to be busy, but I had never expected so much to happen so fast.

* * *

On that December night in 1963, I stamped my feet a couple of times, pulled my coat closer to my neck and jammed my cold hands deep into my overcoat pockets to endure the brisk air of the winter evening.

Frank Sinatra Jr. had been kidnapped and the two dozen newsmen, cameramen and reporters standing around me had been on the story from early morning, right up to these cold, post-midnight hours. We had raced around the city to phone booths where the kidnappers had called from, to places where the ransom money had been picked up and to different police stations where we hoped to pick up some official news about late developments.

We all knew that something was about to happen. We had converged outside the Bel Air home of Frank Sinatra. Throughout the evening, different news crews and reporters showed up at the scene to see if the big break in the case would take place here.

There were countless rumors flying around: that the ransom had been paid, that Sinatra Jr. had been released, that he was already inside with his Dad, that the suspects were still at large, that they were in custody and that Frank Sinatra was about to come out of the house with his recently released son. Unfortunately, as far as we could tell they were all rumors.

All of us were discussing these fresh and stale rumors. Everyone seemed to think the climax was at hand. There were too many secret things going on and each reporter's news instinct brought him here to the home to try to get the main elements of the story as they unraveled.

We had little official information about the kidnapping. Many news leaks had occurred but could not be confirmed. Frank Sinatra had not talked to the press and there had been few statements by police officials.

We maintained our vigil in front of the house for about two hours, when a couple of closed vans pulled into the driveway and several men in tuxedos got out. They swung the back doors open and started pulling out tables, benches and chairs. They brought out tablecloths and candelabras. They set everything up on the damp grass next to the street. They dressed the tables with linen napkins and silverware. Then they brought out trays of meats, cheese, fruit, salads and breads. They poured hot coffee and stacked china plates on the elegantly tailored tables.

The outdoor buffet was for the shivering newsmen. The men in tuxedos were waiters from Chasen's in Beverly Hills. Dave Chasen, the owner of the famous restaurant, was on the scene himself to make sure the buffet was just right and to see that the reporters had all the food and drink they wanted.

Chasen said that Frank Sinatra had seen the large number of reporters outside his home. Everytime he looked out, the crowd was getting bigger. He knew it was cold and that everyone must be getting hungry. Chasen said he got the call from Sinatra to get the formal buffet up there as soon as possible. He was told to set it up on the lawn and try to make the reporters a little more comfortable.

It has been many years and memories tend to fade, but I do believe the candelabras were lit and the light helped the waiters serve the food and let the reporters see what they had on their plates.

I will always remember the elegant way Frank Sinatra fed the press that night his son was freed!

There is a vague postscript to the banquet. The Bel Air Patrol helped Frank Sinatra Jr. get away without talking to newsmen. When he was released by the kidnappers, the Patrol hid him in the trunk of one of the patrol cars. They took him to their office about a mile away. They put him in a friend's car and he left the scene. We never did catch up with the freed kidnap victim that night.

I was talking about the generous gesture with a cynical reporter friend who was also there that night. He wondered if that catered dinner was a diversion to get Sinatra Jr. away from the cameras and reporters. I still think it was a delightful gesture from Frank Sinatra, who has had more than his share of run-ins with the press. And besides, the roast beef was delicious.

*　　*　　*

Days later I looked back at the events of those turbulent weeks and began to realize that vast changes had taken place in my professional life. I had been appointed news director on December 1, 1963. The Baldwin Hills Dam collapsed and Frank Sinatra Jr. was kidnapped in the weeks that followed.

Only two weeks earlier, on November 22, 1963, I was in the newsroom preparing one of my daytime newscasts when I heard the ominous, staccato ringing of the bulletin bell from the UPI newswires. I jumped up from my typewriter and raced to the bank of chattering teletypes, one of the few times in my life that I heard a UPI 15-bell flash. The urgent sound of the chilling bells was accompanied by the printed word "FLASH" on the teletype paper. I stared at the wire machine in disbelief. The word FLASH was followed by a two lines: "PRESIDENT JOHN F. KENNEDY WAS SHOT IN DALLAS,

TEXAS...."

In just moments, I was in front of a television camera reporting the shooting. I only had a few lines of wire copy in my hand and had to keep on talking. We knew the President had been rushed to a hospital. We knew that he had been wounded, but we did not know how badly.

In our time and our America, presidents are not assassinated. That happened in the days of McKinley, Garfield and Lincoln, but not in modern times. It was a situation that could not be confronted with conventional wisdom. The chance that President Kennedy might die from an assassin's gun was not possible to accept while I was on the air. I was broadcasting for about twenty minutes, ad-libbing around the small amount of information I had from the United Press teletypes, when I was told by a voice off camera that President Kennedy had died from gunshot wounds. I delayed for a moment, looking off camera at the newsman who was giving me the devastating information.

The gravity of what he had told me was like a blow to the head. I said to myself, "Can I say this? What if it is not true? Are you certain?"

He handed me the wire copy and I read it, "President Kennedy has just died of the gunshot wounds."

I kept talking for another five minutes or so as a few more details came across the teletypes. Then, in a completely unprecedented act of cooperation, the television networks permitted us to join them in their coverage of the assination.

As KTLA picked up the network feed, I concluded my part. I had been on for about 20 minutes. The television coverage of the assassination of President John Kennedy went on for days. It was one of those rare moments in television when every station in the country was broadcasting the same story; the tragic developments in Dallas. The world seemed to stop as the nation mourned its young President.

I was only a small participant in that historic moment, but it was an experience that will always be with me.

Many say that this was a defining event in history. What had been would never be the same. What would happen would always be affected. The death of President Kennedy and the grievous mourning of a nation spilled over into everyone's lives. His death seemed to be the watershed between the old world of the 1950s and the turbulent times that followed.

13.

THE SIXTIES RIOTS:
THE NATION IS SHAKEN

Decades, like people, are difficult to classify in orderly categories. They never seem to fit the time frame they are supposed to. The 60s were shaped by two different forces. One era was a continuation, a carry-over from the 50s, with troublesome undercurrents flowing and bubbling, but the threatening rumbles remained under the surface.

After the assassination, a deluge engulfed the nation. New forces bulged to the surface and became part of the mainstream and shaped the new era of the 60s. It was "out with the old and in with the new." In a brief time, the spirit of the old 50s was jettisoned and the new age began. You can imagine what it was like to become news director during this chaotic time of sweeping change.

Looking back, it is easy to tick off the events that moved the 60s into chaos, but it wasn't clear to me then.

When Stalin died in 1953, it marked the beginning of a new era in the Soviet Union. There was some hope that a new, peaceful relationship might be established with the free world, but it soon became apparent that the Soviets planned to continue their old, hard-line policy.

In 1954, in the Far East, the French lost a long, bitter and frustrating war against the Viet Cong when Dien Bien Phu fell. An armistice was signed and the French pulled out their troops, leaving a festering vacuum in the area.

The United States and mainland China came "eyeball to eyeball" over the tiny offshore islands of Quemoy and Matsu. It almost ended in war, but the crisis subsided.

The H-bomb became a reality in 1954.

The Israeli-Egyptian War in 1956 resulted in United States peace keeping forces being deployed in the Mid-East. The powder keg was being filled with more explosives.

The United States experienced a great wave of prosperity with more real income for most people than ever before.

Nikita Khruschev became premier of the Soviet Union in 1957. He made a favorable impression on world leaders, renewing hope that relations might improve between the superpowers.

Sputnik stunned Americans in October of that year. Sputnik II was sent up in November. The Soviets had beaten us into space and the United States had to play catchup in attempts to get a satellite into orbit.

Our Marines went ashore in Lebanon in 1958 to smooth the trouble waters in that faraway land. Our force was so overwhelming, the crisis was eased and the Marines pulled out.

Fidel Castro came to power in Cuba in 1959 and the United States had to learn to live with a communist power just off our coast. The same year Vice President Richard Nixon and Premier Nikita Khruschev had their famous kitchen debate in Moscow. Both men argued in public about the strengths of their two nations. Cameras were rolling and people around the world saw the two men as they aired their views. It was a sign that although our countries disagreed about many things our leaders could meet and talk. Maybe there was some chance the mistrust between the two nations could be eased.

Beverly and I were in the Soviet Union shortly after the Nixon visit. While we were there, the Soviets announced that President Eisenhower would visit Moscow. The President was probably the most respected man in the world at that time and was nearing the end of his two-term presidency. There was great excitement . Russians on the street, recognizing us as Americans, would tell us how pleased they were about the news. They were genuinely moved that the American President was going to visit their country.

The smiling people would repeat "peace and friendship" over and over again. It was a time of great hope and possibilities. It was exhilarating to be there in the middle of it and get the positive feedback from the average Soviet citizen about Eisenhower's plans.

The trip was not to be. Instead, a high flying U-2 plane was shot down over Soviet air space. Eisenhower played down the significance of the flight. The Soviets said it was a spy plane. Eisenhower denied it. Premier Khruschev called him a liar. The Soviets showed the wreckage of the U-2 on television. They captured the pilot, Francis Gary Powers, and put him on trial. He was on a spy mission. He was tried, convicted and sentenced by a Soviet court and spent time in a Russian jail.

The prestige of President Eisenhower plummeted and the Khruschev charge that he was a liar stuck with him for the rest of his presidency. The U-2 spy plane incident ended any chance that the two countries could resolve their major problems. The tension between the two superpowers continued to build until the harrowing, dangerous days of the Cuban missile crisis when the world moved to the brink of atomic war. We plowed through those terrifying days and tasted the possibility of nuclear destruction. We lived on the edge of oblivion for those perilous hours. We had a chance to reflect on what we had and what we would lose.

I remember standing in front of a bank of teletype machines in the newsroom at the climatic moments of the missile crisis. Bill Stout was next to me. We did not talk, but just stared at every single word being formed on the wire machines that told us that the Soviet ships were still heading towards Cuba.

Later the wire machine bulletins flashed the word that the Soviets had turned around and pulled back. The Soviet missiles bound for Cuba would not land. The Soviets came right up to the brink, but blinked. We did not budge. The United States' blockade of Cuba continued.

The first indications that the United States might get involved in Vietnam could be detected in the Eisenhower and Kennedy administrations. The United States moved to fill the vacuum that the French had left in Vietnam. The long road to war in that troubled land was underway.

The State of California,which had built one of the largest university systems in the world in the previous decade, was not ready for what was to happen. The unbridled optimism of the 50s soured into self questioning, exhaustion and disbelief at what was taking place to many in the 60s.

The dream seemed to shatter. The boys who came home from World War II, who worked so hard for their families, for their home and for their jobs, couldn't understand what happened. Where had they gone wrong?

College campuses across the country were quiet and settled during the 50s. Critics said the students were not interested in anything but themselves. They were in college to get a degree, a job and find a soft spot in the world for themselves. But things were changing.

Many tired of the old ways. They didn't like the business world and the impersonal demands of industry. A job was just something that had to be tolerated. Many kept on working just to get that weekly paycheck that was vital to the wheels of progress. Many people seemed bored with what they were doing. Many felt their work was far too insignificant but went along with it because they had to.

People were slipping deeper and deeper into debt, but few retrenched. Things had been going along for so long, there was no reason why it would not continue.

Children seemed happy enough. They had money, cars, friends and time to do what they wanted. Maybe they were not interested in the rat race that their parents were caught up in, but this was always the case when you compare generations.

New concerns rose to the surface, things like juvenile delinquency and drug use. Fortunately, it always seemed to be other kids in other neighborhoods who were to blame.

We were always protective of our news audiences in the 50s. We were selective and careful about stories we covered and the words we used on the air.

We never used the word " rape." We said "assault." We never talked about venereal disease, prostitution or personal behavior. We never talked about abortion, homosexuals or people living together. We never said "hell" or "damn" on the air.

If a news story on the UPI teletype contained any material the audience might find offensive, it was clearly marked at the start with a slug that read, "Editors note contents." This was to protect radio newsannouncers who might read the copy cold and find themselves reading a story that they wouldn't have aired if he knew what was in it.

Some television programs did daring interviews with prostitutes, pornographers or drug users. The guests were hidden by shadows or masks and were called only by their first names. They were paraded on the screen like freaks in a sideshow. Broadcasts like this were called sensational and not considered real news programs.

There were undercurrents everywhere that foretold change, but they had little effect on the actual content of day-to-day television newscasts.

I was a combination news director-assignment editor during these years. Each day, I had to deal with these new forces making news for the first time.

I remember a popular nightclub for young people on the Sunset Strip. It was Pandora's Box, built on a triangle of land at the corner of Crescent Heights and Sunset Boulevard in the heart of the Sunset Strip. I wasn't interested in any social causes when I sent camera crews up there. I was there because the Sheriff's Department was having trouble handling the large disorderly crowds. It happened frequently so the Sheriff had to show strength and arrest those who got out of line. It became a symbol of what was to come. So many young people poured onto the Sunset Strip that they, in effect, took it over. Over a brief period of time businesses and restaurants began to close, unable to keep open because their customers were being driven away by this new group of undesirables.

Pandora's Box became the center of the problem. It was soon closed down by officials amidst the hooting, shoving and pushing of the mob. The establishment won this one. The building was bulldozed down. Our cameras recorded the action. The vacant triangle on the Strip is still there today, the notoriety of its disruptive past long forgotten.

The young troublemakers were dubbed hippies. They became news-worthy because they did things and got in trouble. We soon discovered a new source of news. Our camera crews were busy recording the day-to-day encounters over issues that varied from curfews and causes to anti-war demonstrations and campus unrest. Hippies were unpredictable and they got our attention.

We got to know the ringleaders, who kept us informed. There were demonstrations every day on countless different college campuses and in front of government buildings in the city.

A beautiful blonde, Tiger Slavick, frequently briefed us on some of the black civil rights marches. Our terminology began to change. Negroes were now called blacks. Mexican-Americans were called chicanos. The women's movement was growing and demanding attention. There were "sit-ins" at the Board of Education to protest injustices. Unfair housing practices were under attack from the new demonstrators. Long lines of protestors marched back and forth to show their anger.

Protestors roared and shouted at school meetings, shutting them down and then walking out. College "free speech" areas were ablaze with colorful speakers and chanting students demanding redress.

Underground groups like the "Weathermen" threatened violence. Extreme racial groups fought the police. Our camera crews were trapped in a full-scale gun battle that erupted outside a black extremist headquarters on Central Avenue in Los Angeles.

Others used intimidation to show their latent power and their disdain for the news media. Reporters and cameramen had to be searched by members of extreme groups before they were permitted to go inside and cover the news story.

Chicanos rioted in East Los Angeles. Tear gas and gunfire was part of the pattern. Angry, brutal clashes broke out and threatened the entire community.

Many different forces were emerging. Many noble and worthwhile causes were being brought to the attention of the public. Though events were disruptive, there was no way they could be lumped together and called a single force. The term hippie could not be applied to many of those who took to the streets.

As an assignment editor, I didn't have time to look at the worthiness of the causes. I just concentrated on their newsworthiness.

Los Angeles was spared much of the tragic violence that plagued San Francisco, but we had our share. Each day turbulent events in the city were covered. Each night we showed what had happened on our newscasts. It went on day after day. Violence was almost the norm, but it was still the headline news of the day.

Our Telecopter overhead covered the stories. Our camera crews were in the middle of much of the action, but somehow we all got through most of the decade unscathed.

The anti-war demonstrations grew more desperate as the number of students about to be drafted increased. It was a convulsive situation that seemed to boil hotter each day.

When President Lyndon Johnson appeared at the Century Plaza Hotel in Los Angeles, thousands of organized anti-war demonstrators showed up to protest the policies in Vietnam. It erupted into a full-scale riot that broke out while the President was inside the hotel.

The 60s were not a pleasant time. I do not recall it with any fondness, but I was in the middle of it, while the local combat zone moved from one location to another.

Looking back, we can see that many positive changes were made because of what happened on the civil rights marches through the South and the human rights protests across the country. Unfair practices were rooted out, because so many people took to the streets to gain fairness for all. Each cause was separate, but they used similar tactics of protest: marches and demonstrations which dominated our attention.

During that decade we were plagued with an outbreak of violence when a series of brutal crimes hit the city. The Charles Manson gang went on a killing spree unheard of in a civilized society. The murders of actress Sharon Tate and her friends at her luxurious home shocked the world.

We covered the developments with disbelief as more gruesome details became known almost daily. Our reporter, Dick Hathcock, worked the story methodically as the Manson gang was captured one by one. He was on the case for weeks uncovering strange developments in the investigation before the murderers were finally arrested.

We had camera crews covering the arrests, the trial and the "side bar" stories as the Manson gang was gradually broken up and put behind bars. We did frequent interviews on a street corner next to the Hall of Justice in Los Angeles where the women of the Manson clan who were not in jail, set up housekeeping to protest the imprisonment of their leader. It was bizarre and foolish, but newsworthy.

We had to cover the first serial killers, who were called the "Skidrow Slasher" and the "Hillside Strangler." They killed dozens of people over long periods of time before they were finally arrested.

It was ironic that the Skidrow Slasher, who murdered his victims in flophouses and back alleys, was able to avoid capture for so long. When he was finally caught, it was because he dropped his wallet with his name in it at a crime scene. He tried to get away too fast.

I remember going to the site where two victims of the Hillside Strangler were found. It was on an overgrown gully, high on a lonely hillside overlooking a wide section of the city. I remember standing there, looking out over the flatlands and hills beyond, and seeing in the distance locations where the bodies of five other victims had been discovered.

When the Hillside Strangler was eventually found, his auto body shop was in that general neighborhood.

*   *   *

Ken Graue was running down a Westwood street as fast as he could. The demonstrators had turned mean and were racing after him. He had his undeveloped news film in his hand and he was trying to keep it from the extreme members of the mob. Some of them did not like what he shot and were determined to grab it away from him.

People stopped on the sidewalk and looked in amazement as this grown man in a suit and tie came racing past them and an angry group of jeans and T-shirt clad college students roared by a few seconds later.

Thanks to the congestion on the streets, Ken was able to make a desperation detour into the lobby of a theatre and hide behind the popcorn machine. He had saved the film and probably his neck.

When we screened the film back at the station, we couldn't see anything different from what we had shot dozens of times before. The crowd was apparently in an ugly mood that day and decided to take out its anger on the nearest television reporter.

The late 60s had many surprises for newsmen. There were angry marchers, anti-war demonstrators, picket lines for countless causes and college campuses boiling over with discontent.

It was a strange time to be an assignment editor. I remember on many mornings, when I was scheduling stories for my film crews, I would check to see where the riot for the day might be.

Southern California had its hot spots, as there were in almost every city across the country. The University of California at Los Angeles had a belligerent, active anti-war group. Their free-speech area was always ablaze with firebrand speakers calling for an end to something. California State University at Los Angeles offered some perilous times for news crews. Los Angeles City College and Southwest College were bubbling with tensions.

Two good friends of mine from the radio station at USC decided they would not go into the pressure-packed world of commercial broadcasting. Instead, they decided to pursue a more sensible direction: getting their advanced degrees and remaining in education. Despite the added years of study in graduate school, Jay and Glen were pleased they selected the ivy halls of academia. It was a gratifying endeavor and far less hectic that day-to-day broadcasting. They both got their doctorates and moved quickly up the academic ladder.

Both reached the top of their profession in the late 60s and became presidents of community colleges: Jay Gresham of Southwest College and Glen Gooder of Los Angeles City College.

They arrived at their campuses just as students rebelled. Broadcasting was never as turbulent as the schools they had to run. They were at the center of the storm the entire time they were at the helms of their institutions.

It was a strange world in those days. There could be a riot on campus one day and peace the next. Some students might barricade themselves in one building protesting some issue, but classes would be going on in the hall next door.

I remember sending a news crew to Gooder's Los Angeles City College.

I told the cameraman to keep a low profile. If something was going on, we would cover it, but we were always careful not to inflame it.

The story this day was a barricade at one of the campus entrances. Our crew hid behind a gas station across the street and watched what was going on. They spent a good part of the day there, but nothing happened.

I felt we were responsibly covering the news. Our sources told us something would happen, but we did not let our camera crew help trigger an incident.

I later learned that, while my crew was hiding on this side of the campus, other television crews were on the school grounds in plain sight of everyone, covering a news conference in the auditorium. In those days of riot coverage, it was sometimes difficult to know if we were covering the news or causing the news because our cameras were there.

Governor Reagan was holding a Regent's meeting at UCLA when some group unleashed a massive demonstration against him and the college administrators. They were banging on doors, shouting obscenities and creating near-riot conditions.

Cameraman Ed Clark, in the middle of the demonstration, recommended we send the Telecopter, because, as he said, "This thing might explode into a major riot."

I had the copter up in the air and on its way to UCLA in a matter of minutes. The campus at UCLA is so large, with beautiful green, flowing lawns, gardens and fields that the copter crew could not find the building where the demonstrators were haranguing the Governor and the Regents. They flew over the peaceful scene for 10 minutes before they finally spotted the cluster of students bent on disrupting the meeting.

How ironic! The big story of the day was on the turbulent UCLA campus, but from the air everything appeared calm and pastoral. We had to search to find our demonstrators. The copter offered the right perspective, the campus was calm, but the small group of student demonstrators captured the news.

The hippies, the dopesters, the dropouts, the anti-war demonstrators, the protestors, the changing local issues and the college campuses that seemed to be the center of the action, kept assignment editors busy during those revolutionary years.

At one point during the Cambodian incursion by U.S. troops in the Vietnam war, tempers reached the flash point. It seemed as if a revolution was possible. Angry students from so many schools were almost psychotic in their fury. They were so outspoken that their message was lost. They took to the streets. They held mass meetings and shouted their slogans into the wind.

The University of Southern California had been relatively quiet during these times, but the latest action stirred students there into action. However, their approach was radically different. They invited the newsmen to lunch.

It was an unusual but effective approach. They were well organized and their calm efforts paid off. USC had a large group who felt strongly about the "immoral action" of the government and they wanted to get their position across.

The lunch was held on campus and several newsmen were seated at each table. Each of the tables had a student spokesman who could talk on a one-to-one basis to the newsmen about the righteousness of his causes. It was an interesting give and take between the newsmen and concerned students.

Their beliefs were so strong and their frustration so apparent, I came away from the briefing sessions feeling the station should give them some kind of a forum to express their case. Up to now there had been no worthwhile debate because face-to-face encounters merely turned into shouting matches. I tried a novel approach.

We took our cameras to USC and taped an emotional and very one-sided discussion among the students. We ran the students' presentation on the air for 20 minutes. We had also invited some national administration spokesmen to the studio and they listened to what the students had to say. Then, they came on the air live and gave the administration's rebuttal to the students' arguments.

In the following segment the same students, now in another studio, responded live to the administration's position. By keeping the two sides separate in different studios, we had a debate without the irrational fury that marked similar discussions. Administration officials summarized the evening and tried to point out areas of agreement.

A successful series, it ran for two hours each night for a week and became a rare chance for the students to give their side of the story. Until then, they didn't believe anyone cared enough to listen to them. In turn, they had a chance to hear a rational reply from the administration. It was an interesting give-and-take that covered policies being followed in Vietnam and what should be done in the future. The administration sent out some top people from Washington for the series, but since it lasted five nights, we needed more local experts to augment the administration spokesmen. Everything went rather well until the fourth night, when the spokesmen for the administration's position were the chancellors from several local universities. This seemed very appropriate because of the turbulence on their campuses.

The students were well-mannered and effective that night. They made their points with directness and conviction. They were against the war and they wanted the United States to just pull out.

Much to my shock, the chancellors agreed with almost every point the students made. My carefully balanced show had tilted all the way to the students' side and everyone on that broadcast backed what they were saying.

The next night I made sure my foreign policy experts were more in line with the government's position.

I did learn, during that entire series, that if you talked to the anti-war demonstrators on a one-to-one basis, they were pleasant, logical individuals who believed strongly in their cause. However when you put them together in a mob, it could be frightening.

I recall one demonstration of UCLA students who decided to stage a sit-in on Wilshire Boulevard to bring their cause to the attention of the media. There were hundreds of them sitting in the middle of the street completely closing down the flow of traffic.

Police moved in with their riot gear. The Los Angeles Police Department used a firm but gentle technique devised by Police Chief Tom Reddin. They would go up to each individual and arrest them quietly one by one. They would be assisted to their feet and walked to a nearby bus where they would be booked. It was an effective strategy, because any problems would be caused by the demonstrators not the police.

I remember being there during the arrests and seeing UCLA basketball star Bill Walton sitting on the boulevard. I was next to one of the lieutenants and I said, "Be very careful when you pick up Walton. He has a big game tomorrow night."

I still meet many former demonstrators, now in influential establishment positions, who recall meeting me at some of the near-riots during the 60s.

In December 1965, there were some big changes at KTLA News. George Putnam, who had been broadcasting at KTTV since 1952, moved to the station. He was an immediate hit and KTLA had another successful news era with Putnam at the anchor desk.

*   *   *

A chorus of 50 people was assembled on the news stage when I walked into the studio. Several wooden risers had been elevated in a semi-circle so that viewers could see the national costumes of the singers, each representing one of the captive nations. They sang the patriotic songs of their homelands with love and fervor. They were all American citizens but looked as if they were from Lithuania, Latvia and Estonia. They had the physical qualities of the Czechs, Hungarians, Poles and Ukranians. These were the people of the captive nations; the ones who had escaped.

George Putnam had invited them to appear on his newscast this night because this was "Captive Nations Week." It had been observed since the Eisenhower Years, but now the U.S. government was no longer giving it any special recognition. George felt that by ignoring "Captive Nations Week," after so many years of observing it, we were turning our backs on millions of people held behind the Iron Curtain. This was his protest to the President and the Congress.

It was a moving presentation. Women wore their white bonnets, colorful sashes and full skirts of lace and cotton. Each was garbed in the distinctive style of her country. Each design was different, proclaiming the individuality of the homeland. Men in their national costumes sang proudly beside them.

Their songs brought back the painful memories of the families left behind. They reinforced the message to the viewer, that people still could not leave their countries but lived as captives under the brutal heel of the Soviets. George thought this was a very important message and couldn't figure out why the President and Congress didn't think so, too.

He did cover the major news stories on the broadcast that night, but the main content of his newscast was the chorus and the message that these are the people of captive nations and that we should not forget them.

Although quite conservative, he was the most popular reporter on television for the minorities of Southern California. He tried to tell their stories and point out their problems. He always accentuated the positive. He became a champion of causes. He put his personal effort into many fights to right some wrongs. He tried to stop what he considered to be serious ills from spreading further into society.

He was emotionally effected by the issues of the day. He tried to help the underdog, the person who never got a fair deal from society. He did this early in his career and he did it often. He was one of the first television journalists to reach out to different communities and to try to help them with their problems.

There are former gang members who are grandfathers today who were helped by George Putnam. He worked with them. He visited them. He knew them. He helped them break their gang cycle. He was doing this 10 years before the civil rights efforts of the mid-1960s. He was helping Black reporters get jobs in television years before the broadcast industry caught up with him and started to hire minorities.

He stood for the old values. There was right and wrong, good and bad and we were supposed to take our stand. He had a loyal following in the ethnic communities.

He was very concerned when some of the activist young people of those communities took radical stands against what their parents believed. He was hurt when those radicals considered him unfaithful to the cause because he disagreed with what they were doing. He battled them and their ways throughout the turbulent 60s.

George was crusading against drug use when it was little known to the vast population. Putnam was warning about the spread of drugs among young people before others had any idea that drugs might be used in their neighborhood, on their block or in their family. He did editorials, commentaries and news stories pointing out the dreadful consequence of a drug-infested society.

George got very involved in his news coverage. He could not sit back and watch things crumble around him. George was a crusader of the old school of reporters who tried to change things for the better.

People loved him for it. "Give it to them, George..." "We're behind you all the way..." "Keep up the good work."

His mail was voluminous. He touched a chord in viewers and got them involved. He had the ability to vocalize what they were thinking and became their spokesman. No issue was too small or localized. If there was something wrong, it should be righted.

He was for law and order and was enthusiastically pro-police. He built a large and dedicated following among law enforcement. He understood the problems they were facing and he stood for what they were trying to do. He confronted, head on, liberal forces who he thought were trying to make it tougher for police to do their jobs. The police were among his most loyal supporters.

Anytime I was out on a story, I would always hear from officers, "How's George?"

"Say hello to George for me. He's doing a great job."

"Putnam knows what is happening. I'm glad there's someone to tell others what's really going on."

"Putnam's the best."

Everywhere I went, someone would ask about him. George was always at the center of controversy. His large audience was comprised of those who couldn't stand him and those who thought he was the fairest and brightest reporter on the air.

George was the great communicator, before that title was ever applied to anyone. His vibrant enthusiasm, commanding appearance, and booming voice blended to make him a major force in television news. He not only delivered the news, he cared about it and got involved in his stories.

He aired his personal feelings and comments on "One Reporter's Opinion." He called it his mid-spot. It always came half-way in the broadcast. He delivered it with conviction and made it the highlight of the entire newscast.

Here, he dissected the controversial issues of the day, and took sides. Because his stands drew such widespread interest, he converted the last section of his news broadcast to an open forum for the studio audience. He called the segment "Talk Back." Pro and con opinions bounced back and forth from the audience. "Talk Back" was always filled with tension. People were there to speak up on issues they felt strongly about. There were some great arguments between George and the audience. He stood toe-to-toe with those who disagreed with him and battled it out.

Hal Fishman and Larry McCormick, who did the newscast with George, were also on "Talk Back." The three of them faced the audience and tackled the volatile subjects of the day. It was a new and refreshing departure from the usual newscast because it gave people a chance to react to the news that had happened that day.

The "Talk Back" segment was videotaped and played back again later in the night. Barry Shiff, a commercial airline pilot and good friend of Hal Fishman, tells of the night he watched George Putnam and a Marxist from the studio audience engage in a wild and angry debate. George was verbally hammering away at the man, when Barry and his friends had to turn off the set to go out to dinner. Barry said he was astounded when he returned home several hours later and turned the television set back on. There was George still shouting and arguing with the Marxist agitator, just as he was doing a couple of hours before. It took Barry several shocked moments before he realized that he was watching a videotape replay of the violent argument that he had seen earlier.

George Putnam has been a positive force in television since the early 1950s. He made people aware of what was going on about them. Although people have criticized him for his stands, he is easily one of the most respected news broadcasters ever to step in front of a camera.

One of his finest hours was during the coverage of the Deadwyler inquest in the mid-1960s. There had been a long period of racial unrest in the city. The tensions seemed to be slackening and there was hope that everything would be returning to normal. Then the Deadwyler incident happened.

A car was racing through South Central Los Angeles at high speeds. Police spotted it and chased the vehicle through the city streets. It turned into a high speed pursuit. It ended with a confrontation with police officers and one man in the car was shot and killed.

As details of the chase became known, the event sparked widespread resentment. A woman in the car was being hurried to a hospital to have a baby. The driver had used an emergency sign that was often used in the South. He had connected a white piece of clothing to his antenna to show that he was going on an emergency run. The local police were not familiar with the procedure. The driver refused to stop although he knew the police were chasing him.

Because racial tensions had been high, this event threatened to touch off further serious disturbances. There were emotional rallies and demonstrations in the black community and genuine concern that riots could be triggered again in Los Angeles.

On the first day of the inquest, people surged in the corridors outside the courtroom. They became loud and unruly when they were not able to get into the hearing room. All of the scenes were shown on the newscasts that night. We had all been through the Watts riots and many feared that could happen again if people didn't get the full story of the investigation.

Lloyd Sigmon, a Golden West Broadcasting executive, asked me to find out if there was any way KTLA could televise the inquest to reduce tensions in the city. I called District Attorney Evelle Younger and told him of Lloyd's concern.

"Stan, I have been thinking the same thing. I was wondering if there was any chance that some station would televise the inquest," the district attorney told me on the phone.

"We are ready to go right away." I relayed Lloyd Sigmon's instructions. Evelle Younger made a few quick calls and phoned me back in minutes, giving KTLA permission.

Cameras were not allowed inside the courtrooms in those years. Since inquests were proceedings conducted by the coroner, they were not considered court trials. Officials in the coroner's office were more lenient in giving permission for television cameras at their hearings. However, permitting live coverage of an entire inquest was something entirely new.

The inquest was transferred to the largest courtroom available. Two television cameras were brought in and KTLA started several days of live coverage. The telecast had a soothing effect on the city. People were able to watch the developments as they took place. Nothing could be covered up. The whole story unfolded in front of the cameras. People could see what was happening and emotional tensions began to subside.

Johnnie Cochran, attorney for the Deadwyler family, was an outstanding spokesman. He was a respected leader of the black community and one of the major reasons that tensions relaxed. He handled the case with great dignity and competence. He was a fair, but hard-probing, lawyer in the courtroom.

Although this was only an inquest, it took the form of a trial on television and the audience viewed it as such. I worked with Putnam on the long telecasts. KTLA pre-empted the entire morning and afternoon broadcast schedule to bring the inquest to the viewers. George and I had to fill in during the recesses, to keep the viewers up-to-date on what was happening and explain the inquest process.

As people watched the telecast, it became apparent this would be a fair and full inquiry. Televising the drawn-out sessions and the questioning of the officers involved proved to almost everyone watching that the results would be based on all the facts available.

The officers were found to be blameless in the incident and those who followed the proceedings seem to agree with the findings. KTLA added another first to its list of innovative telecasts. The broadcasting of the Deadwyler inquest showed the importance of television cameras in the courtroom to keep people informed when highly volatile issues are before them.

* * *

In 1967, George Putnam switched stations again and returned to KTTV. His old station gave him a contract he could not refuse. KTLA selected the well known and popular police chief of Los Angeles, Tom Reddin, as the new anchorman.

Putnam was a strong, flamboyant broadcaster. His personality carried the newscast. The newsfilm was always secondary to his appeal. When Reddin became anchorman, we put more emphasis on "the picture" to take advantage of his reputation as one of the city's most important public figures. His expert handling of the dangerous hours during the Watts riots impressed the people of Los Angeles and it was our strategy to keep important issues of the day at the center of each news broadcast.

We had a relatively small staff during those years, which meant that everyone did several separate jobs in the newsroom. Although I was news director at the time, I spent my mornings exclusively as assignment editor. This gave me a chance to get a jump on the news day. I was able to see what was happening; get a good hold on developments and send camera crews to the important stories.

Looking back on those years, I now see I spent too much time covering what I considered the important news. I did not worry about whether it was visual or not. If the story seemed important I sent a camera crew. This was the purist's position in television journalism, but it created problems for the over-all newscast. Put five important stories together and you would, more than likely, end up with five "talking heads" following each other on the broadcast.

The plague of the talking head was being reckoned with during those years. It originated in the traditional news conference. Most news people believed at that time that if there was a news conference, you should be there to cover it. It was being held because some spokesman had something new and important to say. The news conference syndrome became such a habit that I often found myself sending a crew to the Los Angeles Press Club to cover a news conference at 9:00, another one at 10:00 and a third one at 11:00. Most of the other television stations would be there as well.

It was difficult to realize that other stories more visual and less important were going on out there in the real world and that we should spend more time looking for them. We did features and light stories to break up the chain of talking heads, but we did so reluctantly. I often questioned if some light, pleasant story was really news, or was it a cream puff, a meaningless feature, some public relations stunt.

Sportscaster Dick Enberg summed it up best when he complained about the timing of his sports section in the newscast. He said, "I always follow the animal story from the zoo."

Our station manager, John Reynolds, gave me the best suggestion on how to handle a problem like this. He said that a newscast is like a special meal. There are meat and potatoes for the main course, but there should also be the appetizers, dessert and all the other niceties of a meal. It should be prepared well, with the right trimmings, atmosphere and be complete—a piece of advice I always remembered. When I looked at some visual story that didn't have the importance of meat and potatoes, but could be served for dessert after dinner, I covered it.

Pictures are the vital element in a television newscast. It is important to take advantage of the visual possibilities of the television screen. One of the stories I did was almost too visual.

For many years, the Los Angeles Police Department did not use dogs to flush out suspects. There was a time when the image of a policeman using a dog was reminiscent of the early civil rights marches in the South when dogs were misused in controlling crowds. However, a group of LAPD officers wanted to prove how helpful dogs could be in finding hidden suspects. A dog could search a warehouse in minutes where officers might take hours to complete the same task.

The police department decided on a pilot program. Each dog was thoroughly trained by its master, who was an officer. Each dog lived with the policeman, was part of the officer's family, would play with his children and would go to work with the officer at night. We did a story on the start of the K-9 Corps. We watched the officers put their dogs through a series of training exercises. They searched deserted buildings, responded to various commands and were always under control. It was a visual story.

I wanted to show how gentle they were at home with the officer, how they were loveable pets for children and how they were members of the family. I worked out a scene for our story where the dog would put his paws on my shoulders and I would pet him as I closed off the segment. Police dogs are big; when they stand on their hind legs they can place their front paws on your shoulders. Their heads are then almost eye-to-eye with yours.

Cameraman Joe Dylan gave me my cue and he started rolling his camera. I gave the command. The dog stood on his hind legs and placed his paws on my shoulders, his mouth open and his tongue hanging out. At that moment, somehow, I moved and stepped on his hind paw. The dog let out a loud howl, looked at me eye-to-eye and lunged at me, his teeth very close to my face. Then his forepaws slid down from my shoulder and he walked away.

The film shows the startled, tear-filled look on my face as the dog growled, gnashed his teeth and instinctively defended himself. Phil Leask, the editor who put the story together, rolled the color film frame by frame for me. In slow motion you can see the dog's reaction to the hurt of being stepped on. He opened his mouth and in a devastatingly threatening way, almost bit me before backing off. The dog's training saved me. He responded to the hurt in an animal fashion, but caught himself because of his discipline.

I have watched those dogs over the years in awe and wonderment as they catch suspect after suspect in dark, strange places. I certainly understand why so many thieves and robbers give up when they see the K-9 Corps on the scene.

The advent of color film made us all realize the extreme importance of the picture in telling a story. We were able to expand our horizon and look for subject matter that we would have ignored before.

One of the continuous problems I had as news director was isolation. I was so much involved in today's newscast and today's problems, I was unable look ahead at what was going to happen in the industry. It was just as difficult to look around at other stations and keep close tab on what they were doing. While I had my head buried in the production of each broadcast, there was much going on I was not aware of. Color film was becoming commonplace. We used it only rarely, usually footage from Vietnam. New techniques to make the news program more visual were being introduced. Full-time artists were being added to staffs to make the programs more attractive to viewers. More reporters were being added and the scope of news was being expanded. Despite all the changes, I was remaining primarily in a meat and potatoes world.

Unfortunately, I was too well trained in the local station syndrome. If it is new and costs money, we don't have a budget for it. Expenses had to be kept down; we had to make do with what we had.

My tunnel vision in those years kept me at my desk. I had my Telecopter crew on duty. We did live coverage of stories almost every day, while other stations were just starting to experiment with it. We were doing reasonably well and given the extreme limitations of my budget, I felt I didn't have much to learn from the others. I was a perfect example of a person trapped in the present and not realizing that changes were about to explode around him.

I had heard of electronic breakthroughs, but thought they were the concern of the engineering department. I was one of the first news directors in the country who used a mini-cam crew every day. It was the one we used in our helicopter. I did not see the time when all cameras would be mini-cams.

If someone had suggested it then, my first reaction would have been they cost too much and we can't afford them.

I had trouble getting money from my budget to keep my film cameras repaired and operating. I had only one film editor and his assistant to edit all of our film. I had a live Telemobile and a live Telecopter, why should I need more?

We had one transmitter for our live units at the time and I figured that was enough for any station. I did not foresee that almost everyone would have three or four in the near future.

It was 1970 and things were not going too well. I heard rumors from the front office that changes might be made. It was a great shock. I knew no one could do the job better than I, but that uneasy feeling that is a precursor to something actually happening gnawed at me.

*   *   *

Sitting behind the assignment desk in the newsroom always made me jealous of the reporters who went out to do the stories. They did what I wanted to do. I put up with newsroom assignments because the work had to be done and I figured I could do it better than anyone else. However, when I had a chance to go back into the field I was delighted.

A desk job was work, reporting was fun. Field reporting is the best part of television news, the real world and where I wanted to be.

Now, with the clear vision of 20/20 hindsight, I can see the reasons for the changes that took place over the years. When I left the news director spot, the biggest correction made by my successor, Bill Fyffe, was to triple the news department budget. Television was an expensive business and it was necessary to spend money to make money. His was a sound and daring move after my years at the helm when the less you spent, the better you were doing the job. Bill asked me to stay on his staff as a general reporter. Although I was still stunned by the bleak turn of events, I accepted his offer. It was the best thing I ever did.

14.

SUPER BOWL SUNDAY AND A NEW CAREER

It was good to get away from the station for a few days. I was concerned about the developments there and this weekend was a good chance to put things into perspective. There are times in your career when everything seems to be drifting, stagnant and ominously quiet. Sometimes ordinary things rescue you, pull you back to reality and point you in the right direction.

The loud cheering on the television set in the den could be heard all over the backyard, but no one was listening. The Super Bowl was about to kick off, but the people in the Chambers house were all doing something else.

Nineteen-year-old Dave was in his music studio above the garage, practicing arias from his current opera production at college. He was hitting the big notes well. The opera was to open the next week.

His voice boomed out in the backyard as 21-year-old Beverly sunned herself in the bright January morning. The sun was hot, the temperature over 80. She was wrestling with a stack of books on the Balkans crisis leading up to World War I and was not doing too well. The opera aria, the sun and the dull text was not conducive to the retention of subject matter.

She watched her father vacuum and brush a winter swimming pool that hadn't had any real care in almost a month. The water sparkled at times as the algae, leaves and dirt were sucked from the pool.

Two-year-old Elizabeth sat on the side of the shallow end and braved the chilly water with her tiny feet daring her wary father to do anything about it. The two worked watchfully and silently on the terms of their truce. He was close by, in case she slipped, but she knew she was not to be there by herself.

Five-year-old Edward used the net at the end of a long silver pole to scoop up stray leaves that sprinkled the surface of the water. It was a haphazard effort, lasting only until boredom motivated him into another project;

walking the ivy path to the pump and filter house behind the pool to find old cars and trucks he might have left there last summer.

Twenty-three-year-old Stan was bundled up in his father's bathrobe and pajamas, still unable to snap back from the ravages of winter flu. He sat at the kitchen table barely listening to the game on the set in the den; instead he was engrossed in the *Times* sports section while sipping a hot mug of chicken broth.

Seventeen-year-old Nancy had left the Chambers house on Windsor Boulevard in Hancock Park to do her weekly volunteer job at the soup kitchen on skid row. She would miss the Super Bowl.

Mother Beverly was cooking sausages and eggs at the stove while cradling a phone on her shoulder. Her mother was calling with the latest family news.

The fragrance of the breakfast food brought in 16-year-old Jim, who was completing a project that had extended over most of the weekend. He was replacing the glass panes in eight separate windows in the house. He snitched a sausage and a piece of buttered toast as he walked through the kitchen.

Our dog Barney, half German shepherd and half collie, chewed on a rubber toy doll on the back porch while waiting for someone to open the door so he could get into the backyard.

Eleven-year-old Mary Ellen had left earlier to go to mass with her girl friends. They were still exhilarated and delighted by the success of the big birthday party the day before. She had some shopping to do at the drugstore and wouldn't see the Super Bowl.

Twelve-year-old Margaret was washing dishes almost as fast as they were brought from the table to the sink. She had put through several loads with more to come. She knew Barney had to be fed.

Seven-year-old Bobby and 15-year-old John were up in the park playing football with the neighborhood kids. They would have their own Super Bowl up there.

The aroma of hot coffee and good cooking permeated the house. There was some laughter, but everyone was quiet and relaxed as they enjoyed the informality, the community and the summer-like day they had inherited this January Sunday.

The sun was warm and delightful. The sky was summer blue and the trees a spring-like green. Everything blended into a quiet happiness that seemed to be everywhere. Nothing too important, no major problems, no great challenging conversation, no grasping with issues and victories, just slow warmth that glowed and radiated happiness.

That was our Super Bowl Sunday. I liked it more than the game. Time stood still. Things were captured and relationships were cemented a little more.

It was a good Super Bowl Sunday. And Miami won the game, or did we?

A little elbow room like this gives you a chance to reflect on other things as well. No job can be fulfilling all the time. News is a people-bruising business. If you've been knocked down, let the pain wear off and get back up. This morning with your family is the shining real world. Enjoy it, there is so much ahead. The emotional hurt will heal.

The news business is ever changing. If you keep on the bright side, fine-tune your attitude and keep plugging ahead. You can carve a new career. What more could you ask for than going back to reporting?

It happened fast! Elections, fires, earthquakes, encounters with hundreds of people involved in the news. I was out there every day with my cameras and crew. There were a few bonus stories.

One of my favorites was being the "Action Reporter." It stirred up a lot of viewer interest and gave me a chance to get a new perspective on people I met while covering news stories.

* * *

He was in an Army uniform. She stood beside him. She wore a big hat over her 40s hairdo. Their picture in the frame was tinted in that style so popular in those years. Coloring made the picture more lifelike. The gentle pastels of that wartime era preserved that moment in time. It was a warm reminder of what was. After all those years, the picture still remained in its position of honor on the mantle in the living room. Next to it was a tinted baptism picture, then another black and white likeness of that little girl taken with first-grade classmates.

Tinted pictures of young men in Army and Navy uniforms and pretty girls of another era were on the mantles of a lot of homes that I visited during the early 1970s.

I was in more living rooms than an aggressive insurance salesman. It was all part of the station's attempt to show viewers that we cared about them and would help them whenever we could. In addition to my new reporting duties, Bill made me the "Action Reporter." Several times a week, I would visit houses of people whom I had helped. They had sent us letters complaining of some problem that they were having. When we were able to solve it, we would bring our cameras into their living rooms and have them tell us how things were resolved.

It was quite impressive. People would write to the Action Reporter at the station, outlining details of what was wrong. Carmel Denton, who was the entire "Action Reporter" staff, would get to work on it and in a few weeks, she would usually resolve the difficulties.

She solved a wide variety of viewers' headaches, ranging from mail orders that never showed up, to lost veterans and social security checks. The list was lengthy and varied, but Carmel always seemed to find a solution. It was an ideal consumer segment in the news, because each night something was resolved. It showed that the station would make every effort to help its viewers.

In those living room camera sessions, I would interview the person who wrote the letter, find out what the problem was and listen to them tell me what happened when the Action Reporter entered the case. I personally had little to do with the actual process of getting things resolved, but I was the hero on the spot when the accolades were handed out.

Our conversation on film would usually end with, "...nothing happened until I wrote and the Action Reporter got to work on this. In two weeks, a nice letter came from the company telling me that everything was settled. I want to thank you and KTLA for all you did."

This repeated itself night after night, with more gratitude expressed each time. People were beginning to believe I could do anything. Actually, I couldn't do anything; it was all Carmel.

The formula was elementary. We would get a letter outlining the problem. Carmel would copy it and send it to the president of the company along with a form letter from the KTLA Action Reporter. That was all. The president would make sure the letter got to the person in his company who was responsible for the problem and he would usually take care of it. It is much better to resolve these things than let them fester. When an inquiry comes from your president, you tend to investigate the circumstances more quickly. It is amazing how things can be corrected when the person at the top asks you to clear something up.

We corrected so many complaints, we would use only the more interesting and visual items on the air. Those that were special, visual or of real human interest were broadcast on our evening newscast as an example of how the Action Reporter could help our viewers.

I was doing my regular news reporting every day and the "Action Reporter" segments were just something extra. We completed so many of them, we kept a geographical file with the names and cities of the various people we had helped.

Carmel would find out what area I was assigned to do a news story for that day. She would go through her file of completed "Action Reporter" cases and give me addresses of people we had helped. If the film crew and I finished our news assignment early enough, we would go over to a house in the neighborhood and film a person and listen to his story of how the Action Reporter helped.

Whenever I had time to talk, I would ask about the pictures on the mantle. Those conversations were usually rewarding. You get to know people quickly when you are talking about their pictures and their family of a few years ago. I always wondered why particular pictures remained up there and all the others taken over the years are relegated to albums, drawers or hidden boxes. Those old, faded photographs were high moments of a young couple just starting out. The first baby was often there to join them, but the later pictures were spaced over the years.

Often their daughter's wedding picture was there, or their first grandson, or a family vacation or a recent snapshot tucked in the frame of an older picture. Those memories were enshrined on the mantles and I was able to share in the stories that they told.

As the years went by, the tinted pictures began to disappear. New, bright, sharp color photographs took their places, as sons and daughters took over the homes. There are more pictures around today, most of them very good. I always take a close look at them when I do interviews in living rooms. I'm not the Action Reporter anymore, but I do enjoy talking to people about their family and finding out where everyone is.

* * *

The mid 1970s were great travel years for me. Out of the blue I was sent to Japan, Guatemala, Canada and England. Trips like these always add great zest to your life. It is not that routine local stories are dull, but overseas trips are always a challenge. It's going through customs with 20 pieces of luggage and not losing one of them. It's trying to ship your videotapes to Los Angeles on the weekend and finding out that it can't be done in the country you're in. It's visiting the ruins of Tikal in the Guatemala jungles and standing over the tomb of Oliver Cromwell inside Westminister Abbey in London, or getting close-up film of Her Royal Majesty, Queen Elizabeth II as she greets her subjects.

Dark wooden beams crisscrossed the ceiling and the white straw-and-plaster walls of the pub. Ornate pieces of brass hung as sentries from the rough oak mantle. Overstuffed chairs and couches formed a homey half-circle in front of the newly lit fireplace.

Waltzing flames were caressing the crackling logs in the soot-charred hearth of brick and stone. The flickering light brightened the bricks in the back of the firebox, blackened by the hundreds of fires of yesterdays—it was a time to enjoy the warmth of the fire and be engulfed by the moment. The damp coldness of the outside melted away as you gazed into the hearth and listened to the kindling pop and crackle.

Why would anyone leave this setting to go out into the cold overcast of the English countryside this dreary October afternoon in 1975?

We had left our camera crew, Gil Donaldson and Sy Klein, in a small open boat slowly cruising down the Thames. Her Majesty was making a ceremonial visit to the small island of Runnymede as part of the celebration of the signing of the Magna Carta by King John and his noblemen 760 years before.

Earlier that morning, she boarded her open craft at Henley amid the proper pomp and circumstance and sailed down the Thames. Thousands of residents turned out in each riverside village to greet the Queen, to give her a festive and special welcome as she passed through their town.

This was an ideal opportunity for us to film a news story on the beautiful English countryside, see the excited townspeople turn out to honor their Monarch and get close-up film of Her Majesty as she greeted her subjects.

The only way to do it was in a small, open boat cruising alongside the Queen's yacht. There was only room for a cameraman, soundman and a pilot who would guide them along the way. The British boatman knew the royal protocol and how close he should get to the Queen's open boat on the slow-moving cruise down the Thames.

The other two members of the news team from Los Angeles were disappointed we could not be aboard and view royalty close-up. We did the next best thing. We drove our car along the route to the various towns. We would stand in the crowd and watch the enthusiastic reception the townspeople gave to the Queen. Then, as the royal party departed, we would jump back in our car and drive to the next village.

Needless to say, we would always arrive considerably ahead of the royal flotilla, so we would stop and go into the town pub and wait for the small task force to arrive.

My producer, Lew Rothbart, and I would enjoy the frothy taste of English ale. Our host, Bruce Higgens, who was driving us to Runnymede, seemed to enjoy showing us the various taverns along the Thames. He would regale us with the historical importance of each pub.

He was a tall, sturdy man with a light pinkish face and a shock of blonde hair that was never quite combed. Bruce helped us on our news assignment in Britain. He was a fount of facts and stories about local history and kept us well informed as we followed the Queen. He drank sparkling water while Lew and I enjoyed the ale. This was an ideal setting for Lew. He always had a sparkle in his eyes and this setting triggered a memorable list of one-liners that expressed the unlikely contrasts of our situation. He found Bruce the perfect foil for his gentle barbs of humor.

It was warm and comfortable for the three of us in our pubs, but it was cold, damp and drizzling for Gil and Sy in their open boat. The camera crew had to be hearty and brave to stand up to the harassing elements. The moisture kept fogging the camera lens. Gil Donaldson had to keep wiping it dry during the entire trip. His lens paper was used up quickly and his handkerchief was almost as wet as the lens as he tried to battle the moisture.

When the film was later developed, the dampness on the lens created a soft, warm, gauze-like tone. The film gave the Queen, the flotilla and the countryside an unreal quality, as if they were something out of the past, a strangely medieval picture.

The film magic did nothing to raise the spirits of the freezing camera crew. The biting cold and the pervasive dampness grew more severe as each town was reached. They huddled together in the bobbing boat with no protection from the elements except their thin California jackets.

On the other hand, Lew Rothbart and I grew more mellow as we visited country pub after country pub. We had no problem enjoying the English ale and appreciating the pageantry and excitement as we watched Her Majesty being welcomed.

Flag-waving schoolchildren lined the bridges and the river bank. The local town band played military marches. When we passed through Eton, the rowing team in single and two-man shells, joined the naval party and escorted Her Majesty for many miles.

One of Bruce's friends had invited us to his cottage for the end of the ceremonial cruise. We enjoyed the warmth of his Runnymede retreat, while our camera crew kept filming.

Several neighbors also had been invited to the handsome cottage that rested on the tip of a small island in the Thames. It was a perfect spot to get a close-up look at the Queen. Her boat would pass right in front of the house. She would be so close, you could almost reach out and touch the royal craft.

Two young mothers with their year-old babies were among the guests. Although they had lived in England all of their lives and had seen the Queen on several occasions, you could share the excitement they felt about seeing her here on their island.

It was a small, sophisticated crowd in that living room with the floor-to-ceiling windows that looked out over the river. A glowing fire kept the room warm. When the flotilla came into sight down the river, there was a mounting tide of excitement in the room. Several went outside, down to the bank 30 feet away. Others stayed in the warm room, but planned to go down to the river when the boats got closer. The mothers, with their children in their arms, decided to stay with us in the comfortable living room so their children would be warm.

As the parade of boats came nearer, more of the guests went outside to get as close as possible to the Queen.

There were finally just four of us left standing in the room: my producer, Lew Rothbart; the two mothers; and me. The tension and excitement of the moment was just too much for the mothers.

"Would you mind?" asked the tall brunette as she handed me her baby. I took him with a feeling of surprise and concern.

"How nice of you two," the other mother said as she handed her child to Lew.

"You are sure you don't mind?" the brunette asked as both of them quickly walked out the door and half-ran down the bank to the river.

Lew and I were startled, but rose to the occasion. We looked to each other for support. We bounced and jiggled our charges on our shoulders as we peered out the windowpanes of the closed doors and watched the flotilla pass by.

We could see our camera crew bundled up in their open boat. Gil Donaldson was wiping the lens of his camera.

Within five minutes, the chattering, smiling, ecstatic guests came marching in out of the cold, still enthralled by the moment they had just enjoyed with the Queen.

The English mothers took their babies from the shoulders of the American strangers. They were still too excited from the experience to even say thanks.

It isn't every day that Queen Elizabeth visits Runnymede.

Gil and Sy nursed colds for the rest of the trip, but Lew and I had a delightful time in England. We had enjoyed our brief countryside stops in Henley, Hurley, Marlowe, Boulter's Locks, Maidenhead, Shepperton, Chissick and the visits to the pubs, Belles of Ouxley and the Fox and Hounds. We saw Barclay Square, the Mayfair District, Captain Bligh's Tomb at St. Mary's of Lambeth and the wartime headquarters of General Dwight Eisenhower. We learned all of the famous historical dates that we could handle and enjoyed great dinners at the Rules Restaurant and the Tower Hotel.

The news stories that we filmed were visual and creative. The tube rides were cheap and easy to navigate. We had to cut short our visit to the Tower of London because of the plane flight back home. It will be my first stop on my return to London.

We had rented a car for the trip to the airport. There were four of us and 13 pieces of luggage with all our camera gear. We gathered outside the Tower Hotel at a reasonable hour to give us more than enough time to get to Heathrow Airport.

"I'll help you with these last bags," Sy said to the doorman. Sy insisted on putting everything in the car just the way he wanted to.

"This bag on the sidewalk has my passport in it, so leave it near the top. I'll need it at the airport," Sy said as he gave the doorman a pound note.

"I have my passport in my coat," Lew Rothbart said as he got in the front seat.

"Me, too," Gil added.

I felt the bulky envelope in my coat pocket as I got in the back seat next to the far window. I find it reassuring to have my passport with me all of the time.

The driver was relaxed, having a brief conversation with one of the other drivers outside the hotel. When he saw that all four of us were in his car, he slowly walked over and got behind the wheel.

We talked about the trip, how successful it was, how we were confused by the money exchange, how much we liked to walk in London and how we looked forward to the flight home.

It was a very scenic drive to the airport. We seemed to take some unfamiliar turns, but we were new to London and did not know the short cuts that the driver was taking.

The scenic drive was much longer than anyone of us expected. We began to worry about when we were going to get there. Our flight time seemed to be getting closer and closer. I privately wondered if our driver could be lost.

We were late and we could now see that our driver became very much aware of it. He started driving faster. He kept looking at his watch. He must have been lost. But we finally made it.

We jumped out of the car the moment we arrived at the airport, gathered our luggage and ran to the ticket counter. They had been expecting us, but it appeared that we were too late.

"I'm afraid you have missed the plane," said the Pan Am representative who hurried out to meet us.

"That's not possible. We have to be in Los Angeles tomorrow," Lew protested.

A thin, austere woman in a Pan Am uniform came out from behind the counter. "The plane has already boarded," she said.

"We have to make it," Lew pleaded.

"Are you willing to run?" she asked.

"Let's go." I joined in picking up the one piece of luggage I had put on the ground.

"Do you have your passports?" she asked.

"We sure do," Gil answered.

"Let's see them," she looked at all of us. "There isn't any time to spare."

We all pulled them out for her, except Sy. He was looking frantically for his suitcase, the one last seen on the sidewalk next to the car at the hotel. It was not here.

"I can't find my bag," he said.

She looked perturbed, but didn't say anything.

"I can't believe it's not here. Maybe it is back in the rear of the car," he said.

The three of us had ours in our hands. She said, "You'll go. You'll go. You'll go..." then she looked at Sy, "You stay."

He couldn't believe what had happened.

"Let's go. Follow me," she started to run across the busy terminal building to the gates.

"Sorry, Sy. Get the next plane," Lew called back as the three of us, bags in hand, raced after the Pan Am woman threading her way through the people crowding the terminal.

It was the last time we saw Sy in London. We ran at a fast pace through the main lobby, down a long corridor, up some steps and to the boarding gate that was just closing.

"Can I get three more passengers on board?"

"You just made it," the ticket agent said as the plane's door was about to close.

"Hold everything," she called out, "We have three more passengers."

Two flight attendants poked their heads out from behind the door and looked startled, but invited us on board. We had made it. The thin, austere Pan Am woman had run a fast course and got us there in time. We thanked her and boarded the plane, all worried about Sy. He arrived in Los Angeles the day after we did.

He said the Tower Hotel sent a car to the airport to pick him up. They took him back to the Tower, found his bag, gave him a free room with dinner and provided him with another free car to take him back to the airport the next day.

He survived the ordeal, thanks to the Tower Hotel staff. Even Pan Am took pity on him because he missed his first flight. The same Pan Am agent who ran us to our plane helped Sy get "upped" to first class so he would be more comfortable on the non-stop flight from London to Los Angeles.

I never found out the name of the gracious lady who gave us such an unorthodox escort at a high speed through Heathrow. I can still see her running ahead of me like a champion, dodging passengers, turning corners and running up stairs, while never missing a stride. I truthfully couldn't keep up with her and neither could the others. She wasn't even out of breath when we finally reached the closing door of the plane. I will always remember and appreciate that extra effort that got us home on time.

The fact that we must have looked ridiculous and turned many heads in the airport terminal as we ran across the lobby didn't bother us a bit. We just reaffirmed old British beliefs about "crazy Americans."

15.

THE SEVENTIES:
MEAN STREETS, MURDERS AND MUGGINGS

The country staggered into the 70s, battered from the blows of the 60s. Changes had been unleased that would plague the nation for years to come. The heated anti-war fever was contagious. The Vietnam war continued to take its toll on the nation's morale and disenchanted veterans started coming back to mixed welcomes at home.

A troubling gas shortage startled the nation. Desperate drivers waited for hours in long lines at the gas pumps. The shortage turned some Americans away from their gas guzzlers to Japanese cars that offered more miles to the gallon.

Inflation was brewing, bubbling and exploding throughout the country and a growing recession was stirring up trouble. President Nixon stunned the world twice; his surprise trip to China and his resignation in disgrace in the wake of the Watergate investigations.

Sky Lab and the Voyagers were rocketed on their space missions and John Travolta became a bright, new star with his film, "Saturday Night Fever." Martina Navratilova from communist Czechoslovakia dominated the tennis world and O.J. Simpson from USC was the football star.

There were the Sandinistas in Nicaragua, the Ayatollah Khomeini in Iran, a Soviet expeditionary force in Afghanistan and a dozen wars and revolutions creating serious trouble throughout the world.

One of the most telling developments in this country was the rise of violent urban crime.

* * *

Graffiti was scrawled over gray walls and on tired, old buildings. These were hideous marks of street gangs which disfigured almost every surface in some old neighborhoods. Irregular block letters were etched in messy spray paint.

Inmates had taken over the jail. Delinquent students ran the school. Gangs had run the residents off the streets.

Fear and sympathy had somehow blended to let street gangs rule their special turf. How could a society allow outlaws to spread their ugly banners, defacing walls and homes?

But, somehow, it did.

The bodies of two people lay under white sheets sprawled on the street. They had been standing by the curb, drinking beer and working on their old cars, when rival gang members sped by and opened fire. The two young men fell dead on the spot. Another revenge gang killing shattered the late afternoon in this deteriorating section of East Los Angeles.

Homicide investigators and members of the Los Angeles Police Department's gang section were already there when television news crews appeared on the scene. Neighbors huddled in small groups by their homes, in the streets and by the yellow plastic ribbon that had been stretched from tree to tree to keep gawkers from the crime scene.

It's often difficult to talk to possible witnesses in situations like this. There are those who are shocked, angry, vengeful and helpless. Others look upon the invasion of the police and press as a circus setting up tents in their neighborhood, and they don't like it.

There is a lot of childish waving into the television cameras. Many are pushing and shoving to get behind reporters who are doing live shots on their afternoon newscasts from the murder location. There seems to be little concern for the two boys who lie dead in the littered street. The bodies are next to a broken-down car with the hood up and the driver's door open.

The traffic control officers try to keep order and move the crowd away from theinvestigation scene. Youngsters move back and forth, mill around and shout out smart remarks at the officers. Then they dip into the crowd and disappear.

Homicide detectives go about their investigations measuring the locations of the bodies and ringing chalk marks around spent bullets they found in the gutter and on the curbs.

Other officers sweep the area for witnesses. Most of the investigators are Spanish-speaking. They knock on doors, talk to witnesses, get a feeling for what happened. They compare notes and gradually put together a mosaic of information on another gang killing.

Television reporters are often limited and restricted in their coverage. Most of the people who saw what happened are taken from the scene to be interviewed at the police station.

Just the same, we talk to people to see what we can find out. To my surprise my crew and I found a girl who lives two houses away, knew the two boys and saw the drive-by shooting. She agreed to be interviewed on camera.

"Doug and Ricardo were fixing the car. There was the sound of a car racing up the street. I turned and looked. It slowed down as it passed the two guys. I think there were four or five shots. The guys in the car screamed something. They burned rubber and sped away. The two guys standing next to the broken-down car fell to the pavement. One of them, Doug, tried to reach up to the car door, but he just toppled into the street again."

"Could you see who was in the car?"

"Sure, they were all Brown Doggers. That's a bad gang. I know two of them from last year in school. I know who they are."

"Thank you," I stopped the interview.

By this time, all the children in the neighborhood were jumping up and down behind the girl, waving, making faces and trying to get in front of the camera.

They kept on chanting, "Put me on TV. Put me on TV."

We stopped the camera, thanked her again and walked away from the shoving, waving youngsters. Several followed me.

"When's this on TV?"

"What Channel is this?"

"Put me on TV."

Then, they started to disperse and followed my cameraman and soundman as they went back down the street to get other pictures necessary to tell the story.

No other camera crew had discovered that Amelia was a witness. I walked back to the young teen age girl.

"Amelia, can I talk to you for moment?"

"Sure," she smiled.

"You have to be more careful what you say about gangs. You just told me you know who the killers are. That could be very dangerous. Tell the police, but no one else."

"Those Brown Doggers don't scare me." She tossed her head.

"If they think you know who killed the two boys, they could cause you a lot of trouble. Never say you can identify the killers. I won't use it on the air, but others might."

She just looked at me.

"No hard feelings?" I asked.

"No, none," she answered.

"Thanks," I said, "Thanks for the interview. I won't use that part."

She smiled at me. "I'll be more careful."

Later, as the coroner was taking the bodies off the street, I watched Amelia on the steps of her house, looking at the sad scene. Her brothers and sisters and her parents peered out the front door and through the windows.

I looked at all the neighbors, the graffiti, the youthful exuberance and all the sadness. I wondered if Amelia might tell others she knew who the killers were. I know that no reporters would run a sound bite like that, but if only one did, Amelia could be the next victim.

As I walked back to our camera car, I kept thinking about it. We have a responsibility to the person we interview. We must use good sense and good taste in determining what is used on the air. We want the best and most interesting sound bite, but we can never jeopardize the safety of a person who might have told you too much.

Is that censoring the news? Is that holding back something that people have a right to know? I don't think so. I believe it is just good news judgement. The police have to know, but I don't think others need to.

You do not encounter many situations like this, but when you do you must be cautious.

The best suggestion is, "If in doubt, don't."

You must check everything out to make sure it is accurate. Don't shoot from the hip just to beat your competitors on other stations. Be sure first—otherwise you could hurt a lot of people.

I felt uneasy as we drove away from the graffiti-scarred neighborhood. I knew there would be other gang killings and little girls like Amelia could easily be among the fatalities.

As we drove along looking at the graffiti on the small homes and walls, I kept thinking how mean the streets can be. Life goes on as normal, but there are those who try to rip it away from us.

We have drive-by shootings as one gang seeks to revenge the violent act of another. They fight it out for their old traditional turf in the neighborhood, but they compound it now with their battles over the right to sell drugs on certain street corners. The number of gang members has risen dramatically. In Los Angeles alone, police have targeted thousands of gang members who they consider hard core. However, sending them to jail often makes the hard core even tougher. They learn the vicious ways of prison and take that attitude onto the streets when they finally get out. The streets have become very mean.

It is not just the gang members, but the street punk who makes his cocaine money by stealing stereos from cars, television sets, jewelry, guns, videotape recorders and other valuables from homes. He hits during the day when no one is there, makes a fast getaway and turns his loot into instant cash. It happens every day in many parts of the city.

It is a frustrating and helpless feeling to do a story on recovered stolen property and actually see several hundred victims who were ripped off. Standing in the midst of the victims you can feel the human toll these burglaries take. This was just one night of the public display of the stolen articles. Thousands actually visited the display room at the Van Nuys Police Station to try to locate their possessions. Many did, many could not.

Each victim had his own story of how terrified he was to come home and find his place ransacked and his stereos, television sets, jewelry and silver gone. The threatening question was always there. Would they come back again, break in when they were at home? Would they have a gun? Would they use it? These victims were of all ages, all colors, people from every background, brought here by a common experience of having their homes broken into.

The police had arrested several burglars and recovered all this loot. Hundreds of rings, watches, bracelets and pieces of questionable value were spread out on tables for the visitors to view. There were computers, typewriters, tires, guns, vacuum cleaners, lamps and every variety of appliance you can think of lined up in rows waiting to be claimed.

Identifying your stolen property was difficult. Would you be able to pick out your stolen videotape recorder from a dozen others? Homeowners, who had filed burglary reports right after the thieves hit, had the best chance because they described the stolen property before it had been recovered. Now, it could be checked by the police and returned.

The discouraging thing was that the police knew this would only continue. They had recovered a lot of material, but more was still out there. Street thugs use the appliances as barter. Taking an expensive stereo from a convertible by ripping the car's top, jamming its dashboard and causing $500 damage might bring $20 from a local fence.

I remember one story on recovered stolen property in which thousands of car stereo units were stored in a warehouse floor-to-ceiling high. There so many, police officers took most of the day loading trucks with all of the stolen items. They had been taken out of parked cars and were valuable to the thieves because they easily could be turned into cash.

As bad as the street crimes are, the robbers and muggers are the most feared. They strike with random violence and prey on those least able to protect themselves. They use the knife, the gun, the chain or the lead pipe and care nothing about the victim, only his money.

The sound of a gunshot brings real fear to the streets. It is always unexpected. It freezes the blood. You are covering a story doing what you usually do, then something happens and the adrenalin surges through you.

We were at the scene of a barricade at a Western Avenue motel.

Officers had moved all the newsmen across the street because of the danger. The suspect had an open window and had fired out of it several times earlier in the day. It was dark now and they were fearful he might aim at the clustered newsmen and cameramen.

I had left the group to call the newsroom from a pay phone down the street. I could see all of the cameras and reporters on a side street using the edge of the corner building as protection.

The blast of a gunshot seared the night. I saw all those stoic newsmen dive for the ground. It was pure reflex. Only the cameramen acted differently. They kept their cameras high so they would not be damaged when their bodies hit the sidewalk. Cameramen instinctivly protect their cameras at all cost. The newsmen were scattered on the ground for a moment, before they realized no one was hurt and the gunman had missed his target. They slowly got up and retreated to a safer position. I was down the street out of the line of fire while I watched the frightening, but humorous action.

While no one was hurt that night, the suspect was killed the next morning when he tried to take hostages out of the motel and make his getaway.

Violence is unexpected. One moment you are walking along. Everything is normal, then it happens. The incident was really my own fault. Beverly and I were about to cross a street when a fast-moving car came to a quick stop next to a car waiting at the signal. The driver started shouting at an Asian woman inside. Two children and another woman were also in the car.

The long-haired driver began a tirade against the woman for cutting him off. The blast I later received was being spewed on her at the time. It looked as if the angry man with gold rings in his ears might really get violent and harm the woman. I decided I had better try to deflect his attention. He came at me like a Doberman guard dog with fire in his eyes erupting from the hate unleashed in his heart. He spewed the "seven words" at me in staccato flashes of disjointed fury. He repeated them, combined them, mixed them up in random blasts 10 inches from my face with his eyes drilled into mine. It was a babbling rage of obscenities that had no perimeters, control or reason. It lashed and lathered, roared and quivered. His hands flailed and bounced with every syllable to give vent to his venomous wrath.

The seven words soon lost their impact and dribbled away the fury they were supposed to expound. The rapid repetition of the sounds sucked the force from his ability to express his rage. He needed 700 times the seven words to rant the magnitude of his uncontrollable temper. Their impact was withering in the extremes of overuse. He lost his shock value and he became a caricature of a wildly insane man. His eyes shrunk in the surge of poison that flowed through his system unchecked by any reason to restrain it. When there are no checks, the system can erupt wildly because there is no limit to reach. It fumed with complete abandonment, until there was no physical strength left to call upon. There is no relief from the bitter surge that exploded inside and demanded the ultimate retribution, whatever that is.

He was an over-the-hill punk rocker still lashed to the childish mentality that had tied him into a ball of ignorance and contempt. His dark and greasy shoulder length hair framed his evil-filled face. His torn and dirty T-shirt was damp from the perspiration of the exhibition.

He turned to walk away, a bulky comb sticking out of the back pocket of his tight dirty jeans. He reached the door of his car. Instead of getting in, he opened it and yelled down the street another version of his all-consuming hate and vengeance. He was not a nice man.

There was no doubt his blast ripped away that cocoon we all wrap around ourselves that creates a feeling that it can't happen to me. Well it did, and the fury left me exhausted and surprised. The violence of the street whipped within inches of my face and somehow, I escaped—shaken and demoralized, but unscathed.

One time when I was walking on a street in New York City and came across a frightening situation in the middle of the sidewalk, I was successful in defusing it. Two cab drivers were head to head, yelling and screaming at each other, just moments from blows.

I walked up and asked if they could tell me where the Plaza Hotel was. They stopped midstream in their argument and both gave me detailed directions. They then broke off their argument and went their separate ways. My intervention had given them the chance to back away and get out of the brewing fight that neither wanted.

It worked that night, but the technique flopped miserably in Los Angeles. This time, I made the mistake of accusing the angry punker of stopping in the pedestrian crosswalk, making it difficult for Beverly and me to get by his car. Instead of deflecting him, I became the sole brunt of his frightening tirade. The woman driver of the car, who had triggered the outburst, just slowly drove away while I was getting the verbal barrage.

Another day we were walking at a brisk pace down one of the streets in our neighborhood, when a tan car pulled up next to us. I thought he was going to ask me directions to some house on the block. I walked over to the car that stopped at the curb next to me, its motor still running. Suddenly, a teenage boy threw open the door and started to charge out at me.

The driver shouted, "Jam them."

I told Beverly to run. I began to move away from the car. The boy looked at me, glanced back at the driver and got back into the car. They sped away. The boy's hesitation probably saved us from getting mugged or at least robbed. We got their license plate number, but found out it was a stolen car.

Events surge and retreat so fast they are over before you realize that you were trapped in the middle of them. Beverly and I have a set schedule that includes a three-mile walk. We have breakfast at a small garden restaurant called The Four Coins, about a mile and half from our house. We enjoy the morning air, the green lawns, the beautiful homes and wide streets. The walk is refreshing and invigorates us for the rest of the day.

We arrive at our garden restaurant after the breakfast crowd and before the lunch hour, so we have the Spanish-style patio to ourselves. Beverly doesn't have to cook breakfast. We are able to be together and talk without interruption for the better part of an hour. It is therapeutic and delightful. We even have old-fashioned things like hot oatmeal, bran muffins and rye toast.

A Spanish fountain with ornate scrollwork and gargoyles in the middle attracts the resident birds. The pond below has been filled in with red Colorado stones rubbed smooth by time. They are always wet and slippery. We have a mossback hummingbird that stops to sip water and perch in the stream that dribbles off the side of the fountain. He spends a few moments there with us almost every day.

Our table is one of many that circle the fountain. Four tall olive trees offer a perfect haven for the wrens that hunt and peck for food all day. Ivy and other green perennials climb the courtyard walls to give you the feeling that you are in Barcelona, Lisbon or Casablanca, or some other exotic Mediterranean site. Blooming plants and small bushes are everywhere. They seem to thrive in the oasis although it is just a couple dozen steps off Wilshire Boulevard.

It is such a haven of peace and quiet that it offers a refreshing contrast to the fast-paced life we live on the other side of its walls. Or so you would think.

The travel agency on the second floor overlooking the patio has been robbed twice. Once the owner and his wife were held at gunpoint while the robbers gathered the cash from a week of work.

The dress shop on the first floor was hit overnight and the stock emptied. The burglars returned later in the night to finish up the job and take all of the merchandise they had to leave behind the first time. It was simple for them. They just cut through the wall and opened the store so they could take what was left.

J.C., a local musician we see at the patio often, was walking in front of his apartment building when a robber pushed a gun in his face, forced him to lie down and took $45 from him. March Fong Eu, California's secretary of state lives in a guarded residential neighborhood nearby. She was beaten and robbed in her home by a bandit who broke in. There was a robbery of a video store nearby. Police arrived and chased the men. Both of them were wounded in an exchange of gunfire.

There have been purse snatchings on the street, hold-ups and muggings in the neighborhood. A lot of street people like to walk the boulevard. One killer murdered five of them and wounded two others in our neighborhood in less than a month. However, a witness saw him stab his last victim to death and followed the killer, who had the murder weapon still on him. The witness spotted a patrol car, flagged it down, pointed out the murderer to the police and the officers arrested him a few blocks from where his victim died.

We go on with our daily routine because we feel it can't happen to us. When you live in the city you have to be optimistic and risk the consequences. It is worth it.

Mean streets are all over, not only for television reporters who are out there every day because of their jobs, but for everyone who lives in the city.

Sometimes situations develop that are comical as well as serious. All of the local TV stations were staked out on a story in South Central Los Angeles; the camera cars were parked at a street corner and the crews were waiting. As you know, there is a very fine line between humor and tragedy. I was sitting in the front seat of our camera truck. A man had been trying to get my attention through a closed window. He had borrowed money earlier and now he was a pest. He just opened the door, reached over me, picked up the portable scanner on the seat and ran off. I was too startled to do anything.

Dave Lopez, a cameraman from KMEX-TV who later came to KTLA, saw him running and tried to stop him. He ducked as the man took a swipe at him with the scanner radio in his hand.

My cameraman, Martin Clancy, and I were too stunned to do anything. We sat there in the front seat and watched the man take off in a dead run across the street.

"Let's follow him in our van," I called out to Martin.

"I'll have the station call the police," he answered as he turned the key in the ignition, started the van and pulled out onto Figueroa, just as the running man, looking over his shoulder, disappeared down a side street.

We drove slowly, working our way through the traffic to get into the left turn lane.

"Ken Davis, this is EJ-2,"

"Go ahead EJ-2," was the immediate reply.

"Call the police, tell them that a radio scanner was stolen from us and we are following the suspect down Figueroa just south of Vernon."

"Are you okay?"

"Yeah, we all right. Call them! Now he's running east on the first block south of Vernon."

We turned down that street and saw him down at the end of the block, still running and looking back. He disappeared behind the house on the corner.

We picked up speed, turned the corner where we had last seen him and drove on by. I saw him hiding behind a gold Cadillac. We passed him, cut in a driveway and started to turn around. He was now retracing his steps, running back down the street. He passed the Channel 9 mini-van that had joined in the hunt. They saw him and started to turn around.

The Channel 2 mini-van stopped in the middle of the street, as the suspect ran by. The Channel 4 mini-van was waiting for him at the corner. He saw the van ahead and ducked in between houses. A boy about 12, who was watching the chase, ran over to the breathless man, who had slowed to a jog. The young boy grabbed the scanner out of his hand, then ran straight down the street toward us. The man ran up a driveway and into a backyard.

The boy looked back and saw the man disappear, then he stopped running and walked over to the KMEX-TV cameraman who had been chasing on foot, and gave him the radio.

It was over. We got the radio back. We just let the suspect go. We saw him come out from behind a house and continue his run southbound on Figueroa.

We all assembled at our original location and traded stories about the chase. I was calling the station to tell them what happened, when I heard the tail end of a police radio broadcast, "...the suspect is being chased by four television news crews."

That was enough to put fear into anyone.

I thanked everyone for the help. Clancy gave the little boy $5 for being a hero and I checked my scanner closely to make sure it was working properly. It was.

The bizarre situation must have looked like an old silent movie. White television vans with their dishes and antennas on their roofs, turning corners, backing up, making U-turns and almost crashing into each other, chasing a man running down the street.

We all laughed about it and knew we were lucky to get through the experience without anyone getting hurt. It shakes you when you think what might have happened if the man got desperate and was armed. We were all carried away by the moment and responded naturally, but the risk was real.

It would have been best for all if we just let the man take the scanner and run down the street. We could have filed our police report and that would have been that.

The frightening part of the mean streets is that everything is normal, then in an instant it is forever changed. With no warning, something violent happens and what was before is gone forever and in a twisted instant your life can be shattered. Your world breaks and falls apart. You have to rebuild it all over again, and learn to live it in an entirely different manner. That is the reality of living on the mean streets. You don't think that anything can happen to you, but it can and you have to be prepared to live with the consequences of the violence.

That twisted instant randomly explodes in traffic accidents, shootings, muggings, drownings, falls, and countless other moments of tragedy that are our human experience. We all know the fabric of civilization is a delicate gauze that binds things. It is fragile and it can be torn so easily. People have to protect this delicate webb and work to mend its tears.

If we ever give up on this, our whole structure can collapse around us. The streets are mean, but we don't have to be.

*　　*　　*

One of the most difficult times for reporters is when they must visit a home hit by tragedy. There is no way the moment can be softened. It is hard, and trying for all concerned, but often necessary.

It is especially painful when the house you visit is the home of a boy who police believe is a murderer. How do you talk to a mother or father about their son who has just been picked up and is accused of committing several murders?

It's a difficult situation for the reporter. To tell the story properly, you must have an on-camera interview. In most cases, the parents refuse to talk and you have wasted a lot of time trying to get the story you know ahead of time you will probably not get.

A newspaper reporter can go to the house and try to get some comments from the parents standing behind a half-open door. Even if they are reluctant to talk, they will often say a few things the reporter can include in his newspaper account. However if your assignment editor feels it necessary to get the story, you must talk to the parents and try to get their permission to go on camera.

I had to go to the homes of two separate suspects in a mass murder. They had been picked up overnight. I had an uneasy feeling as I walked up the driveway, crossed the porch and rang the doorbell.

The shades were drawn at the first house. There were letters in the mailbox and the morning paper was still on the doorstep. I rang several times, but there was no answer. I knocked on the door, one last time, and waited. Then, I walked back down the driveway to my crew waiting in the camera car.

As we drove the two miles to the next address, I radioed my assignment desk, "No one at the first location. I rang several times, but the place was empty."

"Okay, thanks, Stan."

"We're on our way to the next one," I replied.

We drove slowly down the street in a very prosperous black neighborhood. The house was large and well kept. The home was a big white colonial with newly painted green shutters across the front. I walked up a long driveway, crossed over the green, well-groomed grass, climbed the front steps and knocked on the door. After a long wait, it slowly opened.

I introduced myself. The tall, distinguished looking father looked at me and nodded. He opened the door all the way.

"I just wanted to talk to you about your son," I said. "Is he still in custody?"

The father nodded again, "Yes."

You never know what reaction you are going to get. It can vary from anger, violence and frustration to the resigned defeatism of a puzzled and unbelieving parent.

He paused before speaking, "My son didn't do anything. He wasn't worried about anything. I can always tell when he has something to hide. We spent most of the day painting the hallway. When it was time to drive down to the park to pick up his brother, I asked him to do it. He put his paint brush down on the can and picked up the car keys off the table and left."

"Are you concerned?" I asked.

"Of course, I'm concerned. My boy is in jail. From what I can gather, he drove into an area where police had a stake out for someone who looked like him. They arrested him. He didn't do anything. Come in. I'll show you where we were painting."

I followed him into the entry hall and closed the front door behind me. He kept talking as we walked back to the end of the hallway, just where it opened into the breakfast room.

He showed me the partially painted walls, the open paint cans and the drop-cloths still on the floor. "That's his brush over there...on top of the paint can. See, he just finished that section of the wall above."

We talked a while longer and I asked if he would tell me his story on camera, "I'll show what the two of you were doing and you can tell me why you believe he is innocent."

"I know he is innocent," the father replied.

"May I bring the camera in and shoot where you have been painting and talk to you on camera about what you've just told me?"

"Certainly...sure...bring it in."

We ran the interview with the father on our broadcast that night. We showed the unfinished painting job and heard him say, "My boy will be all right. He's done nothing. He couldn't have."

He was released the next day.

*   *   *

I think you grow as a reporter by the experiences that don't get on the air. Those emotional moments are yours alone. No one else knows they have happened. Most are so personal, it is difficult to talk about them. Yet, they are the very substance of your experience and are often called into play.

They are felt when you compare what you are doing now to similar stories you covered before. You may recall striking contrasts, yet they have no place in your current report. But you feel it. Often those remembrances make you uneasy, those living patterns you can't do anything about. They exist, are newsworthy and are covered, but they leave a vacuum inside. They make you want to do something that will change things, but you know there is really nothing you can do. I had those feelings the night I watched a traffic sweep for drunk drivers.

*   *   *

A little boy was clutching a videotape cassette. He wasn't frightened, but he was uncomfortable in the center of the bright lights, the white, hard helmets of the countless motorcycle officers, the red and blue flashing light bars on the police cars and the general chaos around him.

He had been to a video rental store with his family on this warm spring evening. He was the only one to speak English so he picked out the video and paid the cashier to rent the cassette.He was still holding it in his hand, when his older brother slowed to a stop and followed the cars in front of him to a police sobriety checkpoint that had been set up on Santa Monica Boulevard in Hollywood.

The LAPD started these checkpoints to try to cut down on drunk drivers. The little boy's brother had been drinking. The car passed a few officers waving flashlights. It eased up to a few red markers on the pavement and stopped at the intersection.

A tall, uniformed officer wearing a black leather jacket and a white helmet, leaned towards the driver's window.

"We are conducting a sobriety checkpoint to see if anyone might be driving under the influence." The brother did not understand English. He nodded his head. The scent of liquor was strong.

I could see the officer scanning his flashlight through the interior of the car. The boy's mother, his little brother and two other people were passengers in the older model Chevrolet.

I watched as the officer continued to talk to those in the car. He finally motioned for the driver to turn off Santa Monica onto a side street where motorists who were suspected of being drunk were being tested. The driver made the turn and the car stopped in the darkness. The brother got out and stood next to the officer.

"May I have a Spanish-speaking officer over here?" the policeman called out to the command post.

Two officers walked across the darkened street and started testing to see if the driver was under the influence of alcohol. It was a slow process. The brother did badly. He weaved and could not walk in a straight line. He had trouble following some of the dexterity tests. The family just sat in the car.

There was no doubt he was very drunk. He was walked across to a mobile unit outfitted with a breathmobile and other equipment that could confirm the officer's observation. I soon lost sight of him in the crowd and followed my cameraman around as we recorded various shots of what was going on as the checkpoint operated.

Later, I saw the family standing on the sidewalk as their car was being towed away. Obviously, there was no one in the car who could drive it and it had to be impounded at a police garage. Many other cars belonging to drunk drivers were being lifted onto the back of the tow trucks, hooked up and hauled away to the impound lot.

The little boy put his hands on his mother's shoulder to calm her down. She did not fully understand what was going on. She spoke only Spanish and could not comprehend why her son was being arrested. I still see the video movie in the boy's hand as he tried to help his mother.

I knew this was a start of serious problems for the family. There would be a fee to get the car out of impound and money to get their brother out of jail. There would be court costs and a fine for being convicted of drunk driving. There would be the cost of attending driver's school for many weeks, lost time on the job, even the loss of a job. There would be the emotional and humiliating experience of being booked, mugged and incarcerated for hours in jail.

Almost 40 other drivers were arrested and booked for driving under the influence of alcohol that night. Their stories would differ, but the end result would be the same. Society had declared war on the drunk driver after many years of truce.

Drunk drivers were why we had our cameras outside City Hall on a cold December night. A podium with a loudspeaker had been set on a level of the First Street steps in the park surrounding City Hall. This was where festive occasions are often celebrated, giving sharp contrast to this night.

Mothers Against Drunk Driving was holding its annual candlelight vigil. Most of those in the crowd tonight had lost a member of their family to a drunk driver. They carried pictures of their loved ones. They talked of their sons and daughters and how they were suddenly cut down when they were just starting to live. They carried the pain on their faces, in their eyes and in their voices, although the accident might have happened years ago.

Many had been hit in crosswalks while walking home from school. Others had been driving along when a drunk driver roared through a stop signal and demolished their cars and snuffed out their lives. In some cases the drunks had crossed over the double line on curves along the open highway, killing those in the oncoming cars. The stories were catastrophic and heartbreaking. These people holding the glowing candles in the darkness had been wounded for life and would carry the tragedy with them as long as they lived.

I always remember a mother here holding the picture of a little boy in a glass frame that reflected the soft light of the burning candle she was carrying. Her boy had been killed by a drunk driver six months before. She talked about the car accident with resigned bitterness. Her son in the picture looked so much like that troubled little boy at the sobriety checkpoint who was holding the videocassette in one hand and putting his other hand on his mother's shoulder.

You span extremes when you are out there where the real world unfolds. You are sent to a scene because something newsworthy has happened to people. Many have been caught by random chance in a mesh that suddenly wraps tightly around them. Some are trapped and some get free. Being there when things are happening helps you mature as a reporter. You don't know what your next assignment is. Often, it hasn't happened yet. But you wait until you get your next call and your assignment editor sends you racing across town to another human situation.

News is the unusual, the exceptional, the uncommon occurrence that takes place in our daily lives. That is why so much of it is bad. The lucky and average person doesn't get snared in these heart-breaking situations. News is the unexpected that happens. As a reporter, you are often a part of it, but so much of what happens to you doesn't get on the air.

I remember vividly one of those emotional situations unfolding around me that never got on the air. No one even knew it was taking place, except me. I was doing a story about high school security. The script I wrote called for an on-camera close at a school with a football field behind me. I would just stand on the sidewalk next to the field. I would not have to go through the red tape of talking to school authorities and getting permission to go on campus and do the shooting there. I could probably finish the entire sequence in five minutes.

Our mobile unit is not unobtrusive. It attracts attention wherever it goes. The twin transmitting dishes, two feet in diameter, sit in plain view atop the unit attached to masts that can extend 30 feet into the air. There are generator boxes on top, a platform on the roof, twin spotlights, assorted antennae and an all-white chassis that turns heads when we drive by.

We selected the nearest high school, so we could complete the assignment as soon as possible. The story itself had nothing to do with the particular school. It was just the background I needed to tell my story.

This part of town is well known for its gang activity. As we pulled up, we could see a half dozen young men across the street in white T-shirts and jeans. They were standing by three motorcycles and they gazed at us without expression.

Gang members are often sullen, hostile and distant. They mistrust the media and blame reporters for all the negative publicity that gets on the air. However, they usually won't bother you.

They stood in a vacant lot cluttered with debris and broken beer bottles. Graffiti was scrawled on both the houses next to the small open field.

I did my on-camera report two or three times and decided I had what I needed to finish my story. I stood there on the sidewalk going over my notes for the script as my cameraman and soundman collected their gear and carried it to the rear of the truck.

They were behind and on the other side of the vehicle, with the back doors swung open out of sight from my location, so it looked as if I were standing alone on the sidewalk.

As I made a few changes in my notebook, from the corner of my eye I could see one of the young men slowly walking across the street towards me.

I did not want to look alarmed and I didn't want to create any attention by calling out to my crew. I thought I had better just keep on doing what I was doing and wait this thing out. I kept on writing, looking down at my notebook and not giving any indication that I was scared or aware that he was getting very close to me.

He stopped for a moment. I looked up. He walked over the last few steps and smiled, "I'm sorry, Mr. Chambers. I didn't want to interrupt you while you were writing, but could I have your autograph?"

16.

BREAKER...BREAKER...BREAKER

A news beat is not always filled with action. I had to learn to live with big periods of time when little happens, and it is always a shock to the system when you jump from doing nothing into the heart-pumping excitement of a fast-breaking story.

A radio scanner is often the only sound I hear during those lonely hours when nothing is happening. Red, digital zeros run across the narrow screen of the thin scanners sitting on the dashboard of the darkened mobile unit. They look like tiny videogames being ignored. Actually, they are sophisticated radio systems, monitoring hundreds of emergency channels. Each moving to its own beep.

The zeros disappear when a call is picked up and new numbers freeze on the selector screen. They mark the radio frequency captured on the searching scanner. When the transmission is finished, the parade of red zeros starts again.

Three of these units sit in front of me. Night after night, I watch the procession of digits and listen to the eclectic selection of calls. I am looking for that one transmission that might mean a major story is breaking in the city.

I have to wade through countless routine broadcasts and conversations. I sift through bits of static, unintelligible voices and strange digital sounds.

Hour after hour, cameramen Greg Hunter, Jim Toten and I cruise the city streets listening and waiting. The big stories are few. There is much crackling on the scanners. We pick up only partial transmissions at times. Somehow, when it is important, we catch fragments and put the pieces together.

Because we listen to so many channels, it is easy to miss something. Often we catch only a portion of a broadcast and we quickly push the lock-in button hoping the dispatcher will repeat the address.

We are in constant radio communication with the assignment editor in the newsroom who is also listening to similar banks of radios. He is in the center of everything. He can phone directly to news sources and check on reports that might be important. However, he doesn't have the luxury we have of being able to concentrate on the scanners.

He has to dispatch several news crews and keep tab on what is happening moment by moment in the newsroom, handle all of the bubbling questions that are continuously asked in the process of putting a news program together.

The assignment editor has to make the difficult decision and give the final word on whether to go on a breaking news story or not. The important question is what will be going on when you get there? It is the essence of a breaking story.

If it is a fire, is it too far away? Will there be anything to shoot when you arrive? If it is a single-family residential home, the chances are that the fire will be out and the firemen will be cleaning up, getting ready to leave when you arrive. The big fires are the easy ones, they will be burning when you get there. Sometimes fires could be major, but are quickly put out by the firefighters. There is no set answer on whether to go or not. Intuition plays a big factor in deciding.

If the assignment is a traffic accident, will there be pictures to shoot? If you have to drive halfway across the city, what will you see? The visual element is the important part of breaking stories. Without it, we have nothing.

The best advice given to me about covering a breaking story was: If in doubt, go. There is nothing worse than holding back, listening to the emergency radios go on and on about the problems they are facing. The decision is subjective and you can be wrong. However, the worse possible thing for an assignment editor or a news crew is to know about a story and not go because we didn't think we could get there in time. The pain of seeing it on another news channel that night is unbearable.

Talking about a breaker and being on one are two different things. When you are in the middle of breaking news, you know what real pressure is. It is all played out against time.

I know how exciting it is to jump from doing nothing into a fast-breaking story. You battle traffic, try to talk your way through police roadblocks, squint at a map book that is impossible to read and listen to voices that shriek over the radio. You are swept up in a rising emotional tide as you get closer to the scene. When you get your camera gear and jump out of the truck, everything is on automatic. There is no time to think it out. You are carried away by the storm.

I've been through hundreds of them. I remember one night in 1979 when our crew was racing back on the Hollywood Freeway from a murder scene in Westlake in Ventura County.

I was sitting in the darkness of the bumpy front seat of our mobile unit scribbling my copy in a reporter's notebook. My bent knee was a makeshift desk and the bounce of the camera truck made my writing even more difficult to read than usual. Cameraman Dave Moore was driving and engineer John

Fischer was with his electronic equipment in the back.

Although the deadline for our 10 o'clock newscast was close, it didn't pressure me. We would get back about an hour before air time. I had just about finished writing, and in fact had rewritten my copy three times. When we left the busy freeway near the station, I was ready to record the sound track in the front seat the moment we pulled up to the newsroom door. This would give a writer enough time to edit my report on the shooting and schedule it for the early part of the newscast.

As we drove down Van Ness, Akila Gibbs on the assignment desk radioed, "Unit Two, where are you now?"

"We're off the freeway and just about to come on the lot," cameraman Dave Moore answered.

"There's been an accident on the Golden State Freeway. Stand by," she said and then abruptly cut off.

"It might be big," I said, noting the tense tone in her voice.

We kept on driving to the station, past the on-ramp that would take us to the Golden State Freeway. Here was my usual nightmare predicament. If we went right away, we would lose the Westlake murder story. If we waited, we might be too late to cover the freeway accident.

We turned into the main gate at KTLA and waved to the security guard, who raised a wooden protective arm to let us in. Dave Moore whirled the truck toward the newsroom and sped to our parking place at the far end of the lot.

John Fischer, our young, enthusiastic soundman, jumped out of the truck, ran to the back of the unit, picked up a cassette, brought it inside and placed it inside his videotape recorder. I turned on my gooseneck light so that I could read the copy I had scrawled on my reporter's notebook. If we could record the sound track in the next minute or so, we could finish the murder story and still get to the traffic accident.

Suddenly, we heard Akila's voice. This time, it was high pitched and nervous. "They are calling five rescue ambulances to the Golden State Freeway. You had better go."

"Have someone come outside to the truck so we can give you the murder story," Dave snapped back.

I nodded, held up my copy into the light and John said, "Go in five seconds."

I turned off the various radios as John let the tape run for a few seconds before I started to record the audio track.

Our chief news engineer, Jeff Webreck, came running out for the tape. He is the engineer who built our transmitting link and created the sophisticated system we use to broadcast from the field. Everyone helps out in an emergency. He started to open the door, saw we were recording and waited until I finished.

"I'll take the tapes," he shouted. "See you later." He slammed the door.

I turned, waved at Jeff as Dave jammed his foot on the accelerator and we were off.

"News, this is Unit 2," Dave called into the mike, as we careened out of the gate.

"Go ahead, Unit 2," Akila's voice answered.

"Akila, can you find out exactly where the accident is? Is it northbound, southbound, on the transition road? It will help us get there faster if we know exactly where it is." We were already half way up Van Ness to Sunset Boulevard.

"Northbound." She paused. "Did you read that? Northbound."

"Yeah, we got that," Dave turned the corner at Sunset Boulevard and roared up toward Western.

"It's on the northbound Golden State Freeway, just before the transition road to the Ventura. The CHP has confirmed one fatality and four injuries . . . five ambulances at the scene."

"We're on our way," Dave answered as he weaved through the traffic to Los Feliz. He would pick up the Golden State Freeway near Griffith Park.

My radios were quiet. Although I was getting some transmissions on my fire channels, I wasn't able to get more information than Akila had given us. I wondered if my scanners were having a bad night.

We drove past the Griffith Park entrance, slowing down, as the three of us looked down to the freeway to see if traffic had completely stopped.

"Are there emergency shoulders on the Golden State?" Dave asked as he looked at the long parade of stationary red taillights from the cars heading northbound toward the accident scene.

"I think there are," John Fischer said from the darkness of the back seat.

"Shall we try it?" Dave asked as he looked for a place to whip around and squeeze onto the freeway on-ramp.

"It's about all we can do," I answered. "The red taillights are stop-and-go now."

Dave eased past cars waiting to enter the jammed northbound freeway. The accident was about a mile and a half ahead and traffic was at a standstill. It looked as if we were trapped.

Dave worked our mobile unit over to the far right side and moved slowly behind the line of big trucks that careen along this freeway this time of night.

"Why don't you get on the shoulder?" John asked.

"It's too narrow, I don't think we can get through," Dave answered. Tiny beads of perspiration glistened on his forehead.

A high wall bordered the emergency lane at the far right side of the freeway and heavy truck traffic was stalled in the slow lane.

Dave pulled into the narrow shoulder lane and moved slowly past the stalled traffic. It was so narrow that at one point, he scraped his outside mirror on the side of the wall. Trucks on our left and the wall on our right hid our view of what was up ahead. Finally, we reached the chaos and flashing red lights.

Several officers from the Highway Patrol were waving drivers over to the far right lane. The rest of the freeway was completely shut down. Up ahead, dozens of red and blue lights were flashing, red flares were smoking and emergency workers were everywhere.

It was just moments before the 10 o'clock news would be going on the air. John took a quick survey of the scene and realized that by sending a live signal to our transmitter on Mount Wilson, we could televise from here, right in the middle of the freeway.

Dave and John opened the back end of the truck, pulled their gear out, and ran toward the flashing lights and the scene of general chaos 50 yards ahead. John plugged his video cable from the tape recorder into Dave's camera, while Dave balanced his light belt on his shoulder and prepared to start shooting the moment they reached the lighted area.

I ran ahead to get what information I could for the live cut-in. I saw Mike Meadows from the *Los Angeles Times* with cameras hanging around his neck. He is one of the best and most energetic news photographers covering breaking stories in the city.

"Stan, it's a head-on...A wrong-way driver. The other car was filled with people. The dead man is still pinned in there. The others are being treated."

The scene was charged with confusion, but the paramedics and firemen were totally focused on their rescue efforts. Three victims were being treated on the freeway roadway. One was on a stretcher in the back of a rescue ambulance. Firemen were trying to pry loose the side and front of the car where a man was trapped. They were ripping the car apart with the power-driven "jaws of life" that generate tremendous force. It bends and breaks and tears open anything in its path. Firemen were skillfully using the intimidating tool like a surgeon in an operating room. Showers of flying sparks erupted from the spinning edge of a screeching, grinding saw-wheel. It was cutting into the metal of the twisted wreckage.

Mike's camera was flashing as he took countless pictures of the firemen swarming around the scene of devastation. He came over to me. "The CHP got word that there was a wrong-way driver on the Ventura Freeway about 10 or 15 minutes before this happened. They did everything they could to flag the driver down, but no such luck. Here's where it ended."

"Drunk?" I asked.

"No," Mike answered, "Some older lady, disoriented or something. She got on the wrong way and has been driving all of this time, barely missing cars. She was going about 50 miles an hour. She missed all the others and finally smashed into this one."

Just like Mike, Dave and John were videotaping their pictures for our news report. They had dramatic action shots of the quick and desperate attempts of the paramedics trying to help the badly injured victims still lying on the freeway roadway.

"Stan, will you watch the camera and recorder?" Dave called to me as he and John ran back to the truck to get more cable. The chaos grew as more rescue personnel, more news crews and more CHP officers arrived.

Dave was pulling cable along the side of the freeway through the parked vehicles. He carried a huge reel, laying the cable out as he got closer to where I was standing, next to his camera. He had to roll out almost 300 feet of cable to connect the transmitting truck to his camera in the middle of the rescue effort.

John was in the truck, checking gauges and dials, making final tests to be sure our picture was getting to the transmitter and that we were ready to go on the air live.

A CHP sergeant and a fire chief on the scene helped me with more information and confirmed what Mike Meadows had told me.

Dave plugged the cable into his unit, got a picture on his camera and shouted to me, "We're ready to go!"

Meanwhile, the newscast had just begun. I got my earpiece working and could hear anchorman Hal Fishman telling the story of a hijacked Kuwaiti airliner. He said as many as five passengers being held as hostages had been shot.

Now my earphones carried the messages of many voices. I could hear the director in the studio, the engineer in the news center and John Fischer in our remote unit at the scene.

"We're ready to go," I said calmly into my microphone.

"Let's go, studio. We are all set," I heard John say over his radio back in the truck.

I waited for my cue. I watched the splash of colors, the orange, blue and red of the rescue ambulances and the fire engines, the yellow turnout coats of the firemen, the black and white cars of the CHP. They all blended to capture the desperation of the scene as everyone tried to save the victims.

I stood holding my microphone, waiting for the cue, but none came. Again, I spoke calmly but urgently. "Tell the director we are ready and should go right away. This is very important," I called over the mike.

I had the feeling no one was listening to us back at the studio.

Tension was building. Here was a tragic story going on before our eyes and the studio was not cutting to us. Our frustration was rising. What was going on? Were they hearing us back there? Did they understand the urgency of going with us right away?

Again, I told several people I knew were on the line to relay my request to the director and to Gerry Ruben the producer. I knew if they realized what a big story we had here, they would go to us right away, no matter what was happening at the studio.

I kept pressing my side of the story over the communication line. "Studio, tell them to take us."

"They are not going to do it right away," a voice flashed over my earpiece.

"Tell Gerry," I insisted.

"They know all about what you have here and they are not going to take it. Now, damn it, get off the line and keep quiet," he lashed back.

"I won't get off the line. You get off the line. Tell the director to take us," I shouted back, losing my cool.

Tempers were smoking across the line. I could see the story evaporating before my eyes. Already two ambulances had left the scene for the hospital. The turbulent chaos was beginning to be more controlled and quiet. The initial sense that we were right in the middle of things was slipping away.

"Okay, Stan, we heard your last call. We are going to come to you in 30 seconds," a voice shouted reassuringly.

Dave Moore kept on shooting and had sent back many dramatic pictures to the studio during the long delay, and now they could be used in our live report.

"Fifteen seconds."

They were still working on one of the seriously injured victims on the roadway next to me. I was standing next to the two cars that had crashed head on. Firemen were still working all around me.

"Five seconds."

"You're on."

We did an extended report on the tragic accident. It showed everything that was being done to help the victims and we used videotape of what was going on before we went on the air. However, it was not what it could have been and is a good example of some of the frustrations involved whenever you try to go live.

Even though ours is a communication business, communication is one of our biggest problems. I could not convey the urgency of the story to our producer. He did not know the magnitude of what we were covering. He told me later that if he had known, he would have cut to us right away.

The number of people between his ear phone and my microphone blurred our communications. Instead of going on live right away, we were left in the midst of a big breaking story, only to see it evaporate before our eyes. No one was to blame. It was just another example of the possible disappointments when you try to go live. Too many things can happen to knock you off the air. But the feeling of accomplishment when things go well more than makes up for it when they don't.

*   *   *

Flames flowed like a river of fire across the dry Malibu hills. They would leap from tree to tree, exploding as they consumed each one into a cyclonic funnel of black smoke and turbulent orange balls of fire. The heat was so intense, vast acres of yellowish brush that seemed far downhill from the fast moving blaze would all erupt at once. The fire made a violent, hissing roar as it rolled down the hillside, incinerating everything in its path.

Devil winds whipped the blazing canyons and hills as the firestorm destroyed everything it touched. The eerie sound of the wild wind and roaring fire was like a tornado that thundered and cracked across the hillsides.

Our KTLA mobile unit, the Telemobile, was across the deepest canyon from the firestorm as the winds whipped it toward the sea. Firemen at the command post said there was no way it could be stopped until it hit the ocean many miles ahead.

Although we were seeing firsthand the rampaging destruction and feeling the searing heat, we could not take pictures from our location. In 1970 we did not carry film cameras on the Telemobile and, in those years, we had no videotape recorders small enough to fit into a mobile unit. Before we could get on the air and show the devastating fire, we had to find a high peak where we could both see the flames and send a live signal to our transmitter on Mount Wilson.

We knew we had to get ahead of the fire. The road we were on was no place for a mobile unit. A twist of the wind could send the fire racing across the meadows of the valley, down the hillside and through the brush-covered fields toward us.

The map I was studying showed a road several miles ahead that we hoped would take us beyond the fire. It wound its way on the other side of a towering mountain to a communications center atop one of the highest peaks. This would get us ahead of the fire and put us on top where we could get a signal out to Mount Wilson.

We found the narrow road. In a few minutes, the deep canyons and high hills actually blocked out any sight of the fire. The narrow road climbed up hairpin turns to the mountain and brought us to the other side away from the towering smoke clouds. It was a different world here. The only sign of fire was the black cloud in the distance, as we rounded certain turns. It was miles away. This was beautiful Malibu country, wild, unthreatened and heavily wooded. We passed ranches, cabins and barns under construction as we wound our way to the top.

You could tell people were concerned about the fire, but it seemed too distant to be a real threat. Most of them stood outside watching the ominous smoke cloud. There weren't too many escape routes if the fire overran their homes. When you live in the mountains, the threat of a brush fire is always with you. You learn to live with it, and for the moment, there was no fire here. Wind was bending trees and rolling tumbleweeds across the narrow road and through the fields as we got closer to the top.

We entered the empty parking lot of the communications center, found the chain link gate open and were able to drive to the highest point.

Four stucco buildings stood on the plateau atop the peak. One long concrete structure had a dozen or so communication dishes on the roof. A wide parking area provided ample protection if flames climbed the mountainside.

We could see the ocean on one side, the smoke cloud from the fire on the other, and Mount Wilson in the distance, but saw no flames. The three of us jumped out of the Telemobile into the buffeting wind. Roger climbed the ladder on the back of the truck and pulled up the pipe supporting our transmitting dish from the side of the Telemobile. He brought it up slowly, hand over hand. The extended pipe makes a mast about 30 feet high. When Roger got it fully extended, he tried to aim the dish at Mount Wilson. The wind kept rocking it back and forth while Rich was on the radio talking to the engineers on Mount Wilson.

There was the crackle of cross talk on the radio. "I see your picture, Telemobile. Can you pan it slowly?"

"The wind is something else," Rich answered. He leaned out the window and shouted up to Roger, "Pan it to the left."

"I'll try," Roger yelled back. "This whole truck is jumping in the wind."

"They have our signal. The panning might make it a little clearer," Rich shouted.

"I know, I know," Roger mumbled, as he manually tried to turn the pipe a little to the left. The dish atop the pipe was waving in the wind.

"Don't make too big a deal out of it," the voice from Mount Wilson called out on the radio. "The signal is pretty good. Why don't you just lock it in. We'll go with what you have."

Roger tightened the clamp with his hand and came down the ladder, his hair whipping in his face. The truck door barely opened in the gusting wind. He forced his way into the truck and took the back seat. The transmitting dish and the mast holding it continued to bounce and wave in the wind.

"The signal is strong," Rich said as he looked at the monitor.

"Let's get the camera and cable out," Roger answered as he prepared to get out again into the windstorm.

I told the newsroom what we had done. We had a complete view of the mountains. Now, we just had to wait for the fire. The newsroom was in no hurry. They were very pleased that we had found a point where we could get a signal out.

The black cloud in the distance seemed to be growing bigger, but no flames were visible. Waiting for a fire is tedious. You keep thinking you made the wrong decision or picked the wrong spot. Maybe we should have stayed with the fire and at least tried to get a signal out. Maybe we should have tried a closer hilltop. Our doubts grew stronger the longer we waited.

A sheriff's car, red lights flashing, paused at the open gate, then drove up the rest of the hill to our unit. "Where did you guys come from?" he asked as he got out. He had on his goggles and heavy gloves.

"We had to find a good spot to get our television picture out," I answered. "We saw plenty of fire below, but we couldn't get a signal out. We're in a good spot here," I added.

"How long before you can get out of here?" I heard much concern in his voice.

"Oh, we're staying," I called back. "We're going to get some great shots. That fire was really going when we saw it down in the canyon."

"I know it is," the deputy sheriff answered, "and it is coming right in this direction all the way to the ocean. I've been told to get you out of here."

"That's okay, sheriff," I answered as we walked toward each other. "We'll be all right. This is the only place we can get our picture out."

"I'm sorry, you can't stay here," he answered.

"I understand your concern, sheriff, but we'll be all right. There is plenty of flat area up here. The parking section alone will hold back any flames. Don't worry about us."

"Look, when those flames race up this peak on all sides, it's going to be like a blast furnace. Everything is going to go. I don't care about your television signal. I'm not going to let you guys stay."

"Sheriff, this is our job. You worry about those people below. We'll take care of ourselves."

"They're all gone below. I came up here to make sure there weren't any phone company engineers still here. I've got some other people to check on. Will you cooperate with me and get out of here?"

There were still no flames visible. The place looked perfectly safe to me. I was not about to leave. I think the sheriff could tell.

He got back into his patrol car. "Look, I have to check a ranch on the oceanside of the mountain. I'll be back in 10 minutes and I want you out of here." He backed up his car and rode a small dust cloud to the gate.

"Just our luck to get a guy like that at a time a time like this," Roger said, as we watched the flashing red light disappear down the winding road.

"He'll be back," I said as we walked back to our truck.

As we reached the Telemobile, I saw the first flames work their way over a distant ridge below.

"Hello, newsroom, this is the Telemobile, checking in. What's the latest from your end?" I held the microphone close and watched as the flames moved closer.

"We hoped you would have the latest, Telemobile," they answered.

"Well, just as I'm talking, I can see some flames coming up over a hill. They're still pretty far away, but unless the winds change they should be coming our way. I haven't any idea how long it will take."

"Give us a mark on your location again."

"It's the communications peak...the very top. I'm not sure, but we might get some pretty terrific shots here in a while."

"That communications peak is right in the path of the fire. At least that is what the command post is saying. It's going to the sea and you're right in its path."

"You know how those estimates are," I answered. "It goes in the general direction, but it doesn't necessarily mean it's going to burn everything. Besides, we have a big flat spot...a good sized parking lot here. Even if the flames come close, we'll be all right."

"Well, I hope so," the newsroom voice shot back. "When can we do a live spot?"

"We're ready when you are. I can do a spot right now. The flames are still far away, but the smoke is black and it looks huge over the hills."

"Can you be ready in 10 minutes?"

"We're ready now," I answered.

Just as soon as we finished our live report we could see the dust of the sheriff's car coming up the road, still several minutes away. Roger stood in front of the Telemobile looking down the hill at the speeding car, "He looks serious about it. What are we going to do?"

"Let's check the desk," I said.

I went back to the Telemobile, and called the newsroom once again.

"Telemobile, good job on the live report," they said. "That black cloud certainly looks ominous."

"Not as ominous as a sheriff coming up the hill," I called back.

"Is it too dangerous to stay?" The desk asked.

"That's what the deputy says."

"The wire copy says they are evacuating everyone from there. What are you going to do?" the voice over the radio asked.

"We're staying," I paused a moment. "Unless you say differently."

"Let me talk to the others in the newsroom," he answered.

After a long wait I asked, "Newsroom, why don't we just wait a while longer before making any final decisions?"

There was no response.

Roger called up from the front of the truck, "I can see the flames now, they're coming up over the ridge. They're huge."

I studied them for a moment, and I pushed the transmit button on the microphone. "News, I'm getting off the radio for a moment. The sheriff is arriving."

The deputy slammed on his brakes, and ran over to us. "Look, I told you to get out of here. I don't want to waste any more time. Those flames will be here any moment. Now get out of here." He was mad. "I've got everyone else out. I'm not going to be responsible for you guys killing yourselves."

"Let me talk to the newsroom," I answered.

"You're not talking to anyone. You're getting out."

I walked back to the front seat and put the radio mike up to my mouth. "He's back and he's giving me real heat."

"Telemobile, this is news," the voice replied. "We've just checked with top management and the word is...*get out of there.* They don't want you guys hurt and they don't want to take any chance of losing the Telemobile."

The sheriff had walked with me over to the truck and heard the announcement. "Get out or I'll arrest you," he threatened.

"We'll follow you down the hill," I answered.

The two vehicles stirred dust clouds that were whipped higher and higher by the frightening wind as we wound our way down the mountain top and away from the fire.

We drove to Pacific Coast Highway and waited for the flames to reach the ocean. We did several live shots that night as the flames rolled over the mountains and exploded in the dry brush on the oceanside of the hills. In most cases, despite the black, choking smoke that was only six feet off the ground, the firemen used Pacific Coast Highway as a fire break and held back the spreading flames from reaching the beach homes below. Yet despite everything the firefighters did, several beach homes were lost.

We drove back to the communications peak the next day. The fire had run its course and left utter devastation behind. Homes and ranches we saw on our way up to the peak the day before were reduced to burned-out skeletons. The Malibu hills were barren, covered with layers of powdery, gray ash. The narrow, winding road brought us through miles of desolation as we worked our way uphill toward the communication peak. Former homesites were now just rubble. I could remember several before the fire with their owners standing in front and wondering what to do. All of them got out safely. The sheriff did a good job of evacuating the mountain.

When we did reach the peak and drove up to the site where we had parked the Telemobile yesterday, we could see the fire had roared through. All the brush was gone, all the trees burned, it was like the rest of the burned-out mountain we just had driven through. However, the spot where we had parked the Telemobile was untouched. It was at the highest point and the parking lot around it had protected it from the onslaught of the flames. It looked safe today, but I don't know how it would have been yesterday when the fireball climbed the mountainside and its intense heat blistered and destroyed everything in its path. What would the generated heat have done to the Telemobile and its crew huddled inside? Would we have survived? I felt uncertain as I stood there surrounded by the vast acreage of lonely, ashen land. I silently thanked the sheriff for doing his job so well.

So much of what I go through never gets on the air. I cover the story. My cameraman shoots the videotape and captures the visual elements to show the viewer what happened. I write the narration and explain the facts as best I can. The finished report goes on the air and the viewer gets a sense of what took place. But, like the Malibu brush fire, so many things happen that can never be experienced by anyone not at the scene.

*   *   *

My friend Eli Ressler typified the professional cameraman. He always kept his small, hand-held 16 millimeter Bell and Howell at his side. In those days, it was the kind you had to wind up each time you used it. His basic assignment was to be on the spot wherever news was happening in the city.

Eli was driving on the Santa Monica Freeway on a hot August day when the assignment editor called him on the car radio, "Eli, we have a copter on the pad at Santa Monica Airport. A big brush fire just broke out in the Malibu mountains. Structures are threatened," the voice barked.

"I'm on my way," Eli shot back. "Is Wally Smith the pilot?" he asked.

"No, Wally is too far away. I'm not sure who the pilot is, but the copter is waiting for you."

Eli was no more than five minutes away. He saw the helicopter as he wheeled into the airport. He pulled into a space by the security shack, grabbed his camera and raced to the noisy helicopter. Ducking his head as he ran under the spinning blades, Eli jumped into the passenger seat, quickly shut the door and buckled the safety straps over his shoulders and around his waist.

"Let's go along the coast to Malibu," he shouted over the roar of the engine. The young-looking pilot looked at him for a moment, nodded his head and took off.

A black, billowing cloud loomed over the mountains as they left the ground. Neither man spoke as they flew toward the fire. Eli kept checking his camera, putting in new film, cleaning the lens, while trying mentally to push the copter to the fire.

"Go in low, keep the sun behind us and stay out of the smoke," Eli yelled The hesitant pilot responded with a look and a nod, but his squinting eyes betrayed nervousness.

It was a shaky pass, too high to get any good shots. Eli ordered the pilot to go around and do it again. This time was much better, if maybe a little too close. The pilot was a bit unsteady, but the shots were dramatic. Eli was pleased, but he wanted to be sure he had enough footage, so he had his pilot make a half dozen passes before waving him off and telling him to return to the airport.

He noticed perspiration on the pilot's taut face as the copter headed back toward Santa Monica. He looked a little too nervous for comfort.

"What's the matter, haven't you ever flown with a news cameraman before?" Eli shouted over the engine noise.

The pilot turned toward him, a pained expression on his face, and whispered, "Aren't you my new flight instructor?"

*   *   *

The story of Eli's flight is one of the best descriptions of what it is like being in television news. It captures the blows, the encounters, the surprises you might face every day. Learning to live with them is the only way you can survive in television news.

"Expect the unexpected," is one of the best phrases to describe Eli's adventure and the volatility of the news business. When you are out on a story, anything can happen, and it often does. If a reporter is geared to this possibility, he is well on his way to enjoy the events he will encounter in the news world. I believe the unexpected is the main catalyst that helps me thoroughly enjoy my day-to-day work as a reporter.

My friend Eli was probably startled for a moment when he realized his precarious position and how inexperienced his pilot was. However, by the time he slammed his car door and headed back to the studio, he had forgotten his copter adventure and was concentrating on getting the brush fire footage back before the broadcast deadline.

17.

THE EIGHTIES:
PRESSURE AND STRESS

The 80s began with an inflationary recession and bounced into an economic boom. In business, there were mega-mergers, junk bonds and failed savings and loans. Terrorists hijacked ships, downed passenger jets and shot up churches. Drug cartels became headlines as cocaine and heroin flooded the country and inner-city gangs fought over the drug trade.

Iran and Iraq fought a vicious, bloody war. The Middle East continued to be rocked by violence. And the United States agonized over revolutions in El Salvador and Nicaragua and planned a "Star Wars" defense against the communists.

There were assassination attempts on President Ronald Reagan and Pope John Paul II. President Anwar Sadat of Egypt was killed by assassins. Mikhail Gorbachev and Ronald Reagan began their series of historic meetings that brought the Cold War to an end.

I had met Reagan several times while he was governor of California, but the meeting I remember the most was in early 1980, before he officially started campaigning for the Republican nomination. I was at the Los Angeles International Airport covering the arrival of President Carter. It was during the Iranian hostage situation. Students were still holding Americans at the U.S. Embassy in Teheran and the situation was getting worse. President Carter made a brief statement when he left Air Force One and then motorcaded from the airport to some political function.

I whisked the videotape back to our Telemobile and drove it to the spot on the other side of the airport where we could transmit it to our newsroom for broadcast.

It was dark and I was standing in front of the camera waiting for our director to tell me when I would be going live with the video of the president's remarks.

In the darkness I could see a black Cadillac pull up. This location at the airport is where the VIPs are given special escorts to get them on and off the planes. As I stood there in the glare of the television lights, I could see off to the side the figure of a man walking over to our remote truck.

He waved a greeting. "Hi Stan, what's the big news tonight?" It was Barney, Ronald Reagan's bodyguard and driver when he was governor of California. I hadn't seen him for years.

We exchanged greetings and talked a little. "What brings you out here, Barney?"

"I brought the governor here to catch a plane," he answered.

"Reagan, you mean Reagan's here?"

"Over in the car, his plane leaves pretty soon."

"What's the chance of interviewing him on the hostage situation?" I asked.

"Why not? I'll ask him."

I told the station to stand by and said that I might have a live Reagan reaction to Carter's statement.

"Ronald Reagan live?" Was their surprised reply.

"He'll be right over, Stan," Barney called back. "Are you ready now?"

"Can we go right away?" I asked the director over my microphone.

"We're ready when you are," was his answer.

We kept our camera on top of the Telemobile in those days. With it up there, we would always be ready to go on the air when we arrived at a story. Since the camera was so high off the ground, the engineers built a platform on the front bumper to bring reporters and their interviews up to the level of the camera. This was how they eliminated the unflattering angle and were able to shoot the reporters head-on. However, it was quite a high step off the ground to get up to the platform.

"Governor, do you mind stepping up here?" I asked.

It was a higher step than Mr. Reagan expected. His knee hit the base of the platform as he pulled himself up. I could see the pained expression on his face. I could tell it really hurt.

"No, it's fine," he answered as he straightened himself up and prepared for the interview.

Afterwards as he said goodbye and stepped down from the high platform, I could see a slight limp as he walked back to his car.

I worried about what had happened. I was afraid that with that first step, I had almost stopped his campaign before it officially started. I was pleased to see that he made it back to the car with apparent ease. Whenever I notice that slight limp that occasionally shows when President Reagan walks, I think about that night at Los Angeles International Airport.

*　*　*

The sleek white yacht is a converted mine sweeper. The late actor, John Wayne, completely overhauled and refurbished her, making her a showcase.

She was a tourist attraction at Newport Harbor for 25 years. Proud residents would always point out the Wild Goose to their visitors.

"That's John Wayne's yacht."

"Biggest boat in the harbor."

"He's traveled almost everywhere on it."

"I saw John Wayne aboard it several times."

Newport residents took a special pride in the popular actor, their most famous neighbor.

In 1983, Lynn Hutchins, a wealthy lawyer who bought the yacht from Wayne just before his death, had it up for sale for $2 million.

Our news crew clambered aboard the yacht to do a story on the sale. Another news team from an Australian television network was there ahead of us, so I had plenty of time to look around and inspect the luxurious craft.

I enjoyed walking the decks, peeking into cabins and soaking up the atmosphere of this 136-foot beauty. She had come out of dry dock a short time before. Fresh white paint and polished brass were everywhere. John Wayne would have been proud of the way she looked.

Lynn Hutchins introduced himself as I entered the wheel house. I was looking at the pictures of John Wayne and his memorabilia on the bulkhead.

"Wayne wouldn't have approved of all these pictures," he said, "but they add so much to the feeling of the boat, I put them up anyway."

He gave me a brief tour. He showed me the grand salon with its green, felt-covered poker table and upholstered leather chairs. There were plaques and awards behind the beautiful bar.

My cameraman was videotaping the highlights of the yacht at his leisure. Dave Moore enjoys wandering around and shooting the special pictures that catch the feeling of his story. He was enjoying living the legend of John Wayne today.

Hutchins walked me up to the bow, pointing out features as we moved along. "John Wayne carefully screened me before he sold me the Wild Goose. I'm going to be just as careful when I sell it. I'd love to keep it, but my law practice keeps me too busy."

Dave Moore and soundman Ray Lopez joined us on deck.

"We've finished all the shooting. This should make a good story. Are you ready for the interview?" Dave asked.

"Shall we do it here by the wheelhouse?" I asked.

"It's as good place as any. Both of you get a little closer to the rail," Dave motioned us over.

"Beep...Beep...Beep!" My radio pager went off, just as we were getting ready to start.

I fumbled with the small beeper and got it off my belt and placed it next to my ear.

"Go immediately to your truck. We have a breaking story. Go to the truck right away," the crackling voice on the page ordered.

If I did not get the interview, the entire story would be lost. The main thrust of the news story was Hutchins selling the yacht.

"Dave, let's shoot a quick interview."

He had the same idea. He still had the camera on his shoulder and we taped a brief interview with the owner, enough to save the story.

We picked up our scattered gear from the deck and carried our light stands, cables, extension cords and various other items and made a hasty retreat down the gangplank. I yelled back a "thank you" to our host when I reached the dock and started to jog to our camera truck.

I knew we had made the right decision. You have to be lucky in the news business. There are times when you gamble and win. This wasn't much of a gamble, just enough to complete the story. Yet, I had gnawing feeling that we might have missed something because of the brief delay.

Our gear was loaded and we were driving away from the dock when we made contact with our assignment editor. Because most television stations can listen to each other's frequency, he did not want to tell us over the air what the important story was and what we were planning to do to cover it.

"Go to Torrance Airport, call me land line from there," he ordered. The call on a pay phone will keep our competition from listening.

"If you can pick up some sandwiches, get them, you may not have a chance to eat for sometime," the voice on the radio explained.

"Sounds pretty big," Dave said, "I'll put on KFWB and see what might be brewing."

The all-news radio station was in the middle of a brief report about an earthquake that had hit the little town of Coalinga in central California. We knew where we were going.

As we made our way through the rush-hour traffic, from the harbor at San Pedro to the Torrance Airport, we listened to KFWB. Their information was still sketchy. They reported that it was 6.5 on the Richter scale, a major quake. We knew it could mean serious damage and a loss of life. The epicenter was five miles northwest of Coalinga. They were reporting severe damage to several brick buildings in the downtown business district. There were a number of fires and all of the telephone lines were down. They were talking about injuries and damage to the local hospital.

By the time we were 10 minutes away from the airport, everyone in the news business was aware of the magnitude of the damage. There was no longer a need to keep our secrets off the radio.

"A brown and white twin Cessna, No. 467N, will meet you at the office at Torrance. Load up and meet me at Tiger Air at Burbank Airport. I'll have the rest of the gear we'll need for the trip," barked our assignment editor, Scott Barer. "Be sure to finish the John Wayne story on the way. I'll have a messenger pick it up."

None of us knew where Coalinga was. I kept notes as KFWB added to the basic facts of the quake.

I wrote in my notebook, "Coalinga is in Fresno County, about 50 miles from Fresno. It is a small town of about 7,000 surrounded by farming land and oil fields."

When we arrived in Torrance, we parked next to the small airport office. As the men got their camera and sound gear together, I ran to a pay phone inside the single-room office. I made the first of countless calls I would make on this trip.

Pilot Steve McKay landed his Cessna and taxied up to the small building. We checked and rechecked the equipment we were loading. If one important piece was left behind, live pictures out of Coalinga might be impossible.

After a brief flight from Torrance to Burbank, we hitched up with Scott at Tiger Air Terminal. He had additional batteries, chargers and the backup equipment in case of technical problems.

We were airborne by 6:45, about two hours after the quake hit Coalinga. With our hand-held radios, we were able to maintain voice communications with our newsroom for some time. They relayed more information about the quake as it came in.

As I said earlier, you must be lucky in the news business and we were lucky, up to now.

There are so many things that can go wrong, but this was an important story and the station was doing everything right.

We were flying away from our radio transmitter at well over 150 miles an hour. That caused some concern, because the farther you get from the transmitter, the less chance you have of maintaining radio contact.

We were still over Los Angeles when our first problem materialized. Pilot McKay turned to us. He had been monitoring the Coalinga situation over his communications radio. "Bad news; Coalinga Airport has been closed down. No one is allowed in but emergency planes. They specifically say, news planes must stay out."

Scott Barer shouted, "What? They can't do that."

He picked up his hand-held radio and relayed the information to the station. "Get the FAA," he called out to the editor in Los Angeles. "I know they just can't close it down."

The pilot continued to mumble into a small microphone that touched his lips. The words were unintelligible because of the loud sound level in the cabin. Then, he turned and shouted over the noise, "I can hear other planes requesting permission to land at Coalinga. The airport there is saying no.

Our hand-held radio was our main hope at this moment. The studio could call all over the country to get us permission to land. Our distance problem was getting more acute by the second. Soon, there would be no communications with KTLA until we landed and called on a public phone. And the word was that no phones on the ground were working.

In between the urgent requests to get us permission to land at Coalinga, the station gave me the latest update on conditions there. There had been another big earthquake, this one also measuring 6.5 on the Richter scale.

I listened and scribbled in my notebook, "Oil field pipe lines have broken and there are some fires, about 50 injured. Some are serious, but no fatalities at this point. At least a dozen old brick buildings in the center of town have been badly damaged. All telephone service is out. The emergency hospital is damaged, no patients can be taken there."

Scott interrupted, "Studio, see if we can land at Harris Ranch. It's a small strip, but is not too far away from Coalinga."

Our pilot shook his head, "Harris Ranch is also restricted."

"What are they suggesting we do?" Scott asked.

"Land at Hanford, about 50 miles from Coalinga."

"We would never get to the quake scene in time for the broadcast at ten." Scott answered, "But it is our only hope."

"I can hear some of the other stations on the radio and it appears they are heading for Hanford," the pilot said.

Scott had his hand-held radio close to his mouth. "Studio, if you hear me, get us a rental car and have a cab pick us up at Hanford Airport." No answer. Radio communication with the station was gone. We had no idea if they heard our transmission or not.

I keep mentioning that luck is important. It felt now as if our luck was changing. This story was slipping away. The main reason for our flight up here was to do a live report from the scene on our newscast. Now, it appears we might not even get up there in time for the broadcast.

This is the moment you have to practice damage control.

If we can't go live, what could we do instead? Here we are, airborne with all the live transmitting gear we need, but we are not going to be able to make the deadline. If we can't show a live picture from the scene, we have to let our viewers know we are trying everything possible to do so. We aren't the only station facing this problem. All of them are. Since the live coverage seemed to be disintegrating, I decided I would try to do some telephone reports.

If I could find a working phone, the station could then show videotape from our news service that should be in the studio in time for the broadcast. They could use my audio report over the pictures. This is the kind of story you can't let slip away.

A big orange sun was setting as we began our landing at Hanford Airport. All of us knew our chance of getting a signal out of the earthquake zone was next to nothing. It would take us an hour to drive there. We had to shoot the damage and then, somehow, get a picture out. The station had made arrangements with a local television station to use broadcast facilities. We had to get this story on our 10 o'clock news.

A cab pulled up next to our plane as we started to unload our gear.

"You fellows from KTLA, Los Angeles?" The cab driver called out.

I was pleased. That blind radio call to the station had gotten through. Maybe our luck was changing.

Scott raced to see if he could find a working phone at the airport. He did. He called KTLA News to find nothing had changed. Despite all of their phone calls to FAA offices around the country, Coalinga Airport was still restricted. He told them that we had a cab here at the Hanford Airport. There was a debate as to whether we should get a rental car or take the cab all the way to Coalinga.

I had already started a discussion with the cab driver planeside.

"I'll drive you down there and back, and give you an hour to get your pictures for $130," bargained Leonard, the veteran cab driver we had just met.

Scott was still talking on the telephone. I interrupted, "If we took the cab, we'd have a driver with us to be a guide and he'll know downtown Coalinga too." By the time we got back to the cab, three other newsmen were inside waiting to be taken to Coalinga.

"Come on, fellows, this is our cab."

The tall man in the back seat asked the driver, "Who called you?"

Leonard had live customers in the back of his cab and he didn't want to lose them, "I don't know."

"Let's all go together," the one sitting in the front seat said, trying to compromise.

"We can't," I said. "There are four of us and all of our camera gear." I became a little impatient, "Look, we're all wasting time."

We stood there. I was only too aware of the seconds ticking by. Would we get the break or would they? We couldn't afford to lose any more time. Finally, a tall and obviously senior and experienced reporter in the back seat, ducked his head out of the open door and started to get out. "We're not going to steal your cab." He sighed, "You can have it."

Other cabs began to arrive as other planes started to land. We tore off, leaving the other reporters and camera crews to negotiate their own deals to Coalinga.

We were crammed into the old car, which had seen better days. The shocks were just about gone and the rough country roads continuously bounced and shook us as Leonard raced to Coalinga.

The cab's radio squelched with distant sounds. We could pick up pieces of conversation from other cab drivers who gleefully told about the exorbitant fares they were charging the rich newsmen for the trips to Coalinga. About 30 minutes out of Hanford we stopped at a small grocery store. The crew bought day-old sandwiches and cans of soft drinks.

I was surprised to learn the store's telephone was still working. The clerk agreed to let me make a collect call to the studio. I decided to make one of those "damage control" phone calls. I had picked up a lot of new information about the quake. I could do an audio report from this little market in case we struck out completely in Coalinga

Amazingly, the operator put our call through immediately. Lady Luck was on our side.

Or was she? The newsroom picked up our call right away. They liked the idea of the call. But there was a long delay as they tried to get my phone call recorded. I had called in on a number that was not hooked up to the recording equipment. The engineers had to do a lot of rerouting to get it on tape so that it could be played back on the news broadcast.

As I finished, the producer said, "Be sure to call back at 10 o'clock, straight up."

"I'll try, but, as you know, all of the phones are out in Coalinga."

"Try, Stan," Larry Tomlinson said, "Hal Fishman will set up the full quake story and as a part of it, he wants to talk to you live."

I glanced at the clock on the wall. I wondered if we would even be in Coalinga by 10. There were reports of damage to the roads leading into the city.

"Larry, first thing when I get there, I will try to find a working phone. I'll have the crew shoot the damage, but I'll call you right away. Tell the soundman in the studio to be ready for my call."

"Good luck." Larry paused for a moment, "Hey, good news, Stan, I've just been told we will have about three minutes of quake footage coming in on a feed from KTVU, Oakland. We can use your audio over those pictures."

"Great, I'll call you at 10." I hung up and ran back to the cab. Everyone was inside waiting; Coalinga was still a far away.

Back on the highway, Leonard accelerated and bounced us toward the quake damage. I quizzed him about the city and got another shock.

"I've been driving here in Hanford for 17 years, and I have only been to Coalinga twice."

"There went that advantage," I said to myself.

Time was slipping away, but Leonard kept looking in his rear view mirror. "Never can be too careful about the Highway Patrol. They'll nab you every time."

"We're okay tonight," Scott said, worried about Leonard's cautious speed, "All the CHP are in Coalinga working on the quake."

"Well, you never can tell," Leonard answered, as he carefully drove along the dark country road. We got through the first road block without any trouble. The flashing red lights at the corner and the large number of police vehicles there worried us for awhile. There was always the possibility that the road would be impassable.

As we arrived, the city was very dark. Most of the power was off, but the streets were busy. Cars and trucks were moving everywhere. Police had set up road blocks and people were being turned around before they even got into the city. Police and deputy sheriffs were at every corner waving flashlights, worried about looters. Security was tight. An officer directed us to the command post near the center of town, where most of the devastation was. From there, sheriffs would escort teams of newsmen to the scene. No one was allowed to go into the downtown area alone.

A quick check with other reporters revealed that we were, in effect, restricted to the command post. If we wanted to go downtown, we would have to wait for the sheriff. Every so often, he would take a group of cameramen down to the damage area. The escort was strict and newsmen were allowed only into certain sections. Fires smoked a few blocks away. One burned all night long, but cameramen were never allowed close enough to get pictures.

We split up at this point. We had our hand-held radios and could communicate with each other over short distances. The camera crew of Dave Moore and Ray Lopez went with producer Scott Barer to the command post waiting for their turn to be taken downtown. I started a search for a working telephone for my opening report on the broadcast.

I kept asking people if any phones were working.

"No, they're all out. No light, power, gas or phones."

Another lady, still visibly shaken by what had happened called out, "Someone told me that the pay phone on the corner two blocks away is still working."

I was at that phone in a couple of minutes, but it was dead, the receiver hanging by its cord.

A loud voice behind a flashlight stopped me as I walked away, "What are you doing here?"

I had already answered that question a half dozen times in my search. The officers were always polite but firm. No one was supposed to be on the street here. However, after I told each one of them what I was trying to do, he usually had a suggestion. One officer even gave me two locations, both were dead.

The last one was surrounded by rubble. It was next to a damaged motel. The manager sympathized with my plight and said she heard some of the phones at the shopping center a few blocks away were working.

I passed one other phone as I jogged to the shopping center. Its receiver was dangling on its cable.

"Another dead one," I thought.

I picked it up. There was a tone. I dropped a dime, dialed the number, but the phone was silent. Nothing.

Scott called me on the radio, "They say we are going to be taken into the damaged area in a few minutes," he said. "Any luck on the phone."

"No, still trying."

I ran the rest of the way to the shopping center and I was puffing pretty hard as two friendly officers waved me through the lines. In the darkness, I could see tilting houses jarred off their foundations, toppled chimneys that were now just a pile of scattered bricks on the ground. Debris from the broken homes littered the sidewalks and streets.

As I turned a corner, I saw the shopping center with its lights on and a bank of phones with people lined up in front of them. There must have been six individuals at each phone waiting patiently for their turn. I knew I would never complete my call to Los Angeles if I had to wait for all of them.

I knocked on the doors of some of the businesses. Most were closed, but owners let me in. They wanted to be helpful, but their phones were out.

I finally went over to the phone banks and explained to the people standing in line my problem. I was able to work my way up to third in line by repeating my deadline plight over and over. Most were sympathetic, but others would not give up their spot.

The girl in front of me said, "No, my mother is sick in a hospital in Fresno and she must be frantic worrying about me. I've got to call her and let her know I'm all right."

I looked at my watch. My hopes of getting through were dwindling.

An NBC reporter was on one line talking to her desk in Los Angeles. A wire service reporter was thumbing through his notebook as he talked on the center phone. A man was dialing over and over again trying to get a working line on the third phone. Another reporter from Bakersfield was impatiently fifth in another line.

The NBC newsman talked for another 10 minutes. The girl in front of me got on the phone and dialed over and over in vain. She could not get a line. She put in her dime, dialed and waited. Nothing. Then she would do it over again.

Several people moved up in the second line. The girl on the phone there got through. It was a break for me. That girl was the sister of the girl in front of me. She gave me the receiver and talked to her mother on her sister's phone.

My dialing was unsuccessful. It was very frustrating. The dime would go in, nothing would happen, then I would try again.

I laughed to myself. I wanted to hang up and join the crew about to go into the quake damage area. Viewers expect their television newsmen to be right in the middle of the story, not blocks away in a phone line.

Scott called me on the radio, "Stan, we're inside. The damage is unbelievable. Any luck on your call?"

"At least I'm dialing, Scott, but nothing is happening."

I kept dialing. "Is it worse that you had expected?" I asked.

"Every building I see is badly damaged. Skip loaders are working the debris. They are still looking for people trapped. No fatalities yet, though."

I continued to dial as he talked, but it was the same story. A dial tone . . the buttons beeped their tone...a wait...a busy signal and nothing.

I had already missed my live report at the top of the news. They would have to use my earlier call from the fast-food store. As the minutes slipped by, I knew my chance was slim to get in before the end of the broadcast.

Then, 10 minutes before the newscast would be over, all of the digits beeped right and a voice came on the line. I had reached the studio.

During the next commercial, they put some of the videotape of the damage on standby. Hal Fishman came on the phone and we planned our strategy.

"I'll ask you some general questions, Stan. We'll roll the tape we just received from KTVU. It's great stuff."

The broadcast went well. There wasn't even a hint of all the problems that plagued us during that black night in Coalinga.

It was ridiculous I had to be blocks away from the damaged center of town on a pay phone, relaying information from Scott Barer. It was absurd I was in a shopping center parking lot instead of at the quake scene. If it hadn't been for our hand-held radios, there would have been no way to get the latest information. Ours was one of the first live reports to Los Angeles, but this shows you some of the frustrations of being a live reporter at a breaking story.

No matter how important the event, unless you can communicate with your studio, you are not going to get on the air. You have to be there with a working transmitter and crew, or at least be in a parking lot with a telephone that works. And it always helps to have a reporter like Hal Fishman in the studio, on the other side of the telephone call.

*   *   *

Hal Fishman's hands locked desperately on the plane's controls as he battled the shuddering jet being buffeted by the storm-driven winds. The experimental aircraft was thrashed about in the sky. It bounced and groaned as Hal struggled to keep it on course in the fury of the summer turbulence. There was no visibility. Raging storm clouds smothered the cockpit in a capsule of darkness. Only threatening, sporadic flashes of lightning illuminated the faces of the two pilots.

Hal and Richard Hunt were flying a single-engine jet called the Super Pinto. They were trying to set a new speed record following the path of the 1927 Lindbergh flight from the Santa Monica Airport to the airshow in Paris, France. To do this they put so much fuel in the tanks, the plane was a flying bomb. A problem in the project's planning forced Hal and Richard to take many shortcuts to make the deadline. It was quite an unusual set of circumstances for Hal, who was always a careful and meticulous pilot.

The tiny cockpit was crammed with needed gear. Everything else was fuel storage. This violent weather was an ominous sign. It was more than the small jet could take.

They were at 33,000 feet, somewhere above the little town of Las Vegas, New Mexico when it happened. There was a silent alarm, the jet engine stopped and the plane went into a glide.

"Mayday, Mayday," Hal yelled into his radio transmitter. "Does anyone out there hear us? Mayday, Mayday."

A traffic controller responded, "We read you. Identify yourself. Tell us where you are."

"We've lost the engine. We're the Super Pinto," Hal shot back.

"I see you on the radar. You are near Las Vegas, New Mexico. You should have no trouble reaching the airport runway on your other engine."

"We only have one engine. We are in a glide now," Hal snapped back.

The tower was silent for a moment.

Richard grasped his parachute and shouted to Hal, "I think we'd better go. There is too much fuel in the tanks to fool around any longer."

The vast empty desert and mountains were below. Hal nodded and checked his parachute. Both men signaled that they were ready.

Hal reached for the emergency lever on the canopy, ready to fall out into the violent skies. He pulled it hard. The lever didn't budge. He yanked it, jerked it, put both hands on it and pulled. The canopy would not open. He shook it violently. It was stuck.

"Super Pinto, Las Vegas is under you." The voice of the tower continued.

Hal dipped the small jet into the darkness below. To be a good pilot, you have to be lucky. As he lost altitude, there was a slight opening in the clouds. His heart pumped hard as his eyes actually saw the Las Vegas airfield through the life saving break in the storm clouds.

His plane was a wounded single engine jet. How could he glide it to the field and land the flying bomb with all the fuel stored inside?

Somehow he brought it around, got on a glide course and came speeding in for the landing. The plane was not built for this, but he was going to try to make it happen. He hit the ground hard in the middle of the airstrip, jammed the brakes and continued to plunge ahead. The plane was almost out of control. It slowed slightly, then spun around, skidded and screeched and finally stopped in a rocking fashion. They had made it. The Super Pinto sagged on the landing strip, but Hal and Richard were able to walk away.

Instead of a hero's flight to Paris, Hal had to settle for a Greyhound bus ride back to Los Angeles.

That's about as close a call Hal Fishman has ever had while at the controls of his aircraft. He has set 10 official speed and altitude records, has flown around the world twice and has covered countless news stories flying his own plane. After his family and his flying, his next love is broadcasting.

Hal Fishman has been anchor of "News At Ten" since the mid-1960s. In a business where news ratings can dip and disappear over night and new anchors move in and out with the regularity of a television commercial, it seems as if Hal has always been there.

News is a perishable commodity. It is written on the wind and is consumed by the broadcast each day. The only constant, the main continuity for the viewer, is the man at the anchor desk. He is the familiar figure who is there each night, the one who ties everything together to make sense out of the news scene.

Hal is an exceptional broadcaster, the steady force who has made "News At Ten" the successful local news program that it is.

He is more than a newsman; he is an information center. Hal is an ad-lib system who can speak on any subject. He believes in knowing as much about everything as he can. He is a trained observer of his times. He brings his academic expertise to the television screen and delivers the news with the same authority he displayed in the lecture halls.

He is an individualist who refuses to follow the pack. He is a known factor in the news business that always seems to be changing. Hal is seen nightly by millions of viewers via satellite all around the country.

Hal once taught political science at California State University at Los Angeles. He is an academician with a pragmatic flair. He is a teacher who believes that television is the most effective classroom available. His academic background and authoritative presentation are a rare and effective combination. When you add more than three decades of television news broadcasting to his credentials, you see why he is an effective, credible newsman.

He has reported all of the major news stories in Southern California first hand. He anchored much of KTLA's marathon coverage of the Watts riots in the summer of 1965. His ability to ad-lib, to master large quantities of changing information and to communicate accurately to the audience, has been widely acclaimed. During the riots, his reasoned reports did much to forestall wild rumors running rampant through the city. KTLA had its copter overhead showing what was happening and Hal was interpreting the events, separating fact from fiction. It was a great service to the people of Los Angeles who lived through those trying times.

He spent the night at Good Samaritan Hospital in 1968 while doctors were trying to save the life of Robert Kennedy after he was shot by Sirhan Sirhan. He broadcast the details of the tragic story as they became known throughout the night and morning hours.

He has been at the anchor desk during the long hours when KTLA covered fires and floods and other disasters that hit Southern California on a regular basis.

He has a photographic memory that serves him well. He is always able to quickly grasp the essentials of a developing news story. Viewers are able to keep up with the important, changing details because of the clarity of his presentation.

When the news of the assassination attempt on the life of Pope John Paul II hit the wires and details were sketchy, Hal was live on the air with the first information.

Producer Gerry Ruben called out to Hal, "Just ad-lib about the Pope for about five minutes while we get more details."

Hal did just that, without any change of pace in his delivery.

Hal was in the middle of his newscast one night when an earthquake jolted the city. Without a break in his delivery, he switched from broadcasting a newscast to doing an extended earthquake report. He kept on talking about the quake and interspersed it with the latest information coming into the newsroom. Viewers stayed with him for the full report. He ended up with maps from the walls in his news office showing faults that run through Los Angeles. The report continued until it was determined that there were no major injuries nor damage to buildings. We finished with a live report from the seismology lab at California Institute of Technology, where the severity of the quake on the Richter scale was determined and the epicenter was located.

When major stories break, Hal often airs special reports on his newscast. He might take six or seven minutes to give viewers some of the important details they would not get elsewhere. That extra information, in addition to the videotape from the scene and constant reports on late developments, make his newscasts more than a headline service.

He has the instinct to say the right thing at the right moment and is never at a loss for words. During the disastrous brush fires that burned hundreds of homes in Laguna Beach in October 1993, Hal was on the air continuously for 10 hours. He anchored the tense broadcast that showed the devastation all over Southern California. He had a detailed grasp of the hundreds of facts and figures that were constantly changing throughout the day and night.

Also in October 1993, when the world waited for the jury's verdicts in the riot-connected beating of truck driver Reginald Denny, Hal discussed legal ramifications and minute details of the law with lawyers and law school deans for hours as the jury prepared to announce its verdicts. His reasoned and reassuring comments helped to prepare the viewers for the controversial verdicts.

His commentaries have won many awards. He writes them when he feels they are necessary, not because they are formatted into the program. He has been able to shed light on a lot of confusing situations.

He is at home on the lecture circuit, among the complicated details of important news stories or in the cockpit of his plane. He is well known in aviation circles and presents many stories that keep viewers abreast on recent developments in aviation.

Through the years, Hal has been there every night with the news. Viewers enjoy watching him and depend on his accurate, dependable reports. He has been a constant in a changing field of newscasting.He is one of the major reasons that "New at Ten" is the highest rated prime time newscast in the history of Los Angeles television. It has been that way for the past quarter of a century.

In January 1994, he recieved the "Broadcaster of the Year" award from the Society of Professional Journalists.

18.

TO WIN OR LOSE:
AN EMMY

The moments before the envelope is opened and the winner announced are filled with anguish and exhilaration. They are the watershed of the great emotional divide. On one side is the abyss, on the other, the sweet mountaintop.

Somehow the sight of the graven images which personify the award is intoxicating. There are dozens of statuettes lined up in a neat row waiting to be claimed by the winners. The open globe held by the nymph-like figure is multiplied across the stage like the reflection in a series of mirrors. They are for the winners. A mask covering deep hurt is the only award for the losers. There is a thin line dividing victory and defeat, but once the moment passes and the hollow words ring out over the ballroom microphone, the results are cast in cement. To the losers, it is as if they never had a chance. There was no real reason to have hoped that they might have won. To the winners, there is recognition from their peers that they are one of the best. The glow will subside and the hurt will heal, but both will have left their mark.

One of my most memorable experiences at an awards ceremony had nothing to do with my receivng an award, but the mark it left has endured. Emmy awards are an industry celebration where the best are honored. The dinner presented by the L.A. Television Academy is held in a luxurious environment at a prestigious hotel. Tuxedos are rented and new gowns purchased for the big event. It is a night to see friends and be a part of something very special to the television industry.

I was one of the presenters for the evening. It was a simple assignment. All I had to do was to read the list of nominees, introduce them, open the envelope and announce the winner.

I arrived early and went to the presenters' table where a stunning woman in a white formal gown greeted me and gave me several pages of script.

"These will show you what will be happening on stage before you go on. You can follow them and when your cue is read by the emcee, go out on stage and make your presentations," she explained.

I looked at the several pages as she discussed them. I saw the paragraph where I was introduced and scanned the list of nominees I was to read.

"Now, if you follow me, I'll show you where you will be just before you go on stage," she said as we walked from the back of the crowded ballroom through a small passageway. We passed stacked chairs and table tops leaning against the wall, as we made our way backstage.

"The script here is just to show you what will happen. Your actual script will be on the back of the envelope containing the name of the winner. You'll get that just before you go on stage," she explained.

Even though the program would not begin for another hour, I sensed a controlled chaos backstage. There is always something electrifying about being behind curtains when an audience sits the other side.

I met several Academy members who were there to make things move along smoothly. It was well organized and I thanked them for the briefing that would make my job so much easier.

Dinner was delicious. I looked at my pages of script several times while I enjoyed the chicken Kiev and fresh string beans. I was impressed with the organization that made me feel so confident.

The program started about 20 minutes late, but it moved along smoothly and the winners made short speeches. The pacing was impressive. I followed the program carefully. When it was time, I excused myself from the table so that I would arrive back stage several minutes before my scheduled presentation.

I walked through the same passageway with the stacked chairs and leaning table tops. It was much more crowded this time. I clutched the sheets of script in my hand, knowing I would leave them on a table once I got my official list of nominees taped to the back of the winners envelope.

I was received warmly by different officials just off stage. Nominees were being lined up in order, so they would go out as their names were called. Other presenters were just leaving and I could see the emcee on stage introducing other participants. My nervousness grew.

"I'll stick the list of your nominees on the back of this, just as soon as we confirm who is here," a young woman holding a stack of white envelopes, told me.

She showed me the small piece of scotch tape that she would use. I put my folded pages of script on the desk and watched the emcee on stage through the narrow opening of the curtain.

I was startled to hear him introduce me. I wasn't scheduled for several minutes. I looked at the young woman who was still holding the scotch tape, but who had not yet received the list of nominees present. She looked at me and handed me the envelope.

"Just use your old script," said another fellow standing there, trying to solve the emergency that had just developed. To my embarrassment, I heard the emcee introduce me again. I grabbed the folded pages on the table and briskly walked on stage, late for my second introduction.

I walked to the podium, thanked the emcee and started talking to the audience. I looked down at the pages I had brought with me to find the names of the nominees. I shuffled them a bit, still searching. There was a pause, but it wasn't serious. I shuffled the pages again. I desperately looked for the names. I couldn't find them. I can remember seeing words and sentences, lines and marks, but nothing made any sense. As hard as I tried, I could not see the list of six names. Beads of perspiration broke out on my forehead, when I realized that I must have left that page with the names on the table back stage.

I often have had a dream like this. I am usually ready to go on the air, sitting at the anchor desk, but the teleprompter is not working. I decide to use my script and not worry about the teleprompter, but when I look at the pages in front of me, they are the wrong ones. I shuffle and squirm and frantically try to find the copy for the newscast in piles of script pages in front of me. It goes on for a long time, but I am never able to find the right copy.

I was living that dream, on stage, before a thousand people at the Beverly Wilshire Hotel. I kept thinking that this could not be really happening to me. I have always tried to be the dependable one, who always has everything under control, who is never flustered by anything, who keeps a cool demeanor no matter what is stirring inside. My image was cracking and reeling.

After what seemed an eternity, one of the Academy executives walked on stage and handed me the official list that was supposed to have been taped to the envelope. The crisis ended. I read the names of the nominees, shook their hands when they came on stage, then opened the envelope and announced the winner. I felt shell-shocked throughout.

My ordeal was only half over. While Elliot Fons of KCBS took over the microphone and thanked the Academy for his Emmy in the "Camera Crew Hard News" category, I drifted off to the side of the stage and asked for the envelope that I was to read for the next presentation. They handed it to me, but the list of nominees was not taped to the back of that envelope.

I desperately looked again through the wrinkled pages I had crushed in my fist during the recent ordeal. I couldn't find these nominees either. The stage manager helped me scan my script, but he struck out as well. Elliot was walking off stage now to the applause of the audience. I knew I had to go back to the microphone and announce the next nominees, but I didn't know who they were.

The stage manager said, "Take my script, but be sure to give it back to me right afterwards."

I walked back to the microphone. I did not know at the time that there had been a slight mix-up in the sequence of presentations. My nominees were not ready to come out on stage, so when I announced their names, nothing happened. No one came out. I didn't want to make anything out of it. Things were bad enough. I went on to the next names, they didn't come out. Then as I finished, several nominees rushed on stage, breathlessly and frantically, just in time for me to announce the winner.

I was dazed as I walked backstage and through the maze of people waiting to go on. Everything got back in order and the rest of the evening went smoothly. My daze continued as I walked past the folded chairs and leaning table tops, to the ballroom and back to my chair in the darkened room.

Beverly took my hand and said, "You were very good, dear."

No one else talked to me. I just stared ahead and watched the ceremony, not hearing a word.

I had picked a monumental moment to make a catastrophic mistake. There is nothing like having a thousand of your peers in an elegant ballroom before you, while you live the recurrent dream that has haunted you for years. The terrifying experience that unfolded in countless dreams, was a reality tonight. The pages before you contained your script, but you could not find it. You shuffle and squint, but the words are not there. Unfortunately, there was no dream to wake up from, this was the real moment. I kept looking at the stage, but not hearing a word.

I was silent for the better part of the evening. I was one of those nominees for "Best Live Reporting." At the appropriate time, I went to the rear of the ballroom and met the others who were also nominated for the Emmy in this division. There were three programs in this category. My former colleague at KTLA, Tom Capra, then news director at KNBC, was there to accept the Emmy if his station won for its coverage of the Baldwin Hills brush fire. Another good friend, Bob Dunn of KCBS, was the third nominee for his coverage of an oil refinery fire.

A pretty young woman in a red dress held up a sign to show us where to assemble. Several from KTLA news would share this Emmy: Jeff Wald, the news director, Gerry Ruben, the producer and Jon Fischer, the cameraman for our coverage of the Baldwin Hills fire. If the station won, we would all get one of those elusive symbols of victory. We lined up next to the young woman and then followed her out of the room, down that narrow passageway with the chairs and tables to the small backstage area where I had been before. I was still stunned, but the thought that I had a chance of winning the "Best Live Reporting" category buoyed me a little. My thoughts went back to last year at this time and the surprised delight when my name was announced as the Emmy winner for live reporting. The dark cloud of the earlier episode was still hovering over me and I couldn't shake it, even as I was introduced as a nominee and walked on stage for my certificate.

I joined the other nominees as we all went off stage and waited for the presenter to open the envelope and declare the winner. I walked a short distance down the narrow hall, the others from KTLA stood in the wings. I was too far away to hear the voice of the presenter, but I could tell from the expression on the faces of my KTLA colleagues that someone else had won the Emmy. Tom Capra and KNBC were the winners.

I tripped over one of those stored chairs as I walked through the narrow passageway back to the ballroom. I don't think I would have minded losing if it hadn't been for the embarrassing experience earlier. I somehow thought that an Emmy victory would take the sting out of the script debacle.

We had to wait for a long time before valet parking brought our car up the driveway. Lots of people tried to leave as quickly as possible.

Ours was a 20-minute wait. When our car did arrive, I tipped the attendant and took my place behind the wheel. There was a general background noise of car doors slamming, engines running and people saying good night.

I closed my door as the attendant opened the door for Beverly on the other side. I put my hand on the gear shift to drive out of the crowded driveway, but it would not move. The gear was stuck. I pulled hard on the gear shift sticking out of the steering wheel casing. It would not move. I gently tugged at it. Nothing happened. I looked at the long line of cars waiting behind me. I was blocking their exit. I pulled the shift hard and almost broke it, but it remained locked. I heard engines rumble around me and felt practically defeated. How could something like this happen? My car was stalled in the main driveway of the Beverly Wilshire Hotel and dozens of people were behind me trying to get out.

Beverly always remained calm in emergency situations like this. "Is the engine on, dear?" She asked.

It wasn't. The sound I thought was my engine rumbling came from the other cars. The attendant had turned mine off. I was embarrassed once again, but relieved. I turned the key, the engine started and I easily shifted into drive and we pulled away.

It was an evening to forget, but doing so seemed impossible. Later that night while I was taking off my Tuxedo jacket, I felt the wrinkled pages of the script in my pocket. I took them out and put them on the dresser. As I was removing my bow tie, I looked down at one of the pages. I could not believe what I saw. There was my cue and there were my words. Everything I was supposed to say was there on the page. Somehow, with the pressure and with the shuffling of the pages, I missed the entire script although it was in front of me all of the time.

I went to bed and tossed and turned through a sleepless night. During those half-awake hours I replayed over and over again, the agony of the moments on stage with nothing to say to 1000 people at the awards ceremony.

It seemed I had lost more than an Emmy.

The irony of that Emmy night experience is that the year before, on the same stage, I was there with my head in the clouds. It is another example of the roller coaster ride that runs through any career in television news.

At that dinner, I received the Governor's Award, another Emmy and a nomination. All but one of my children were there to see their father center stage. My news director, Jeff Wald, sent a limousine to take Beverly and me to the affair.

Earlier in the day I attended ceremonies for my son, Ed, who graduated from Loyola High School and later I went to my daughter Margaret's graduation from nursing school at Mount Saint Mary's College. The whole day was clogged with about as much soul-stirring rapture as I could handle. There was such an emotional high that I was sick for four days after it was over.

I was especially pleased to get the Emmy for best live coverage of a breaking news story. It was a report on a tragic schoolyard shooting where a gunman opened fire into crowds of children, then boarded himself up in his house across the street from the grammar school. Many were hit, one was killed and the entire school was terrorized by the berserk gunman.

Many heroes disregarded the gunfire and rushed to the fallen figures of the little children and carried them to safety. Police officers arrived on the scene moments later and the man ran inside his house. Countless rescue ambulances were called in. The wounded were treated on the school grounds and then taken to local hospitals. The entire city was shocked by the tragedy. The area around the suspect's house was cordoned off and a long stand-off began.

Sam Chu Lin was our reporter at the school. He was with cameraman Bill Knight and soundman Bob Zimmerman. They covered the rescue efforts and talked to eyewitnesses of the shooting.

I was with Tom Branagan and Ray Lopez that day. Although the action was over when we came on duty, we were sent to the school to help the crew that had been working the story. The interviews had been completed, most of the action had been shot, there was little for us to do.

Because such a large area was involved, we kept two crews there. Sam Chu Lin was down the street from the suspect's house. We were across the school grounds near the administration building, in case anything should happen. We were there several hours doing very little.

Since ours was a live unit, the station decided to break into programming and do a report from the scene. When the coroner brought out the body of the little girl they would put us on the air. It would be a very short cut-in, but there would be time enough for me to bring the viewers up-to-date on what was happening at the school.

Tom Branagan had the camera resting next to his leg. He planned to put it on his shoulder when we went on the air for the brief cut-in. We were waiting much longer than we had expected and Tom excused himself to go to the men's room in the school building. The campus police would not let him go in.

We saw one of our friends who was a member of the board of education and asked him to get us permission so Tom would be able to go in. He came back in a few minutes, a little embarrassed, "Sorry Tom, they say the whole school is a crime scene and they can't let anyone in." That summed up the power of the press at this location. We were kept out and there were no exceptions.

In a few minutes, there was action inside the hallway and we knew that the little girl's body was about to be taken out. I told the station to get ready for the cut-in. They came to us live just as the coroner rolled the gurney out the door. I started talking giving a description of what was happening. Tom followed the coroner pushing the gurney to his wagon. A half dozen other cameramen were in the street getting pictures, but we were the only station live at the time.

The action was over in about two minutes. I kept on talking and was waiting for a "wrap-it-up" order from the director over my earphone. I heard nothing, so I just kept on reporting.

When I still failed to get the cue to end my report, I asked Tom to follow me with the camera as I walked to a point where we could see the gunman's house. It was on the street that bordered the far side of the school's play yard. The picture gave a full perspective to the viewers. They could visualize where the children were and where the man was when he started firing.

While I was on the air, I saw members of the L.A. SWAT team moving into position around the house getting ready to forcibly enter the gunman's home and they were right before our live camera.

Before I realized it, we were in the middle of SWAT's operation to get the suspect out. There was action from that moment on. I described the careful, methodical moves of the officers in their battle dress. Tension began to build. The station executives realized they were on-the-air with a major story. A quick decision was made to stay here and follow the action.

Unscheduled telecasts require the approval of a lot of people. Programming has to agree to pre-empt what is on the air. Sales has to give approval to juggle the commercials that are scheduled. The station manager has to make the final decision. Jeff Wald, our news director, had to ease the whole request through the different departments and keep a close tab on the developments at the scene. The decision had to be made right now, while we were on the air. Teamwork paid off and we stayed there until the end.

Tom Branagan had not planned to be on the air for more than a few minutes, so he had not brought a tripod to his location and had to keep the camera on his shoulder the whole time. He stood motionless to keep the camera steady and zoomed in to a close-up of the action. That is one of the most difficult things a cameraman has to do. When you are shooting a close-up from a long distance, it is almost impossible to keep a steady picture. You can imagine the discipline it requires to stand still and shoot a close-up picture of the target house a block away. All this, while you have to go to the bathroom. The lens can do it, but the human body can't.

Action continued before our camera. Tear gas projectiles were fired into the house. The SWAT team, with their guns at the ready, prepared to rush the house and confront the suspect.

The day wore on and we started losing light. Our video camera was an older model and did not have the night-vision capability that newer cameras do. The picture quality got worse and worse as it got darker. We actually lost our picture for a few seconds as our battery ran down and went out of service. Although the action was still going on around the house, darkness threatened to end our telecast.

KTLA works closely with CNN, the Cable News Network. They started continuous coverage over their network soon after we did. Their picture was being received in our control room. Jeff Wald could see that their video transmission was now considerably better than KTLA's. He got on the phone to their offices and requested permission to use their video on our air while continuing to keep my narration. It worked. The quality of their newer model camera gave us a brighter picture.

We were there until the end. The SWAT team entered and discovered the body of the suspect. He had turned a gun on himself shortly after his shooting spree. The tragic day had ended. KTLA had covered the entire story live and our viewers were there to see the conclusion of the tragic events that engulfed the frightened children playing on the school grounds.

I was able to thank everyone who made the teamwork successful that night at the Emmy dinner. Although we lost out on our other Emmy nomination, it too was an example of the hurdles we face and the way we try to handle them.

*   *   *

On the night before the 1984 Olympic Games opened in Los Angeles there was great expectation and excitement. The Games would be a once in a lifetime event and everyone wanted to enjoy those rare moments. Although tickets were sold out to the opening ceremonies, everyone would be able to be a part of them on television.

We heard the initial call on our scanners. So many rescue ambulances were being sent to Westwood, I thought that it was a probably a drill. I had never heard anything like that emergency broadcast.

We left the station immediately, having no idea what had happened. On the way, Susan Kohn, our assignment editor, relayed information as she received it.

"There are dozens injured. A car crashed into a group of pedestrians on a sidewalk in the center of Westwood."

Westwood is a wonderful place to stroll. On summer nights, thousands of people enjoy walking there on their way to a movie, or dinner, or just to enjoy the atmosphere. The community was especially festive this summer. It had been draped with flags and banners for the games. One of the Olympic Villages was located on the campus of UCLA in Westwood. Many of the athletes would be out there enjoying the warm evening.

Susan Kohn's voice came over the radio from the station. "We have videotape from the scene. Bob Tur will meet you there with it."

Westwood is in a little valley next to the hills of the campus and high rise buildings to the south. Because of that, it is difficult to get a television signal out of here. You can get out from some parts of it, but with a breaking story like this, you wouldn't have time to look around for a spot where you could be certain.

John Fischer knew he could transmit from a location about three blocks south of Wilshire Boulevard. The accident happened about three blocks north of Wilshire. We decided, because of the tremendous traffic jam, that he would let me off near Westwood Boulevard and would go to the location and set up a signal. I would run the half dozen blocks or so, try to find Bob Tur with the videotape, and then run to the truck.

By that time, he should have a signal out and be ready to go on the air. Time was slipping by, and it was only a half hour before the news broadcast. I ran at a fast pace through the crowded streets and slowed down after a block or so to a steady jog. My breathing got heavy and I was getting very tired.

When I arrived at the chaotic scene, ambulances were everywhere. Triage teams were taking care of the injured and victims were being moved out as fast as possible to the nearby UCLA Medical Center.

Although hundreds of people milled around, I spotted Bob in the crowd. He gave me the videotape of the rescue effort. Although I thought I was completely exhausted, I got a second wind on my run back to Wilshire. It lasted for a couple of blocks, then I slowed to a fast walk as my heart pounded in my chest and I gulped deep breaths.

I had learned that a car crashed into a big crowd on the sidewalk. It had hit about 50 people. There were no reports of fatalities, but there were many serious injuries.

My thoughts returned to the Olympic Games. Because they were opening the next day, I wondered if this tragedy could be terrorism. I was determined not to say a word about that possibility since I did not know for sure what had happened.

When I got back to our truck I was out of breath, hardly able to talk. It was a few minutes before 10 and the news was about to begin. John Fischer was still trying to get a signal out. He was hopeful, but there were a few things yet to be done.

I was still having trouble catching my breath. My half-mile run had left me completely spent. I was only partially successful. I had brought the tape to the truck in time for the telecast, but I had no idea how I would be able to go on the air and talk.

The problems were settled and we were ready to go at the start of the broadcast. The decision at the station was to run the video tape we sent them, unedited. There was no time to work on it. I put a monitor with KTLA's picture on the hood of the truck, took my cue and started to tell what had happened.

It was a powerfully visual report. The unedited tape looked as if it were live. We did beat all of our competition on the air.

Fifty people were injured, but no one was killed. International terrorism had nothing to do with the tragedy. One person deliberately drove a car down one of the main sidewalks hitting pedestrians as he went. Police figured the driver was mentally deranged, not a terrorist.

Despite everyone's fear that terrorists would try to disrupt the Olympic Games, there were no incidents. The games went off smoothly and they were two of the most glorious weeks Southern Californians ever experienced. The Westwood incident was a terrible tragedy, but not the international disruption it could have been.

There is a postscript to this night. Several years later, I was covering a story at Los Angeles City Hall. My cameraman and I were taking the elevator up to the mayor's office on the third floor. When the door opened a man in a dark blue suit looked at me and did a double-take. I knew he recognized me. I nodded, picked up my tripod and walked out of the elevator. He took a few steps ahead, then stopped and walked back to me.

People often stop to talk to me when I am out on stories, but this man seemed different.

"Stan, you won't remember me, but several years ago in Westwood, about 50 people were injured when some guy rode his car down the sidewalk and knocked a lot of us down. I was one of them."

"I certainly do remember," I answered.

"I wasn't hurt, but they took me to the emergency room with everyone else. I remember you came over there to do interviews. You asked me, but I said no. I was standing by a pay phone going through my pockets to find some change to call my friends to let them know that I was all right. I couldn't find a single coin. You reached in your pocket and gave me all of your change. I'll never forget that."

Then, to my great surprise, he reached in his pocket and gave me all of the change he had.

I was stunned. I stood there with the coins in my hand.

He just nodded, "Thanks, I told myself that I would do this, if I ever saw you again." He walked away.

19.

THE SOVIET UNION'S CURTAIN CRACKS

It was the summer of 1986, in Moscow. A Soviet security officer jumped out of a yellow van that had abruptly stopped on the narrow road bordering the tarmac. He was the deputy chief security officer for Moscow International Airport. A half dozen other men rushed out of the van's open door and followed him. They ran across the asphalt into the muddy ruts of wild grass that grew between the road and the airport runways.

They left footprints of Reeboks, Adidas and Nikes in the mud as they hurried across the rain-soaked field. Each step seemed to sink deeper. Despite the mud and water, no one even broke stride in his effort to get to the pavement on the other side.

The only Pan Am plane scheduled to leave Moscow that day had already taxied the length of the runway, turned, and was ready for take off. One of the men carried a Betacam, another an extended tripod ready to steady the camera the moment it was locked on. A third carried a black bag filled with videocassettes and batteries. The others were just running to stay with the pack.

The wide-body jet was already moving down the runway when the camera was finally secured on the tripod and the cameraman started shooting the plane's departure. He squinted into the eye piece and focused on the 747 as it gathered momentum, roared down the runway and finally lunged into the sky.

If we did not get videotape of this graceful airliner taking off on its flight to Frankfurt, we would have to scrub our story on the resumption of Pan Am flights between the Soviet Union and the United States after a lapse of several years.

Everyone standing by the cameraman was smiling as we watched the plane fly off into the cloudy sky. We had made it in time and saved the story.

*   *   *

The security man in the Soviet uniform, who only a short time ago kept on repeating the Russian word for "problem," had overcome all the problems. He got us to the runway just in time to get the vital shot. Without his help, the story that had taken two weeks to arrange, would have disappeared before our eyes. Our new Russian friend was the vital link in helping us get the essential shots.

This summer marked the beginning of the end for the Soviet Union. Winds of change were blowing breezes of *glasnost* and *perestroika* across the land. Nothing had really changed, but historic forces were beginning to jar the status quo, moving the Soviets to the end of communism. We didn't know it then, but we were visiting the Soviet Union during its last days. The old system was crumbling and revolutionary changes were foaming throughout the land.

I was fortunate to be there at this moment to experience the Soviet Union before the old regime withered away. This is how the Soviets had been for decades. I would be part of some of those last days before the old Russian world changed.

Beverly and I were still standing next to the van on the narrow road watching all this unfold. It was like a scene from a low-budget comic opera to see all of the smiling and hand-shaking going on, then to watch the moods change. The men started concentrating on the new problem of how to get the mud off their shoes.

Everyone hiked back across the rain-soaked field, this time being careful to step on the high grassy knolls and avoid the mud holes. The image of the crew off to the side of Moscow International Airport seemed to capture the contrasts we encountered in covering our stories in Moscow.

The security officer who got us there in time to get the story was the same one who detained us so long in the terminal. We thought he was trying to prevent us from shooting some sensitive security area. We later learned his problem was not hiding some secret site from our camera. It was just the mundane headache of not being able to find a van to take us out on the runway. Because of some bureaucratic foul-up, he was not able to locate the van he had ordered earlier. He was embarrassed about what had happened and was telling our translator there was nothing else he could do. When he heard we had our own van, he was a different person and called for everyone to follow him.

The deputy chief of security was as happy as anyone in our group that we got the take-off pictures. He even volunteered to take us around to the other sites at the airport we might need for our report.

Our airport encounter set the stage for what we would face on other stories in Moscow. The same people who set up the verbal barricades when we sought permission, were the ones who did everything possible to help us get it, once they decided to say yes.

We were warned on the incoming flight that we were not permitted to take pictures at the airport. Yet, our producer, Scott Barer, remembered seeing a network news report from Moscow on the day Pan Am resumed operations there. He put the Pan Am request down as one of our 25 news stories we wanted to do while in Moscow.

Pavel, our official Soviet host, looked at our list and was silent as he scanned the two typewritten pages of subjects. "I think we will be able to do most of these. However, I'll have to write some letters for permission. It will take some time."

"We're not going to be here too long," Scott reasoned with Pavel. "How long will it take?"

"Everything takes time, but I would think a couple of days at the most," he answered.

"That long?" Scott was impatient.

"I'll get some of the letters off tomorrow. I don't think there will be any trouble, however," he reassured Scott.

Scott changed the subject. "Looking at our list, are there any there you don't think we will get permission to do ?"

"It all depends," Pavel answered, "The Metro is one that will cost some money to do."

"You mean we have to pay to do some of these?" Scott was surprised.

"I think they want 300 rubles to shoot in the Metro," Pavel answered.

"Three hundred!" Scott's voice raised emotionally.

"Something like that. I'll check it out."

"That surprises me. I never pay to do a story."

Pavel changed the subject, "This request to do a story on Moscow night life is a problem. They are very cautious about certain topics. You understand, people not wanting to be filmed while they are relaxing. This might be a problem."

Scott listened and thought, "Well, that is not too bad out of 25 requests."

Pavel added, "Taping at Radio Moscow is also a problem. We don't allow cameras inside. We can probably get an interview with television commentator Vladimir Posner at some other location, but not inside."

"We were hoping to catch him as he was broadcasting one of his commentaries from his studio at Radio Moscow, then do an interview with him."

"Let me check," Pavel answered.

"What about the story on Pan Am starting up again from Moscow?" Scott asked, not expecting an affirmative reply.

"I don't know about that one. I'll have to ask the civil aviation people."

"Well, if those are going to take some time, why don't we go down to

Red Square and do a story there so we can get it back to Los Angeles tomorrow?"

"That takes some time, too," Pavel explained.

"What do you mean? It's outside on the street."

"We have to get permission to shoot there," Pavel explained.

I watched the exchanges. Pavel never said, "It's absolutely impossible." Both men were listening to each other trying to figure out the other. Surely, we were going to get cooperation, but no telling how much. We were about to find out just how strong were the fresh breezes of *glasnost* and *perestroika*. We had yet to see this new "openness and restructuring" that was beginning to be felt in the Soviet society. However, it marked the first big opening in the Soviet system and the cooperation of our television hosts was one of the encouraging results.

The next day things began to happen. Pavel told us the story on the Russian fashion industry would take some time, because there were certain important people who had to be contacted and scheduled. The request to show a movie being made would be difficult because there might be nothing going on. We had seen parades of buses taking children to "Pioneer Camp" on the streets of Moscow. We thought that might be a good story, but Pavel said the camps were too far from the city. However, the story on the Soviet space program, the visit to the Kremlin, the taping in the biggest department store in the city, the general footage of Moscow and the nearby museums were approved. We had made a good beginning.

*　　*　　*

Everyone has credentials.

To get into our hotel, the Moskva across from Red Square, you need a special pass given to hotel residents only. The average Soviet citizen cannot enter. Officially, we are told this is to separate them from businesses in the hotel dealing in "hard currency." Many people on the streets want to buy jeans, shirts, shoes, anything American, from tourists. This black market problem is dangerous for both parties. We were warned that one of the most foolhardy things for tourists to do is to trade U.S. currency for Soviet rubles.

The over-zealous reaction caused each hotel to check everyone's credentials when you entered the lobby. If you were going upstairs, you went through another checkpoint where two or three young men in suits and ties inspected your credentials again. If you went to a hotel restaurant there would be another group of young men checking you before they would let you go inside.

When you took the elevator to your floor in the hotel, there would be three other young men sitting in the floor lobby reading books or quietly talking, eyeing you while you walked up to the desk to get your key. Quite often they would be in uniform. Beverly got to know many of them. They said they were there for security, that the man in a uniform was a fireman.

Some of these young men spoke a little English. They became more friendly as they got to know Beverly. They would smile and wave or even get up from their seats to greet us when we left the floor.

One of the men, who was always reading, said he was a student of Oriental culture born in Siberia where his parents still lived.

On Beverly's birthday, the woman who cleaned the floor left a vase with four beautiful roses in our room. It was signed from the "collective on the fourth floor." They became fond of Beverly.

The Intourist staff in the lobby signed cards and wished her a "Happy Birthday." The manager of Intourist in Moscow went out of his way to meet us in the lobby after we returned from a story that day and called to Beverly.

He said, "I want to wish you a happy birthday and hope that you will always remember your visit to Moscow. We will do everything possible to make your stay a happy one."

He even purchased a single rose from the flower girl in the lobby and gave it to her. He emphasized that this was from him personally, and not from his company. He then made hard-to-get dinner reservations for us at the Hotel Berlin, which has subsequently been refurbished into Moscow's premier, luxury hotel and renamed the Savoy.

Our requests for stories were approved rather rapidly. I found out that certain museums insisted we pay a fee if we wanted to tape inside. The Ostenkeno Serf's Museum would cost $100. Although we did not officially ask permission to tape inside the Armory Museum in the Kremlin, one of our other news colleagues was told it would cost him $1000. We did not do many museum stories during our stay.

The Soviets were being cooperative. In addition to the approval on the airport story, we got the go-ahead on "nightlife" and permission to shoot inside Radio Moscow. Indeed, times were changing in the Soviet Union.

* * *

Beverly died February 4, 1989. She had fought cancer for many years, but she more retreated than battled. She discovered a lump in her breast while we were covering the Republican Convention in Dallas, in 1984. Her operation was a success and we had a few more wonderful years together. The children were mostly grown and busy with their own lives, so we had more time together than ever before. She moved through the declining stages with great class and patrician dignity. She began to fade about Thanksgiving 1988. Up to then, through the long ordeal of chemotherapy and radiation, she was her magnificent self. I drove her to the doctor's office several times a week for the treatments. We would sit in the waiting room, holding hands and talking, trying to ignore the reason for our being there. She accepted these inconveniences. She felt there was so much more to living than just these treatments.

She was my assistant producer at the Democratic Convention in Atlanta and the Republican Convention in New Orleans in the summer of 1988. She was always there to experience the stresses, tensions, and yes, jubilations when our live broadcasts and reporting went well.

Our crew always celebrated at the end of each day. Tired as we were, the adrenalin was running high and we relaxed with late dinners at a different restaurant every night. There were plenty of laughs as we replayed what had happened that day and prepared for the challenges of the next.

I remember one hot, sticky afternoon in New Orleans. After a delightful, lingering lunch in the French Quarter, Beverly suggested we walk down to the Mississippi River bank, only a few blocks away. She wanted to see President George Bush arrive in New Orleans. He was sailing down the river on a big paddlewheel riverboat. Scott Barer and I had previously agreed we would have CNN shoot it for us and we would include their tape of the arrival in our news segments that night. But, Beverly got so excited about it that we all decided to go along and wait for the colorful boat parade. John Fischer picked up his camera, tripod and camera-gear bag and we were on our way. It turned out to be the best and most visual story we did on the whole convention.

When the riverboat sailed downstream, you could hear the calliope blaring away in the distance. The riverboat led the way, followed by a parade of private yachts and assorted crafts accompanying the Republican candidate. There were flyovers by antique and World War II planes as the flotilla moved to the riverfront in downtown New Orleans. Many in the crowd along the embankment waved small American flags and beamed emotionally as the boats floated by.

Red fireboats shot multicolored streams of water into the sky creating misty, vapor clouds that added more excitement to the Southern welcome. It was a "happening" and although we were only reporting it, we were emotionally swept up in it. Our cameras told the story.

CNN did cover the last part of the event. They had cameras dockside as President and Mrs. Bush stepped off the riverboat and addressed a crowd of thousands in the humid New Orleans heat. It was here that Mr. Bush finally shared his well-kept secret with his cheering supporters. He announced the name of his vice-presidential candidate.

We were a distance away and couldn't hear the proceedings, but the word traveled on the wind and we were surprised to hear that Senator Dan Quayle of Indiana would be his choice. We were all perplexed; he wasn't on any of our lists of possible choices.

I did remember asking delegates on the convention floor the night before who they thought would be the best candidate. I remember one said, "Dan

Quayle of Indiana." Little did we know how the Dan Quayle saga would unfold.

Later that night in the Superdome, I had a live five-minute cut-in from our skybox above the convention hall. Everything was set up with California Senator, and later Governor Pete Wilson. He had agreed to be a live guest on the program and we remained in touch with his staff during the days of the convention. It was getting close to airtime and there was no senator. Beverly took her post next to the top escalator and anxiously eyed every person entering the hallway. I had gone to the skybox to do the live broadcast, but I was trying now to figure out how I was going to fill the time.

The skyboxes are at the top of the Superdome accessed through a walkway lined with a series of doors that look very much alike. Unless someone in Wilson's party saw Beverly standing outside, they would never be able to find our skybox. We had taken every precaution, but we had missed one, the final assurance that he would be there.

Beverly's assignment was to recognize the Senator and bring him immediately to our skybox. Our broadcast began live to Los Angeles, but without Pete Wilson. Beverly was frantic. Then, she heard rumblings down the walkway from the skyboxes to the right. A group of men came out moving fast and determinedly.

The first man stopped. Beverly said, with a brief hesitation and a plea in her voice, "Pete?"

The man quickly answered, "Bev?"

There was no need to answer. She ran ahead, the others followed to the skybox and made the deadline.

We celebrated at dinner that night so long that we closed the restaurant ourselves. Victories snatched from certain defeat are the ones we savor the most.

*　*　*

Beverly and I learned she was having a recurrence of the cancer just before we left on our trip to Poland and the Vatican in 1987. The doctor assured us it was okay for us to go. We seriously considered cancelling, but the idea of doing a documentary on the Pope, visiting his birthplace in Poland, seeing where he lived, the rock quarry where he worked and where he hid out from the Nazis during World War II, was too exciting. Beverly and I quickly agreed we must go. This would be our third trip behind the Iron Curtain; we couldn't miss it.

Beverly became very involved in the entire trip.

I remember a turbulent, rocky flight from Rome to Kracow on a Polish LOT airliner. The plane bounced in the sky while our party of five laughed nervously as we endured the flight.

We were flying, but all of our suitcases and most of our television gear was being driven to Kracow in our rented cars. The cars had left much earlier and would be at the airport when we arrived.

After an especially severe and unnerving bump, Beverly asked aloud, "Aren't you glad all our luggage is safe down there in the cars?"

In Kracow, our Polish press officer tried to help us find the lodge where the Pope skied while he was bishop of Kracow. We searched the hillside city, and finally he stopped the car and asked a nun walking along the road in her flowing black robes if she had any idea where it was.

"I'll be glad to take you there. That's where I am going," she said. She got into our crowded car and we drove another five minutes to a beautiful building in an alpine setting.

The sisters were not expecting us and the reception was pleasant but restrained. Our press guide talked to two sisters in the yard when we pulled up. They said they could not let us in the house until they spoke to their Mother Superior in town.

Also outside were several other sisters who had just arrived on their first day of their vacation. It was awkward! Everyone just stood around the patio and looked at each other. Then Beverly broke the ice by pulling out a rather large picture of our eleven children and showing them to the sister in charge. They both laughed and enjoyed the exchange. The sisters gave us permission, on the spot, to bring our camera equipment inside and shoot the room where the Pope stayed on his ski vacations.

*   *   *

I tried to put my life on automatic pilot after I lost Beverly. I threw myself into work, and its demands stabilized my aimlessness. I came home after my night shift, turned on Ted Koppel and "Nightline" and fell asleep when it was over. I went to Mass every morning, took a long walk to a little breakfast place in Larchmont Village, read the morning papers and then topped it off with another long walk home. I began to set a pattern that helped me get through the impossible time.

My biggest concern was how the children were taking their loss. I was on the phone with them every day. I wanted to thank them for being so understanding about all of those missed vacations, skipped dinners and picnics at the beach without their father; for being so accepting when I could not be a manager of their little league teams or go to parent's night at school.

Television siphoned away a lot of my time from the family, but it was Beverly who let the children know that it was necessary. It was an occupational hazard of being in news.

It is always a shock to look around at your little children and see that they are all grown. How could this have happened so fast? Now, they were taking care of me, helping me through the days of grief. Beverly and her husband, Don, invited me for weekends at Mission Viejo in Orange County. I had the guest room at Jim and Jane's house at Solano Beach. They took me for long walks along the beach and we watched the yacht races off the pier. Nancy often invited me to lunch at Redondo Beach. Stan, Dave and Ed were always on the phone to make sure dad was doing well.

John and Bob helped me keep the house in repair. They could do all of those nagging things that happen to old homes. It took a lot of the drudgery off my shoulders. Margaret took over the accounting and made sure all the bills were paid every month, even though she was working a full schedule in the intensive care unit of Children's Hospital. Mary was starting a new career in Santa Barbara. I enjoyed my long weekends up there. It seemed like only yesterday, that the two of them, not quite in their teens, would come to KTLA to help me put together my Sunday night newscast. They would help paste scripts together, frame pictures for the broadcast and tidy up the newsroom while I was writing my script. They often borrowed quarters from my co-anchor, Dick Garton, so they could get their favorite snacks out of the food machine.

I remember how my youngest daughter, Elizabeth, helped run our house during those dark days. She was everyone's baby sister, and loved it. She is the only one of the children to go into television news like her dad.

During those long, lonesome walks in the brisk morning air, I often thought about those days when the children were young. The mornings were busy and routine. It was a rush breakfast, a silent carpool to school, signing notes for the teachers, then off to work for me.

I remembered how effortlessly Beverly handled everything. She made those growing years for the children smooth and delightful. She always had the right answer to all their questions.

I did spend too much time at work, but it was good training for the separation that comes naturally as the family grows. I could feel them becoming more independent. It was a continuation of my theory of the open hand. Keep it open, so that the baby can walk and hold your fingers or let go and be on his own.

I think it's important for them to know they are the ones to take their own steps and chart their own direction. We must stay close to those we love, even as they go their separate ways.

My children's love and their lives through all these turbulent years have taught me many things. I am a better, more concerned, understanding and knowing newsman because of them. They taught me how important it is to keep the human spark glowing when I am in the middle of a difficult story. I share the anxiety and sorrow, the bewilderment and futility of others when they find themselves trapped in crisis situations. I am especially vulnerable to their feelings because of the tenderness our family has always shared.

I never had to worry about a generation gap in covering stories because I bridge it every day with my children. They kept me posted on the trends, the vibrations and directions they and their friends live through.

When my mosaic of news stories is completed and brought into focus, my family will have added the bright splashes to the mural that makes sense out of it all.

But, without Beverly, the lonesome path was a struggle.

*   *   *

In 1990, less than a month after the reunification of Germany, I stood in what had been East Berlin and looked West. The Brandenburg Gate with its heroic figures and massive pillars was being refurbished. The Wall had been demolished. All that remained was a series of light standards that cast a yellowish glow on the dreary area.

Checkpoint Charlie, the East German border guards, the gun towers, the drab, graffiti-scarred Wall, were all gone. Now, they existed only in the painful memory of the people or in the powerful videos we all saw on television that showed the process of revolution firsthand.

Television had become part of the process. It had documented the seeds of discontent and helped spread them into a full-blown revolution. Television ushered in the new era with its expanding ability to reach across the continent.

The upheaval was a communications revolution which incorporated TV, videotape, the BBC, Radio Free Europe, CNN, fax machines, copiers, computers and printing presses. More and more people in the communist bloc countries had gained access to these electronic marvels. The communications revolution didn't create the political revolutions, but accelerated them when TV cameras showed a close-up of the first domino as it fell.

Events seen on television ignited the latent feelings of the people which exploded into huge demonstrations in town squares and major cities. Television became the town crier shouting the call to liberty, ringing a bell that reverberated throughout the land. Television screens carried the sounds and showed the pictures. East Germans claiming to be on vacation in Hungary burst across the border into Austria, deserting their homes, their families and their lives of suppression to flee the communist east.

Televised images of the tide of discontent sweeping across Central Europe fueled fires in the hearts of many. Angry crowds in the streets of Poland were seen by people clustered around television sets in Hungary. The stunning revelation that it was happening in Gdansk and Warsaw meant it could be duplicated in Budapest and along the Hungarian border.

East Germans watched the intoxicating tumult on their screens and took to the streets with a mixture of fear and rejoicing. The momentum reached the people of Prague. They couldn't believe what was happening on their television screens. East Germans watched West German television. Hungarians saw the evolving story over Austrian TV. Even the people in the Baltic states could see what was going on in the rest of the world by tuning into television from Finland. Lithuanians, Estonians and Latvians took heart when they were shown the support given to the ideas of freedom on western television stations. People all over the world were sharing the epoch-making moments rocking the very foundations of the old order. People swept on, passed their leaders and changed the course of history.

I was with a group of newsmen invited by the German government to see what was happening in the newly united East German cities and to observe the first effects of reunification. This was also during the final days of the 1990 election campaign and Chancellor Helmet Kohl was a heavy favorite to win. His dramatic monetary exchange plan of offering the economically depressed citizens of the East one West German mark for every two of the nearly worthless East German marks was already in effect. The quick action by the government did much to stabilize the country and resulted in instant economic reunification.

We drove to the dreary, East German city of Cotbuss to meet some of the revolutionaries who had taken to the streets early and were the real leaders of the upheaval against the communists. Theirs had been a heady victory. They had won so quickly they were almost disappointed. When the reality of what they had done finally sunk in, the leadership of the revolution had passed on to others.

I remember a heavy-set man with flowing hair and an intense personality who was a member of the Green Party. He had been one of the early inspirational leaders, but now was just another East German baffled by his newlywon freedom, almost stunned by the rapidity of events. Only months ago, he had led the revolution, but now he was an outsider. Others had taken over and now the former leader looked around and found that he was left standing alone in the streets. The crowd followed someone else and everything had passed him by.

There was a pensive, matronly schoolteacher, with deep-set eyes, who had fought for freedom, but was now deeply concerned about what it would mean. There was a tone of deep bewilderment in her voice as she asked, "What about our government medical coverage? What about our child care programs? What about our jobs? Yes, I'm glad the old way is gone, but I'm fearful."

A studious plant manager sat comfortably behind his desk and talked about buying his company. "There will be many companies like this up for privatization. They are good, but so far few contracts have been signed. It's going to take a long time."

I attended a huge political rally in East Berlin and was engulfed by the incongruous situation of the former East Germans tasting democracy for the first time in this huge convention hall. They were confused, cautious and apprehensive, but most of them were wearing new West German clothes bought with their windfall marks from the government monetary exchange program. They were entering a new life, without knowing where it would take them.

*   *   *

I had a similar feeling that night as I walked the dark, damp streets around my East German hotel. Here I was walking in this section of Berlin that had been patrolled by the East German Stassi police only months before.

I knew my personal life was on the brink of a change. Beverly had died almost two years ago. I relished those 40 years with her, but now she was gone and I knew that I must move on, a difficult reality to face. On this chilly night on the rain-splattered streets of East Berlin, I knew I had made the decision and Beverly had helped me make it.

The unlikely connection went back to 1978 when Beverly and I were in Quebec City, Canada. I was doing a series of stories on the growing disputes between the French-speaking Canadians in Quebec and the rest of the English-speaking provinces of Canada.

I was filming a report in one of the historic old town squares, when Beverly started a conversation with a young honeymoon couple. She discovered they were from Los Angeles and that the bride, Anita, was the daughter of Desmond Hinds, a high school friend of mine. After I completed the filming for the news story, the four of us enjoyed talking about their wedding, our trips and her dad. Beverly and I often reminisced about our chance meeting with them, one of the highlights of the Quebec trip.

*   *   *

Ten years later, after our return from the Dallas Republican Convention in the summer of 1988, Beverly and I unexpectedly met Anita again at a party in Laguna Hills. It was quite a surprise and we enjoyed laughing about Quebec and renewing our acquaintance. Beverly died about six months later.

In 1989, about a year after Beverly's death, I was attending a wedding reception in Laguna Beach and as I stood next to the buffet line in the crowded reception room, I once again met Anita and her husband Mark. A lot had changed since our last unexpected meeting. She had heard about Beverly and we talked once again about Quebec.

After a few minutes of small talk, she became serious and said, "Stan, I want you to meet my aunt. Her husband died a few weeks after Beverly. I think you two would enjoy knowing each other."

It startled me. I had never given much thought about dating again. I thanked her, but brushed off the flattering invitation. Anita and Mark wouldn't take no for an answer and were very persuasive as I tried to ease out of any commitment.

I left them with a vague answer, but Mark ended with a definite invitation. "We'll call you after the holidays and the four of us will have dinner together."

Driving home to Los Angeles that evening I thought, "Imagine, after forty years going on a blind date."

*   *   *

Gege Elder and I hit it off right away. We enjoyed talking to each other, being with each other and it seemed as if we had known each other forever. She was a beautiful, intelligent blonde: slim, vivacious and full of endless energy, a top tennis player, a good golfer and interested in everything.

After being alone without Beverly for almost a year, being with Gege gave me new hope. She helped me put the pieces of my life together. It was on that rainy night in Berlin that I decided that we shouldn't wait any longer. Gege and I should stop looking back to what was, and start moving ahead, getting on with our lives, building a future together.

I arrived back in Los Angeles the night before my daughter Margaret's wedding to Dr. Michael McMonigle at St. Brendan's Church. I was a very proud father as I walked down the aisle with my beautiful daughter on my arm, not realizing that I would be at my own wedding very soon.

Gege had talked about getting married for sometime, but there always seemed to be a reason to delay it.

The next day, while Gege and I were talking about the wedding and the reception, I asked her, "Now that Margaret's married, what about us? When are you going to marry me?"

She smiled.

I said, "Let's do it right away."

She laughed, "Let me look at my calendar."

It was a difficult, but beautiful decision for her. Our new love sustained both of us in our life together.

20.

THE NINETIES:
CHASING SIRENS

An enthusiastic salesman in the late 1940s told me my new television set would be my window to the world. In the 1990s his prediction came true.

The small black-and-white set of the 40s has evolved into big-screen color television, the entertainment and news center of the 90s. Wall-size projection screens in your den or living room are commonplace today, even though expensive. Thirty-two and 35-inch screens are the big sellers among the conventional sets. They offer "surround-sound," motion-picture like quality, and can even show more than one channel at a time. Their performance and quality were unimaginable in the 40s. Turn it on— you'll see more channels than we had sets back the in the mid-Forties.

Television in the 90s shrank the world. CNN televised the bombings in Iraq to the world. Bernard Shaw, John Holliman and Peter Arnett watched through their hotel window and waited for the first wave of U.S. Air Force bombers. They listened and reported the distant thuds of the bombs. They described Baghdad under siege as the explosions ripped buildings close to their hotel.

I watched in amazement at our television screen in the KTLA newsroom, as the wail of sirens announced an air raid. Later, I watched as Iraqi scud missiles streaked like comets across the black sky, vainly searching for their targets, only to crash in fire and destruction.

The world saw the Iraqi war on television, as cameras covered Operation Desert Storm and its aftermath. Reporters and cameramen were on the beach in Somalia to welcome U.S. forces making a secret, surprise landing on the sands of Mogadishu. The Marines were sent to Somalia because television had shown the horror of hunger in the faces of dying children.

The battling warlords of that plagued African country had completely destroyed its economy and civilization leaving the people to starve and die.

The agony of racial strife in Bosnia was shown to the world. The country that had been held together by the brutal force of communism was now breaking apart and bleeding itself to death in its newfound freedom. The images of war were all over the television screens.

These pictures of the world in distress were fed by satellites 22,000 miles in the sky. CNN's round-the-clock coverage not only kept the average viewer informed, but was a source of vital information for world leaders. Khadafi in Libya, Saddam Hussein in Iraq, the offices of presidents, defense secretaries and United Nations officials found it more informative than their latest, closely guarded, secret pouches.

Those signals from the sky are captured by satellite dishes around the world. They are broadcast by hundreds of cable systems that have opened dozens of channels and promise as many as 500. Industry officials talk of interactive television in which the viewer will be part of the broadcast.

C-SPAN opened the world to the Congress of the United States. Viewers watched their congressmen argue and debate from the floor of the House of Representatives.

In the 90s, we see worldwide events as they take place. We become a part of what is happening. We are living through the evolving news stories that affect our lives and change our world.

KTLA has been a part of the CNN television revolution since the start of the cable network. My stories are often fed around the world by CNN. "News At Ten" is on the satellite bird every night and seen by millions all over the world. When something happens in Los Angeles, KTLA's signal can be picked up and rebroadcast by CNN on a moment's notice. When something happens in Los Angeles, the world can watch.

For several days in October and November 1993, CNN broadcast world wide KTLA's coverage of the wild firestorms that hit Southern California.

*　　*　　*

Here I am, back in a news helicopter in a steep bank, on a black, smoke-filled night circling over a cluster of fires and watching the city burn. The hot, dry, devil winds that plague Southern California scooped up an arsonist's torch and spewed a whirling firestorm on the land below. Huge black clouds, reflecting hues of orange and red from the intense flames, boil into the sky over the hills and canyons of Malibu and Laguna Beach. The fires roar out of the mountains, sweep into the canyons and send giant fireballs of destruction raining onto the houses below.

Homes, by the hundreds, consumed by the blast of the inferno that melts and grinds everything—floors, furniture, walls and fixtures— into a gray ashen powder. Only the skeleton of a fireplace and the seared foundation of concrete and rubble outlining what used to be a house.

I feel helpless as I look down from the helicopter at the sites of tragedy and consider the lives that are being ripped apart by the sudden fire. I watch as homes and possessions on the familiar hillsides look like huge campfires in the wake of the firestorms that ravaged them. I wonder if things can ever be the same for those who live through this?

Dozens of these brush fires that broke out while the winds blew in October and November 1993, were set by arsonists who soaked newspapers in gasoline, threw bomb-like mixtures into the tinder-dry brush and let the hot wind do the rest. Some arsonists used sophisticated devices. Others employed road flares or matches with a delayed fuse to give them time to flee.

Officials offered huge rewards, searched for evidence at the scene, hunted for suspicious suspects,and sifted through tips from witnesses who saw someone where the fires began. The arsonists had done their devil's work; almost a thousand homes were destroyed in Altadena, Banning, Thousand Oaks, Topanga Canyon, Malibu and Laguna Beach. This was more than the number of structures set on fire by arsonists during the Los Angeles riots of April 1992.

Even those who fled the violent urban scene have found that they cannot escape disaster. No matter where they go it can find them. Violence, crime, murder, robbery and vicious people continue to take their toll on us all. However, it was not the drug-dealing gang members of the inner city this time. It was the solitary, demented arsonist—who was just as deadly.

We must find a way to combat it. The city staggers to recover as it survives one blow after another.

*   *   *

These are the stories we have to tell. This is what news is all about. News is what is happening today. My executive producer, Gerry Ruben, produces his nightly newscast like a musical conductor. He directs it with flair and enthusiasm. He gets involved and emotional. He knows what he wants and demands the best. He is always on stage. He knows that sound is important, but he looks for the picture. The visual is the most important element of television news and he builds his program around it as he assembles the most important stories of the day.

He is constantly telling his crew, "Keep it simple. Be basic. Key your copy to the pictures on the screen. Viewers have only one chance to get what you want to tell them. In a newspaper, they can stop, look back and check something they have read. In television, if they don't get what you are trying to say the first time, they're lost. Your copy should help viewers understand the pictures they are watching. Don't confuse them."

"Be conversational. Your writing must help the anchorman be natural. Write for the ear. Read your script aloud. Make sure it sounds comfortable. Use simple, basic words. Leave the fancy ones for the novelist. You are communicating. You are telling a story.

"What you write will disappear the moment it is spoken. Your script is 'written on the wind' and will quickly be forgotten.

"News is perishable. It becomes less important as hours go by. If it is yesterday's news, it doesn't belong in today's broadcast. You only use a story again if it has moved forward and has a 'today' news peg.

"What is the latest? What is the most important development in the hours before airtime? Keep looking at the wires. They tell us what has happened since we went on the air. News is what is happening. It is changing and always new."

Gerry Ruben keeps a close tab on his entire broadcast and sits next to the director during it. His minute attention to detail makes the telecast smooth, authoritative and accurate. He directs the presentation from the trenches and responds to the unexpected quickly. His sound news judgment is key to the broadcast.

"Be careful about details," Gerry reminds us: "Are the names right? Is the location correct? Are they spelled right? Be careful. Don't get so busy that you are going to make mistakes. Be fast but be accurate."

A news operation is more than its evening newscast. It is essential to keep abreast of the technical advancements that have inundated the news business in recent years. Newness has almost become a plague, because it can trap you into buying a system or a piece of equipment that could soon be outdated.

Management is still the key for a successful news department. Our station managers through the years, Greg Nathanson, John Reardon, Steve Bell, Mike Eigner, Peter Walker, Tony Cassara and John Reynolds, have given the news operation the support it needs to succeed. It is what makes the entire operation work and has kept KTLA as one of the leading independent television stations in the nation.

The legendary cowboy, Gene Autry, was the heart and soul of KTLA for 25 years. The chairman of the board of Golden West Broadcasting was the kind, considerate owner everyone loved. He was a good businessman, but most of all, he was an outstanding human being. When there were problems, he had good people to handle them; but when they couldn't, he was ready to step in with the right decision. Gene Autry helped the news department soar and later the new owners, Tribune Broadcasting, kept it flying high.

KTLA continued to progress all those years and as the audience steadily grew, "News At Ten" increased its position as the leading local newscast on the air. It kept gaining in popularity as the station developed and maintained a strong news team.

Anchorman Hal Fishman was at the helm of the rebirth of the newscast's popularity. Larry McCormick joined the station in 1971 and is one of the most honored and respected broadcasters on television. He handles any assignment with ease, from anchoring to special events and hosting countless other programs. Los Angeles viewers know him well. Both Hal and Larry have built genuine trust and appreciation among the viewers. Jann Carl, who co-anchors with Hal Fishman, is a bright and resourceful reporter. A graduate of the University of Missouri School of Journalism, she has great versatility and is one of the best anchors in the country. Veteran and popular sportcasters Stu Nahan and Ed Arnold head up the sports team on "News at Ten." They are following in the steps of such KTLA sports alumni as Tom Harmon, Keith Jackson, Dick Enberg, Merlin Olson, Jerry Coleman and the late Don Drysdale.

* * *

I could hear the distant wail of a siren from some rescue ambulance on a mission of mercy. I was listening to my emergency scanners as I do most nights, but very little was happening. I had chased a fire engine earlier that was weaving through the streets with sirens blaring and red lights flashing, but the emergency turned out to be a false alarm. It was one of those slow nights where I sat in the front seat of my camera car vaguely listening to the scattered voices on the radio.

I was somehow thinking about my career as a television reporter. Although there are nights like this, it's part of the job. You just have to be ready when something big does happen. I thought most of my time in television news has been spent skidding on the slippery slides, climbing the tall ladders of success or being content on some plateau in between.

* * *

As a reporter I am mostly an observer of scenes. However, at one barricade situation, I played a different role; one that confused and frightened a colleague next to me.

I was with a photographer from the *Los Angeles Times*. We were both kneeling behind an old abandoned car in a cluttered vacant lot. Although we were well hidden, we could look right into the doorway of a tiny market. We were told there was a gunman inside the small mom-and-pop grocery store directly across the street from us. We normally don't get views as dramatic as this. We had ringside seats where we would be able to watch the police entry effort and we hoped, the climax, when the gunman would be captured and brought out.

The grocery store was a small, two-story building. The family, who lived upstairs, spent many long hours behind the counters of the neighborhood deli and grocery store.

There had been a robbery attempt by a gunman who fired two shots into the ceiling, then ran into the back of the store. The employees and customers were able to get out and everyone was sure the robber was still inside. The police were called in. As other police cars arrived, they were assigned locations around the store in the hope of trapping the gunman inside the perimeter.

One sergeant used a bullhorn several times to order the gunman to come out. The only answer was silence. After a long wait, the officers decided they would have to go in and get him.

The photographer and I had been kneeling silently for a long time, hardly moving, hardly talking, just watching the tense activity build up around the front door. In the middle of all of this, a sound exploded like a gun shot. Instinctively, I stood up, and as I did, I fell to my left into the dirt behind the car. My left leg completely collapsed.

The photographer whipped around to look at me as I dropped. His eyes widened in fear, and I knew he thought I had been shot. I was on the ground before I realized what had happened. We had been hiding so long in that kneeling position that my left leg had fallen asleep. When I got up, it gave way and I tumbled into the dirt. I was shaken, a bit embarrassed, but unhurt.

The photographer reached over to help me. He still didn't know if I had been shot. I assured him that I was all right. I got up with the help of the bumper on the old car. I jiggled my leg, limped around a bit and gradually felt the circulation return.

Finally, we both laughed about it. The "gunshot" must have been backfire from some passing car down the block. I still remember the expression on his face as I was falling. I knew nothing had hit me, but the loud noise confused and frightened me. We resumed our semi-hidden position, but nothing happened. The officers searched the market and found that the gunman was gone.

Another time, I was in the FBI headquarters in Los Angeles looking at a display of pictures taken during bank robberies. The snapshots, clipped together like a chain, were hanging vertically four to five feet down the wall.

The gunmen in these pictures had robbed more than a dozen banks and these photographs showed how each one of them operated. The agents identified each man with a nickname that is characteristic of the way he hits and runs with the money.

Agent John Huess pointed to various pictures and said, "There is the 'paper bag bandit.' He always has a brown bag, fills it with the stolen money and runs. There is the 'baseball capper,' who wears a baseball cap with a different name on its front each time he hits a bank."

He walked over to another group of pictures and continued talking. "The 'jumper' actually leaps over the desks and counters. There may be as many as two dozen such bandits who are wanted for multiple holdups. You can see them in action because they were all caught by the security cameras of the various banks."

John moved to another group of photos and said, "The 'red truck' bandit always escapes in an old, red pickup that he leaves just in front of the bank. The 'sweet talker' is very polite and apologetic, but always gets his money."

I learned as I developed the story for "News at Ten," that the arrest rate is very high for the bank robbers in this group. The agents are able to establish a pattern that eventually enables them to nab the crooks. Nevertheless, many of them go on and on, continuing to hit one bank after another. There was one heavy-set suspect on the wall who had been involved in over 30 local bank jobs. He was very smart, fast and lucky. Twice officers almost got him, but he was able to get away.

I completed my story with an interview with a FBI agent and a detective from the Los Angeles Police Department bank robbery detail.

A week later, I watched a police stakeout of a small house in the Hollywood area. We parked a few blocks from where the police had set up an undercover perimeter, and waited for developments. From the conversations that we picked up over the scanners, we knew the police wanted their suspect badly. From what we could gather, this seemed to be another drug bust.

There were a few people in front of the target house, but no one left it. However at one point, one man walked down the street to a public pay phone. We heard the police move out. When they stopped him at the phone booth, they moved in. He was quickly taken into custody.

We drove our van down the street and shot some of the action through our windshield and got tape of the suspect being arrested. We still could not put the pieces of this puzzle together.

The man in custody was spirited away from the scene. We went back to our corner down the street to wait for the next development. In a few minutes, our scanners indicated that something was going on. We could see that the police did not try to enter the house, but they were moving in on something.

Evidently the man they were looking for slipped out the back door and tried to escape through a neighbor's yard. It was time to move. When we drove around a corner, we saw a man leaning over the hood of a police car, already in custody, his hands cuffed behind him. Our camera was rolling as officers put him in the back seat of the police car. The rear door slammed behind him.

To my surprise the arresting officer was the detective I had met a while earlier in the FBI news conference. I asked him what was going on.

"This is a suspect we've wanted for quite a while," he answered.

"Is this a narcotics operation?" I asked routinely, still very much in the dark about what was going on.

He smiled and said, "Stan, don't you remember that meeting we had last week about the bank robber who was wanted for 30 local jobs? This is the guy."

My suspicion that this was a minor story about a routine narcotics operation turned out to be the arrest of one of the most-wanted bank robbers in the city.

There are so many of these stories. Many of them I have completely forgotten. Others I'll always remember. Steve Weinstein wrote an article about me in the *Los Angeles Times*. His headline was, "20,000 Stories...and Counting. At 70, Stan Chambers shows no sign of slowing down on his night-beat reporting for KTLA."

That's pretty close to the number, and I certainly have no plans to slow down. I enjoyed being in this retrospective mood. I decided that if I had to choose one moment of my career that meant the most to me professionally, it would be the night in 1979 when the Los Angeles chapter of the Sigma Delta Chi journalism fraternity gave me one of its awards.

Now called the Society of Professional Journalists, it presents the Broadcaster of the Year award to working members of the news media. It doesn't normally go to the national anchors or the high-flying network correspondents covering international hot spots.

Sigma Delta Chi gives a journeyman reporter the recognition he may never receive again. The committee selects those they consider the best, not necessarily the best known. My news director, Lew Rothbart, nominated me that year, but I had no inkling I was being considered. The phone call came out of the blue and delighted me. I was the winner without knowing I was even in the running.

The award took place at a black-tie dinner in the Embassy Ballroom of the Ambassador Hotel, the same room where Senator Robert Kennedy was assassinated in 1968. CBS Anchorman Walter Cronkite was the main speaker, Bill Stout of CBS was emcee and NBC's Jesse Marlow presented the award.

KTLA bought tables for members of the news department. My boss Gene Autry invited all 11 of my children to the dinner. I believe it was the first time all of us had ever been out to dinner together. As you can imagine with our family, someone was always away at school, working or sick when we tried to have a family get-together.

At last they were going to be able to see what their father was doing all of those years when he was not home for dinner. We had lived so close to the station that they were used to me jumping in the car and driving up to the "office," as most of them called it.

I don't think the younger ones really knew what I did, except to see me on television. They didn't watch news programs too often, so it was a treat for them when they did see me on the screen during those years.

I had been one of many working journalists in Los Angeles and had covered many of the news beats, but had never been selected for anything like this. The Sigma Delta Chi award was a big turning point for me. The award, at that time, gave direction and recognition to a tiring career. Many in the business had wondered about me. They would see me on a variety of stories on the broadcasts each night. Many believed I did a good job, but wondered why I had remained a local newsman for so long. The conventional wisdom is that, if I were any good, I would have gone to a network long ago instead of remaining a local reporter.

The Sigma Delta Chi award in effect said, "It's all right to be a local reporter. It doesn't have to be a mere stepping-stone to the networks."

You never know where the tides will carry you in the news business, so it is best to be prepared to handle whatever comes up. If you develop your talents as a general assignment reporter, you'll be ready to handle many of the specialties that you could be assigned.

One of the most important things to remember is not to let the story overwhelm you. Even though you are in the middle of riots, brush fires, earthquakes or political conventions, the simple questions of who, what, why, where and when still apply. Answer them and you have your story. Of course, you also need the best pictures possible to make it a good report.

Most of the time, the local reporter will be covering the news stories of the day. He will rarely be called upon to get "the goods" on a local politician who someone has said is "on the take." Mostly he will be covering news in the usual manner, so he should not go into interviews with the attitude that his subject has something to hide.

The reporter must remember he will be meeting his hometown news sources often, so it is important that he be fair and considerate. The reporter should do what has to be done, but avoid being arrogant, overbearing or a bore. His reputation catches up with him after a few encounters and then it precedes him wherever he goes. If he is not fair, his reputation will probably catch up with him at the most inopportune time.

He can ask probing and embarrassing questions in a direct and gentlemanly manner and still be welcomed back the next time. Your news source knows you have a job to do and respects a professional manner. There is no room for temper tantrums, bullying or badgering. The local reporter is going to be a part of his hometown scene for a long time. The contacts he makes and the relationships with people throughout the city are going to help him become an effective and accepted part of his community scene.

I've enjoyed being part of Los Angeles these many years. Looking back, there are few things I would have done differently. I am especially pleased I was able to stay at one station all that time. I never even considered leaving

KTLA in those early years. I was so involved in doing things, I never took time to look around and ask myself where I wanted to be 15 years down the line. With 11 growing children, I had no desire to move to another city and always felt a great loyalty to KTLA.

There is always great competition between stations. I was on KTLA's team. It was like playing football for Loyola High School or rooting for USC. It was loyalty to a place, a cause or a dream. That spirit carried over into television for me and made my days at KTLA more than a job.

In the early years, Klaus Landsberg didn't want us to associate with our competition. We were KTLA and they were the "other guys." My station was something special. My job was to do my best to make it even more special. Through good and bad times I have felt that way. There is much to be said for loyalty. The spirit makes you an integral part of what you are and adds that extra satisfaction when you do something right.

I have always felt I had a big Channel 5 stamped on my forehead and people could see it wherever I went. I think the people at Sigma Delta Chi saw Channel 5 there and gave me the award for that.

21.

THE GRAND FINALE:
SIX POINT EIGHT

We were fifth-row center at the Shubert Theatre in Century City; wonderful seats, a Christmas gift from Gege's daughter, Alicia and her husband, Dave. Gege and I were watching the grand finale of "Sunset Blvd.," the new Andrew Lloyd Weber musical that seemed destined to rival the popularity of "Phantom of the Opera" and "Cats." We were limp from the dramatic performance that had captivated the overflow audience in the theatre.

After the finale, the cheering crowd gave Glenn Close a standing ovation when she appeared at the top of the ornate, winding staircase and descended into the loving embrace of her audience in front of her. She was still Norma Desmond, the aging motion picture star she portrays in the musical production.

This was one of those rare, extravagant evenings when the world was ours. We had spent a delightful weekend together, enjoyed the show and were now on our way to Harper's Pub and Bar across the courtyard from the theatre to enjoy a lobster dinner.

We were to meet my cameraman, Greg Hunter and his girlfriend, Linda Kicak for the after-theatre dinner at the pub. They had tickets for this same night and we decided to celebrate by having dinner together. There was a festive feeling in the crowd walking out of the theatre. Gege and I were talking about how much we enjoyed the performance.

"And it's going to get better when the show finally reaches Broadway," I said to Gege as we walked up the crowded staircase.

"I don't know how they can improve it," she answered.

Harper's was busy, but our table was ready. It was a great evening and we left the restaurant about midnight. Greg and Linda had a long trip to Long Beach ahead of them. Greg and I did not have to be at work until the next afternoon.

Later, as I drove down Sunset Boulevard to our home, I was still thinking how the producers could experiment every night with little changes and additions that might enhance the musical.

It is far more difficult for an author to close the pages of his book. He faces that final deadline, but there's always something else to add or change. I suppose a book is never really finished, but earlier this year, I convinced myself that this book was completed. However, in the still of the night, Mother Nature had another idea.

*   *   *

In the blinding blackness of 4:31a.m. on January 17, 1994, a terrifying rumble roared up from the ground. It was as if demonic hands grabbed the eaves of the house, then tried to rip it apart and yank it from its concrete foundation. As if, in a fit of rage, the giant of the night shook it viciously. I knew it would be only a moment before the shuddering walls, shattering glass, and the creaking, moaning roof would crash down upon us. My wife did the only sensible thing. She pulled the covers up over her head.

Millions of terrified Californians were jarred from their sleep to the same real-life nightmare that erupted ten miles deep in the earth. A subterranean wave swelled up from the depths and exploded throughout Southern California, jarring and twisting the shuddering ground. This was a devastating 6.8 earthquake, ripping and cutting across the land, destroying everything that could not stand up to its rupturing spasms.

We stayed motionless, hearts pounding, heads throbbing until the endless trembling stopped and silence momentarily returned. Then Gege and I jumped up into the impenetrable darkness. I didn't want to cut myself. I remembered the sounds of glass breaking in the blackness as the house trembled about me. I reached for my slippers and got on my hands and knees, and brushed the floor. I had to feel about the carpet to find anything. My slippers, usually under the bed were not there. Instead, I felt books, an overturned lamp, jars and other objects. I felt the edge of my desk, followed a leg down to the soft carpet and found one slipper under the desk. No bits of glass so far. I brushed aside other things in the darkness and continued feeling for my other slipper. It still wasn't there.

On the other side of the bed, Gege probed for her Reeboks. She had the base of her telephone in her hand and was using its tiny green light bulb as a flashlight in the search. She swept her hand through the rubble on the carpet and spotted one of her shoes in the faint illumination.

I found my missing slipper under some books and papers near my side of the bed. I now had my slippers on. As I walked to Gege's side, I stumbled over a CD-stereo player that had fallen off a shelf. I decided to move slowly. Even in the chaotic shuffling of those moments after the quake, I knew I had to leave immediately for the station. If it was that bad here, it must be terrible elsewhere in the city.

We assured each other we were all right. We hugged for a few moments to regain our strength and our sanity. I knew aftershocks were coming and it would be dark for another hour or so before we could judge the extent of damage inside the house. The combination of aftershocks and the gradual discovery of damage could be devastating if Gege were alone, so I persuaded her to spend the day with me.

*　　*　　*

Gege and I tried to find something to wear in the blackness that morning. I reached for an invisible suit, grabbed a handful of ties, hoping one of them would match, took a pair of shoes and a shirt from the closet and started to dress.

We had a disturbing aftershock as Gege stumbled over fallen objects and groped her way to the clothes closet.

She tried to push the closet door open. It seemed jammed. I worked my way over and tried to push it open. It hit a solid object and would not move. I figured something was jammed in front of the door inside. Then I realized the quake made the dresser drawers dance open about six inches, blocking access in the closet. All her clothes were inside.

Gege remained calm despite the closet fiasco. She remembered she left a sweat suit on a chair near the bed. She put it on and was almost ready to go. The only problem was that she could only find one shoe. The others were in the closet.

I offered her one of my slippers and she took it.

So, wearing a tennis shoe and slipper, Gege took my hand and followed me as we felt our way through the precarious darkness downstairs to the car in the driveway.

We found almost no traffic as we drove up Sunset Boulevard. Darkness enveloped everything on both sides of the street. I later learned the city of Los Angeles was completely without power. I couldn't see any damage. In fact I got a reassuring glance at the high-rise buildings in Century City, still serenely standing.

The station was already on the air with earthquake coverage when we arrived. Others, who reached the newsroom earlier, had phones to their ears, notebooks in their hands and computer printouts with the latest news on the quake.

Hans Laetz looked up from his phone call and saw me rush into the assignment room. "Stan, Greg Hunter should be here any minute. Both of you take Unit Ten. Head out to the valley. Look for damage. I think we've got freeway problems."

Weekend anchor Marta Waller greeted us and took a sympathetic look at Gege. For years, Marta has carried a big tote bag around with all the things she would need if a big disaster hit. Some people used to laugh about it, but no one was laughing this morning. She had extra flashlights, batteries, a portable radio and extra shoes.

"Gege, give that slipper back to Stan. I have an extra pair of tennis shoes in my bag. Here!"

Gege was pleased to be set for the day.

Hans kept shouting into the radio in front of him, "SkyCam Five, I know it's pitch black out there, but do you see any damage?"

I picked up a reporter's notebook from my desk and bolted to the parking lot and watched Greg Hunter whip into a parking place.

"I'll be ready in a moment, Stan," Greg shouted. "I called Hans and told him not to let my camera truck go out with anyone else."

He slammed his door shut and raced into the newsroom to get some video tapes and batteries. I could feel the electricity of the moment as others were arriving and running into the newsroom.

"Gege, it's great you're here. Get in the back seat and go with us," Greg said as he juggled a stack of tapes and put them in the truck.

"Why not?" I thought."If Gege is with me I won't have to worry about how she is coping with the aftershocks."

Gege took the big step to the back seat and sat next to the third member of our crew, Carlos Quintero, who was checking out the camera gear. In the early moments after the quake it was difficult to know where to go. I knew there had to be major damage, but didn't know where. We took the Ventura Freeway through the Cahuenga Pass, passed Universal City and headed towards Reseda.

"Unit Ten, there are reports of freeway damage on the 5 Freeway. Head out that way," Hans barked over the radio.

Greg picked up speed and raced faster to our target.

"There's a fire in the Hollywood Hills." Greg pointed to a fiery glow.

"News, it looks like we have a fire here, might be quake-related," I called to the assignment desk.

"Head for it," was the curt reply. "I'll send the copter to the freeway."

"Look at the smoke over there. It's another fire and it looks big," Greg said as he pointed toward the hills.

The black smoke, barely discernible in the dark sky, was developing a reddish glow at its base and seemed to be growing.

"Found a bigger fire. We're heading for it," I radioed to Hans.

"Go for it. Keep me posted." His voice abruptly cut off, then began again. We pulled off on Hazeltine and headed west to Ventura Boulevard, where the fire was boiling into the sky. It was burning through the entire top floor of a long, two story, Sherman Oaks commercial building. The fire was through the roof and pouring out of all of the windows facing Ventura Boulevard. Several fire rigs were shooting streams of water into the blaze. Firemen atop aerial ladders 40 feet high were spraying more powerful streams of water into the heart of the fire as black clouds boiled in the hot flames, casting an orange glow into the night.

It was still dark as I got ready for my first live cut in from the field. All of the windows of the businesses along this section of Ventura Boulevard were broken. Shards of glass were scattered everywhere. The power of the quake had knocked merchandise out of the store windows onto the sidewalks. As I stood there with mike in hand waiting to go on the air, I watched as two individuals picked up items from the sidewalk and put them back inside the broken windows of the stores.

I felt pretty good about that and thought, "Here's a case of reverse looting."

Larry McCormick was anchoring the broadcast from the news set in the studio. "Let's go live to Stan Chambers..."

I did my report, then Larry asked me, "Are there many other fires around you?"

"No, Larry, just these two."

"I understand there are about 40 fires burning at this time," he answered back.

The severity of the quake was beginning to become apparent. I later learned that over 150 mobile homes were burning in Chatsworth, Sylmar and Northridge, near the epicenter of the quake.

I did several reports while it was still dark. Then as dawn broke I could see additional damage. The quake dislodged the inside roof of a Ralphs supermarket next to the fire-ravaged building. What damage the quake didn't do, the fallen roof did. All the merchandise was jarred off the shelves and the shattered roof crushed display cases into rubble. The store was a complete shambles and I broadcast interviews with several employees who were working inside when their world fell down around them.

Later, we showed geysers of water, 50 feet high, erupting from broken fire plugs along Ventura Boulevard.Water was flowing down the street. At another intersection, water was bubbling up through the roadway from broken underground water mains.

Throughout the early hours, people were telling me about other damaged buildings in the neighborhood. I now felt it was time to check them out. We broadcast live from the scene of many of them.

One part of an apartment complex on Hazeltine was picked up and moved three feet off its foundation. It collapsed on parked cars in an underground garage. Some residents couldn't get out of their apartments; cracked plaster, broken stucco and other debris blocked their exits. Neighbors had to dig in and pull the pile of rubble apart to free them.

At another apartment on Tyrone, I saw three people carrying suitcases, climbing out a high front window and dropping down another two feet to the shrubbery in front. Their front doors were jammed shut.

Toppled bricks and mortar were randomly scattered on sidewalks and lawns. Broken walls had fallen everywhere. People stood bewildered in front of their homes, too dazed to start the clean-up.

"Unit Ten, head for the Northridge Fashion Mall. There's heavy damage there," Hans voice came over the crackling radio.

I opened my Thomas Brothers' map book and tried to find the shortest route. We were seeing more and more damaged structures as we drove to Northridge.

Everywhere I went I saw the same tell-tale damage, unreinforced block-walls cracked open and lying on lawns and sidewalks.

"We have an unbelievable picture here, Hans." My radio was inches from my mouth. "This is Unit Ten. We see fire and water on the street not far ahead of us. Evidently an underground water main has broken and a gas line or something, has caught fire. This huge flame is boiling up through the water."

"Thanks, Stan," Hans answered, "but Marta Waller and her crew are already there. We'll have pictures on the air from that location in just a few minutes."

The Northridge Mall was an eerie sight. The huge parking lot was empty. Sitting in the middle of it, like a stranded whale, was the totally destroyed Bullocks department store. Its tile facade in front and back were standing, but the entire roof section and sides had collapsed. The third floor fell on top of the first. A few straggly pillars stood in the rubble, but the structure was gone. A modern building ripped apart by the quake was a shocking sight. The question kept going through my mind, "What would have happened if the quake hit at 4:30 in the afternoon, instead of the morning? There could have been 500 people in that building."

"News room," I called over the radio after my live report from the Bullocks store was over, "One of the people here told me there is a rescue going on at the far side of the mall. A parking structure has collapsed and at least one person is trapped."

"You're clear from Bullocks, head over there," Hans answered.

We drove the streets around the mall, ribbons of yellow tape blocked every entrance to keep people out.

"Hold on," Greg warned as he drove up to a curb and bounced over it and onto the pavement of the parking lot, allowing the yellow tape to remain intact. The twisted wreckage of a broken and tilting concrete parking structure loomed ahead of us. The middle was still standing, but huge sections on both sides were felled by the 6.8 earthquake. There were a half dozen fire department rigs in a cluster.

I jumped out the moment Greg stopped the truck and ran to the crowd of rescuers, reporters and cameramen. I saw my friend, Boris Yarov, a photographer from the *Los Angeles Times.*

He filled me in, "A mall employee was driving a sweeper truck cleaning up the parking structure. He was trapped when the quake hit. He is still alive inside his mechanized sweeper, with layers of concrete slabs on top of him."

A dozen firemen were working around an excavation in the ruin. They were hip deep in the twisted concrete of the fallen structure and were digging through the slabs and other debris to try to reach him. Jackhammers were pounding into the concrete slabs trying to break them apart.

I went on the air live and broadcast the rescue effort. We already knew many people had been killed in the quake, but here was a gallant rescue attempt to save one person who was still alive, but trapped eight feet below the enormous slabs of concrete. Right after the quake, his co-workers heard his cry from under the rubble, they sent for help and firemen had been working for hours to try to get him out.I did several live cut-ins to keep viewers informed about the attempt. Los Angeles city and county fire departments had combined their efforts and were using the latest rescue techniques to free the man.

As I televised from this scene, Warren Wilson was at the site of the fallen freeway sections in the Newhall Pass. I watched his reports as he showed the broken spans and ruptured freeway sections. This was the same area where the freeway had collapsed in a similar quake in 1971. It was also one of the main freeways running north and south through the state.

Marta Waller and her camera crew had now moved to a Reseda apartment complex that collapsed. The third floor had fallen and crushed the second floor causing many deaths and injuries. Firemen carefully worked their way through the debris of the fallen apartment house trying to save those who were trapped and recover bodies of those killed in the aftermath of the terrible earthquake. Sixteen people died in the wreckage.

Bob Navarro reported live on the damaged buildings he discovered in Hollywood, 20 miles from the epicenter. This surprised those of us in the valley. It would be days before the full extent of the quake and its damage would be known.

Jennifer York in the helicopter was over the collapsed sections of the freeway in the Newhall Pass. The pictures were beyond belief. Huge spans of concrete freeways which had been hammered and pounded down by the vertical power of the quake were split open and lying on the ground. Another section of freeway that withstood the force of the quake had trapped four cars on its roadway. The concrete had broken away at both ends. The cars looked as if they were on the deck of an aircraft carrier. This was one of the most traveled sections of the freeway system.

As I continued my broadcasts from the Northridge Mall, the strategy of the rescue played out. Newly developed air bags, which have great strength and were designed to lift a truck off a person, were brought in. As the rescuers opened spaces in the concrete rubble, the air bags would be used to lift another section of concrete. Pieces of wood were sent down and used to shore up the newly opened section. This went on for hours. Move a section of the slab, get under it, bring in the air bags and shore it up. This painstaking process brought firemen to the trapped man about eight feet into the ground. They worked there under the tons of debris and the strong aftershocks while they tried to free him. They were able to get an I.V. needle into him to help stabilize him. They were able to get to the crushed truck, rip off the doors and eventually reach the man, who was critically injured, but conscious.

I was on the air at the climactic moment when he was gently brought up from his broken, concrete prison. Greg Hunter grabbed his camera from the tripod, put it on his shoulder, ran across the parking lot to our camera truck and climbed up to the roof to show viewers, close-up pictures of what was happening.

Firemen lifted the injured man to the surface, placed him on a gurney, rushed him to a waiting helicopter and flew him to UCLA Medical Center for emergency surgery. Greg's camera was live all of the time.

My next report was from a derailed freight train. It was a jumble of tank cars and boxcars thrown about by the force of the earth, some on their sides, others upright and still others tilting on their sides. Railroad repair crews were working to remove the wreckage and put as many of the cars back on the tracks as possible. We drove down along the tracks to do our report, but the Southern Pacific police abruptly turned us away.

"This is railroad property. You have to get out of here," shouted the stern-faced guardian.

It was obvious we couldn't negotiate with him. Los Angeles police officers all over the quake-stricken area had been helpful all day long, but the railroad police had a different agenda. They are very tender about the sight of twisted tracks and derailed engines and tank cars carrying hazardous materials. The train had been uprooted under the Nordhoff overpass. There was a vantage point on the bridge where we could get all the shots of the wreckage that we needed.

The overpass had been closed to traffic after the quake. It is a long graceful span, but the roadway on one side had dropped about a foot at the point where it connected to the bridge. We drove our camera truck up the grade and stopped just short of the span. Greg opened the back door and reeled out about 200 feet of camera cable so that we could get onto the bridge and show pictures of the damaged railroad cars below. Some 50 people were staring at the twisted wreckage. We were ready to go on the air almost immediately, but several other KTLA reporters were doing their stories ahead of us.

I was holding my microphone and Greg was next to me lining up his camera when the damaged bridge started to dance. It was a gentle bounce, but it was a magnitude 5.3 aftershock, and it sent 50 people scattering off the bridge.

I looked at Greg with his camera. He looked at me with my mike. We both decided to stay. The span rocked and swayed for a few seconds, then settled down and it was quiet. I could see puffs of dust on the distant hills. The aftershock had stirred the ground and the dust clouds were beginning to rise.

"Another strong aftershock, and I thought they were over," I said to Greg. "Let's get some pictures of the dust clouds on the hills for our next cut-in."

We were the only two people left on the swaying bridge. Our live report showed the emergency crews draining the toxic substances from the overturned tank cars. Workers wearing special protective gear were hauling long, heavy hoses to other tank cars to transfer the toxic fluids to waiting tank trucks for removal.

My next report showed the back walls of two huge warehouse-type buildings where furniture and various heavy appliances were stored. The walls had split open, hurling merchandise from the exposed storage racks into a huge pile of worthless rubble below. There were mounds of twisted debris—couches, chairs and broken pieces of furniture that had fallen three floors to the parking lot pavement behind the buildings.

As we drove around Northridge and neighboring communities, there were always strings of yellow tape to keep people out. No businesses were open. Empty parking lots were everywhere. For the first time in history, the entire city of Los Angeles lost its power supply. It was soon restored to many areas, but it took hours for different sections of the city to get back on line.

There was no water, no place open to buy food or supplies. Supermarkets were shut down, their employees trying to make some order from the merchandise scattered all over their floors. No restaurants were open. Gas stations could not sell gas because there was no electricity to pump it from their tanks. It was an eerie sight to see the city staggered under the blow and unable to respond. Emergency efforts were successful and in full swing, but the day-to-day necessities we take for granted had disappeared. Buildings, damaged as they might be, remained standing but useless.

My next assignment was in Sherman Oaks. I was told that thousands of people had converged on parks, open fields and parking lots around the city. They huddled in any place they could find to keep out of homes they feared would topple down on them.

I was sent to a small park in Canoga Park where almost 200 people had made a makeshift camp. They built tents of blankets and sheets. They used blue canvas covers to enlarge their shelters. They spread out sleeping bags and clothes, pillows and possessions in their encampments. No one here wanted to go back inside any building while aftershocks quivered and jarred the ground under them. The shaking went on all day long.

Most of those here were immigrants from Mexico, Guatemala, Honduras, El Salvador and parts of Asia. They came from nations with poor building codes, where shoddy construction takes its toll. When the quakes hit in the dead of night in their countries, stone houses collapse killing those asleep in their beds. When you associate earthquakes with the instant deaths of thousands of people, the only sensible thing is to go outside and stay there.

Many others were illegal immigrants who were afraid of going to shelters and having to register with authorities. They feared they would be picked up and deported. Still others were here because their homes and apartments were badly damaged by the quake and they had no place to go.

The scene here reflected what was going on in parks all over the city. Possessions, hurriedly stuffed into parked cars, were being moved to the campsites. Children were running back and forth, playing with each other. A doll carriage stood next to a baby carriage, while fragrant smoke from the family barbecue rose from the hamburgers on the grill. Several of the small campsites had music coming from the portable radios and there were even some small battery-powered television sets showing earthquake damage.

There is a certain amount of tunnel vision when you are covering stories in a disaster situation like this. I know what is going on in front of me, but often have no idea what is going on elsewhere. Late that night, I couldn't believe what I was seeing. I was sent to a 40 unit, residential complex in a rural area above Granada Hills. The quake had devastated the two-building, townhouse complex. There were 20 units in each structure. The quake knocked the upper one off its foundation and dropped it down the hill, leaving it tilting on the hillside. It appeared mostly intact, but was a total loss.

The quake shattered the other structure. It fell onto many cars parked in underground garages. A blazing fire erupted and burned for hours. All the townhouses were consumed in the inferno. As the fire continued to burn, gas tanks of the cars crushed underneath the rubble would explode and feed the flames. Hours later, firemen were still fighting the fire, not able to put it out but still trying to keep the fire from spreading to other structures or dry brush nearby. One of the men standing next to me in the coldness of the night told me of his narrow escape from a nearby house on the ridge.

"I was knocked out of bed by the first shock of the quake. I fell to the floor, then there seemed to be another shake and a huge television set and bookcase fell onto the bed right where I had been sleeping."

As the night wore on, I did several live reports from the burning townhouses.

It was close to midnight. Gege and I were sitting together in the front seat of the camera truck. She was asleep, her head on my shoulder, her hand in mine. The warmth of the front seat was comforting after the brisk night air we had been working in. All of us were silent and tired, waiting for the word from the station that our marathon coverage was over. I had just one more live cut-in to do.

It was great to just sit here and do nothing, after the long, pressure-filled hours of the past day. Greg was napping in the driver's seat, his head bent forward, and Carlos was silent in the back. Dim lights outlined the tilting and burning buildings that were the homes of 40 families last night. Now they were just rubble. They seemed to symbolize the heartbreaking scenes I had encountered throughout the day.

I had a good sleep and was back at work the next day sharing earthquake stories with my friends in the newsroom. The stories were mostly of fear and survival, the same for all of us who experienced the quake and its troublesome aftershocks.

My cameraman, Rod Gilmore, who had just bought a home in Sylmar, lost it in the few seconds the quake shook. He had saved for years to get the down payment and, once he bought it, spent all of his spare time fixing it up.

The morning of January 17 his four-year-old boy, Taylor, couldn't sleep. His wife Manette went into the boy's room to comfort him and fell asleep. When the quake hit, she put her arms around him and hugged him while the house literally shook apart. They were not hurt. When the family got their bearings and stumbled down the damaged staircase, they found the house in shambles, split open, main beams down and a gaping hole in the front wall. It appeared that the house was a total loss. He's rebuilding, but now has two mortgages to pay off.

News Producer Ryan Cowen told me that he and his wife, Nancy, awakened when the quake hit to the disorienting sounds of the pounding and clattering of pots and pans. Nancy had enhanced her kitchen decor by hanging the utensils from the ceiling, and now they were battering each other as the house rocked and swayed. The banging sounds were intermixed with the swooshing sounds of the neighbor's pool as waves of water splashed back and forth and spilled into the backyard. When the Cowens gathered their senses, they went outside to see the black sky bursting with flashes of light.

Ryan said, "It was like a Fourth of July fireworks show at Magic Mountain."

Green, red and blue explosions filled the sky from the nearby power plant. The lights flared brighter. The colors grew in intensity. There was a great flash that made daylight out of darkness. It faded and everything went black as power was lost.

As I talked to people, did my quake followup assignments and read reports of the television coverage of the earthquake, I began to realize the major role KTLA played. The station had helped keep the entire nation informed. Because of the major power failure in Los Angeles, many of the stations had trouble getting on the air. After the quake, KTLA went to emergency power and continued to broadcast via satellite up-link.

When the networks saw the coverage and were not able to get pictures from their local affiliates, they asked KTLA for permission to pick up its signal. All three networks, ABC, CBS and NBC, as well as CNN, broadcast the KTLA coverage.

For many hours, KTLA's telecast of the devastated areas was one of the primary national sources of news. The public's need to know was the important factor, overriding the old constraints of competition and turf protection. The rest of the nation wanted to see what was going on in Los Angeles.

Columnist Marvin Kitman of *New York Newsday*, watching in New York City, wrote that he was most impressed by the coverage of the local stations in Los Angeles, saying New Yorkers got to see all day long what the viewers in Los Angeles were seeing. He noticed how the viewer became part of the story.

"You are there, in the tradition of Edward R. Murrow's radio reports from the rooftops during the London blitz. Except this is live and instant," he wrote. "The news today invites you into the stories. More and more we are participants. We are in all the stories as reporters, fire fighters, rescue workers and victims. We are all of them."

That day, flowers, baskets of cookies and letters of thanks poured into KTLA from other stations that had used our coverage. Once again the station had met the crisis.

In any emergency operation, response time is one of the most important elements. In television, response time is fastest when you are ready.

A few years ago, when KTLA started an innovative morning news program. Its purpose was to capture and entertain local viewers who were used to watching news shows from the East that were three hours old. There is so much going on here in Los Angeles that our own up-to-the-minute morning news seemed to make sense. And it certainly did. Carlos Amescula, Barbara Beck, Mark Kriske, Sam Rubin, Eric Spillman, Michelle Ruiz, Jennifer York and Gayle Anderson have made it a light, humorous, entertaining program.

What it also did was to insure that KTLA's response time would be second to none. The station now has camera crews, reporters and all the facilities necessary to broadcast breaking news around the clock. Jennifer York covers Los Angeles in a helicopter every morning. KTLA station manager, Greg Nathanson, is ready to interrupt all programs to cover major news stories in Los Angeles. The earthquake coverage was our biggest challenge and the station responded well.

Everyone seems to agree that the emergency response for just about everyone was immediate, effective and professional. The firemen, police officers and other emergency workers put the response plan into effect with great precision. Help was there for the injured and protection was for their property. Mayor Richard Riordan has been singled out for providing immediate hands-on leadership during the crisis. He was out there in a sweat suit and tennis shoes from the very start. California Governor Pete Wilson took immediate steps to get aid for the victims of the earthquake and the federal government responded with amazing speed.

The frightening aftershocks kept hammering away at the city in the days that followed. While sitting at my desk writing this chapter on my computer, my world violently shook again. I made these notes as it happened.

*   *   *

{ Jan. 21, 1994. It is 10:39... A jarring aftershock just hit as I write this. My computer monitor is bouncing before my eyes, the house is shivering, shaking and rumbling... Now, everything is still. These jolts are annoying.}

{10:42...Another aftershock! About as big as the first one. The house is vibrating again, windows rattling, everything creaking and shaking as I ride out another one. I've stopped writing.}

{ 10:53...What's happening...we're hit again. Most unusual...Same sounds...these windows are shaking again. I hear a cracking sound in the house. We're all paranoid here in Los Angeles. I'm just sitting here listening to the silence. 10:54... Oops, here goes another one. The house is quivering and rattling. Shakes are hitting one on top of another—a swarm of quakes. The city's psyche is taking a real beating. I had better call the station.}

{ 10:57...I can't believe it. Here's another one while I'm on the phone. Five aftershocks in less than 20 minutes. Unnerving. Assignment editor Hans Laetz wants me to go to KTLA right now and help with the on-the-air-coverage of the swarm of quakes.}

I later learned these were sizeable aftershocks. The first had a magnitude of 4.6. The next two were 4.2 and 4.3 and the last ones were 4.4 and 3.7. All of them hitting in an 18-minute time span.

*   *   *

Scientists have told us that, although this big earthquake measured a magnitude 6.8 on the Richter Scale, the actual vertical ground movement was one of the most powerful ever recorded in the history of California.

The damage was widespread. More than 60 people were killed, 9,000 injured. The damage estimates could be as high as $20 billion. There have been 300,000 applications for government assistance, the largest number ever to seek help after a disaster.

Over 55,000 buildings were damaged, 10,000 of them unfit for habitation, but the city survived and things returned to normal.

Soon after the quake, I had a conversation with an architect as we rode down in an elevator. He said, "I wish you could tell the quake story from our point of view. A 6.8 earthquake hit Southern California and 99% of the buildings survived."

Most of the city was untouched, but as I drove around the city observing different news stories, I could see that the quake did leave many scars. The rebuilding started right away, and some said the earthquake and its countless aftershocks jump-started a local economy that had been flattened by the recession. Thousands of construction jobs were created as people shook off the calamity of the quake and tried to get their lives and their homes back in order.

Los Angeles is disaster prone; it will be ever so. The natural cycle of brush fires, mudslides and floods, high tides and snowstorms, drought and earthquakes, run through our history. Some say it is the price we pay to live here. When you add recession, unemployment and an unfriendly business atmosphere, you would think the city is falling apart at the seams. However, it is important to remember that Southern California is the 11th-largest economic unit in the world. If it were a separate nation, it would be ranked just behind the United Kingdom, Canada, Spain and South Korea. Almost 15 million people live in the five-county area. That's more than all the other states except California, New York and Texas. It is the second largest port city in the country. Some 60 million passengers fly into our airports yearly. Over 25 million tourists visit here each year. And though some companies are leaving the area, others are coming in. Although the defense industries are cutting back and restructuring, we still have more manufacturing jobs than any city in the nation. There are more than Chicago and Dallas combined.

If you drive the freeways at rush hour, you'll experience traffic jams with thousands of Californians on their way home from work. They have jobs, homes, families and opportunities and they share in the great promise of the city. A vast majority of them are here to stay.

Don't sell Los Angeles short just because everything that can happen to tarnish the image has happened. It has taken its hits, but the damage is far from fatal. The area is a dynamic econonic machine that rolls on and on. It still has more to offer than any other place in the country.

The news cycle never ends. One story replaces another.

In February 1994, I was standing in ankle-deep mud on the Pacific Coast Highway in Malibu, watching it ooze across the roadway. The brush on the hills and canyons would normally soak up all of the rainwater, but last year's firestorms had burned all of the vegetation. Now the raging water scooped up the topsoil into a river of mud that overflowed its banks and rushed down to the highway below. The thick flow had already inundated about a dozen beachfront homes.

One owner had just repaired her fire-damaged home. Now, she was hit by the cyclical one-two punch: when there are brush fires, mudslides are likely to follow. She had a foot of mud in the basement of her oceanside home.

It doesn't take long for even the big events to disappear from the headlines and for others to take their place. It is the continuous, fresh mixture of news stories that makes reporting such a challenge. They range from headline stories to light-hearted features. For example, in mid-March 1994, there was a complete change of pace from the quake and disaster stories. First it was St. Patrick's Day. I found myself in the middle of the celebration. I was reporting the bedlam of the singing, cheering and beer-drinking crowd at Molly Malone's, one of the local Irish pubs. The music and noise was so loud, that I could not hear a single syllable that I was pronouncing. The microphone was somehow able to distinguish my voice from the chaos and make it understandable to the viewers at home.

A few days later at the annual Academy Awards, I was part of the army of badge-wearing reporters and cameramen, decked out in black-ties and rented tuxedos, swarming around the stars. Everyone was shouting and waving, trying to get the attention of Clint Eastwood, Faye Dunaway, Glenn Close, Tom Cruise and all the other arriving stars. Many stars did stop for television interviews as they walked the long, red carpet from their stretch-limousines to the entrance of the Music Center in downtown Los Angeles.

In mid-April 1994, I did a live cut in as the quake-damaged Santa Monica Freeway was reopened. Two bridges were destroyed in the January earthquake and the country's busiest freeway was shut down in both directions. There were traffic jams as the freeway vehicles clogged surface streets with infuriated and frustrated drivers. This was a "L.A. rebuilds" story. Construction crews had worked around-the-clock, seven days a week and unbelievably, the earthquake-damaged freeway section had been repaired in only three months. California Governor Pete Wilson, Los Angeles Mayor Richard Riordan and U.S. Secretary of Transportation Federico Pena were at the freeway site to celebrate the opening. They gave the signal and CHP motorcycle officers, with their red lights flashing, led the first cars down the freeway. The nation's busiest freeway was back in business and the symbolic gesture let everyone know that Los Angeles was rebounding from the quake and on the way back.

Also in mid-April, Salvador Pena left the hospital. The man who had his legs crushed and was critically injured when the Northridge Mall parking structure collapsed on top of him had recovered and was able to go home. The firemen who dug through the tons of broken concrete slabs saved his life. The doctors had operated on him and reconstructed his legs, and the specialists who led him through rehabilitation had given him a new life.

In late April 1994, I joined a crowd of several hundred people at the Richard Nixon Library and Birthplace in Yorba Linda. The 37th President had died earlier in the evening and the crowd came here to pay its respects to him.

I reported on the quiet crowd who watched the Marine color guard lower flags to half-mast in Nixon's honor.

On the day his body was brought to lie in state at the Nixon presidential library, I stood drenched in a pouring rain and waited for the arrival of the motorcade carrying his casket. There were threatening thunderheads in the distance when the motorcade neared its destination. The looming, silver-edged, cumulous clouds seemed to get even darker as they slowly moved across the sky. The first sharp flashes of cracking thunder erupted as the black hearse bearing the casket entered the grounds. The rain grew in intensity.

The Marine honor guard and the other military units stood motionless, oblivious to the pelting downpour. I felt very much a part of history as I reported to our television audience this moment. Richard Nixon, who had been a major figure on the country's turbulent political scene since the mid-40s, was being laid to rest here in the mid-90s.

Nothing is routine when you are a television news reporter. The unexpected is always looming.

EPILOGUE

The 1949 telecast of the attempted rescue of little Kathy Fiscus has been acclaimed as one of the landmark news stories in television history. It completely captured and involved its viewers for 27 hours. Those who watched remembered it for the rest of their lives. On June 17, 1994, another landmark television news event absorbed its viewers in much the same way, but this time perception and reality violently clashed on the television screen.

I was reporting the chase of O.J. Simpson by a phalanx of police cars. Forty-five years after the Kathy Fiscus telecast, the impact of live television coverage appeared as powerful and dramatic as ever. I was part of the unbelievably bizarre event that would be remembered by some viewers for a lifetime. Like the Kathy Fiscus rescue attempt, this was a life-and-death story. The 1949 telecast captivated the city, now this chase had people across the nation glued to their TV screens.

The Kathy Fiscus tragedy was the television audiences' introduction to the impact of live news coverage. The 1949 TV screen opened up, reached out, took you by the collar and pulled you into the middle of the ongoing rescue attempt. Emotionally, you became part of what you were seeing. You agonized over the little girl trapped in an abandoned shaft 100 feet below the ground. You didn't know how it would turn out.

A great pall of despair had smothered the city when the exhausted men uncovered her lifeless body. Viewers who had been swept up into the reality of this live television epic, were deeply affected by the tragic loss of the child.

The illusion that watching live TV is a kind of participation in the event was what kept the audience tuned in for 27 hours in 1949. The "you are there"sensation which is only produced by the kind of coverage the attempted rescue of Kathy Fiscus received explains the huge popularity of live TV news. This was not a second hand story being told. Viewers became part of the action as the story developed.

Now, everyone watched with mixed feelings as O.J. Simpson, the Hall of Fame football player and role model for a generation of young people, drove down the freeway, pointing a gun to his head. That this was a life-and-death situation was verified by a suicide note that had just been read over the air. Stations all over the country broadcast the extraordinary developments captured by a fleet of helicopters whose cameras focused on this modern day tragedy. O.J. Simpson, one of the most widely recognised men in America had become a fugitive after being accused of a brutal double murder. This was taking place in front of our eyes and no one could possibly predict the outcome. Once again, a huge audience had been attracted by a living drama. Everyone had to stay and watch, and by watching, take part.

Viewers' feelings were shattered when someone they thought they knew so well was accused of something so monstrous. Polling data showed that 95% of the American people had heard of O.J. and only 3% thought unfavorably of him. I shared the viewers' frustration: as well as we think we knew him, we knew him not. We knew him only from television. I rode this changing emotional tide as I sat next to Hal Fishman and Jann Carl on our set and reported the story. What goes around, comes around. And what a time we've shared over the decades!

From the failed rescue of Kathy Fiscus to the arrest of O.J. Simpson we've been hit by the new element of myth versus reality. O.J. was so real in his television image that we couldn't accept what possibly happened in Brentwood that June night. Many viewers felt betrayed and yet eagerly followed every turn of the chase. Life's complications are ever with us: black and white will always fade to gray.

Where only a city watched in 1949, now an entire nation shares in the human narratives that television news chronicles day by day.

And life goes on.

ACKNOWLEDGMENTS

So many people have helped me on this project. My special thanks go to my mentor, Paul Almond, a very talented and creative motion picture director and producer. He set the deadlines and inspired me to keep going. He was a great sounding board and kept me on schedule until the task was done.

My thanks to my talented news crew who made this a team project. My cameramen, Greg Hunter and Jim Toten, were hands-on with their help. Greg helped with the photography, shooting original pictures and transferring videotape for the printed page. Jim is a whiz who steered me through the computer maze to the final copies of the manuscript.

KTLA's Joe Quasarano gave me valuable technical advice. My son-in-law, Don de Nicola, a great attorney and a talented editor, was especially helpful in the final stages of the manuscript. I turned to him for guidance on many occasions. My good friend from USC days, Bud Stefan, former head of broadcasting at BBD&O Advertising, was always ready to give me feedback when I sent him unfinished chapters.

My colleagues at KTLA were most helpful. Station Managers Greg Nathanson and John Reardon were supportive throughout the project. News Director Warren Cereghino and News Operations Director Craig Hume were always encouraging and were a great source of information when I was trying to track down details of stories from long ago. My thanks to Hal Fishman for being such a good friend and helping me in so many ways, and to Joel Tator for his friendship over the years and for producing the television special on my career, "L.A.'s Treasure: Stan Chambers." My thanks to the former KTLA Telecopter broadcasting team of Larry Scheer and Harold Morby. Harold gave me access to his collection of news pictures taken over the years from the Telecopter.

A special thanks to Pamela Lishen, Reagan Arthur and Michael Hammelburg who helped me in the early days of the project. Many thanks to Amanda Jones of Capra Press and my publisher Noel Young for his patience, understanding and guiding hand. He was the catalyst who put it all together.

I want to express my gratitude to my family, their wives, husbands and children for their support and understanding while I worked long hours at the computer.

And most of all I want to thank Beverly who helped me get started and Gege who helped me finish.

Stan Chambers
Los Angeles, California
June 1, 1994